Public Sector Accounting

FOURTH EDITION

Rowan Jones MA, PhD, IPFA
Birmingham Business School,
University of Birmingham

Maurice Pendlebury MA, PhD, IPFA, FCCA
Cardiff Business School,
University of Wales College of Cardiff

PITMAN PUBLISHING

For Anna, Daniel, Tom and David

PITMAN PUBLISHING
128 Long Acre, London WC2E 9AN

A Division of Pearson Professional Limited

First published in Great Britain in 1984
Second edition 1988
Third edition 1992
Fourth edition 1996

© Rowan Jones and Maurice Pendlebury 1984, 1988, 1992, 1996

ISBN 0 273 61415 0

The right of Professor R H Jones and Professor M W Pendlebury to
be identified as Authors of this Work has been asserted by them in
accordance with the Copyright, Designs and Patents Act 1988.

British Library Cataloguing in Publication Data
A CIP catalogue record for this book can be obtained from the British Library

10 9 8 7 6 5 4 3 2 1

Typeset by Mathematical Composition Setters Ltd, Salisbury
Printed and bound in Great Britain by Clays Ltd, St Ives plc

The Publishers' policy is to use paper manufactured from sustainable forests.

CONTENTS

PART 2   FINANCIAL ACCOUNTING

PART 3   AUDITING

PREFACE

The purpose of this book is to provide an integrated approach to public sector accounting. Accounting theory and practice are drawn together for each of the main areas of financial accounting, management accounting and auditing. Examples from the whole range of public sector experience are woven into the text to illustrate the issues involved.

The book is written primarily for students of undergraduate and postgraduate degree courses of universities and colleges and also for students of professional accountancy bodies. It should also be of interest to research students, to accountants and auditors of public sector organizations; indeed to anyone concerned with management in the public sector.

For historical reasons introductory accounting is taught in a private sector context. We see no need to try (nor do we attempt) to change this tradition. However, it does no justice to the importance of public sector organizations in our economy to leave it to students to translate, unguided, their private sector studies into public sector practice.

Traditionally, also, public sector accounting has emphasized the dissimilarities in the public sector by concentrating on the specific accounting problems of its different segments. We believe that the future of public sector accounting lies in emphasizing the similarities.

We have drawn extensively on our public sector experience and on our teaching of public sector accounting, and we would like to acknowledge all the help and guidance we have received from our colleagues and students over many years.

Rowan Jones
Maurice Pendlebury

CHAPTER 1

The nature of public sector accounting

The purpose of this chapter is to provide an introduction to the nature of public sector accounting. We begin with a discussion of some characteristics of public sector organizations and then offer an overview of the origins of the sub-discipline of public sector accounting. The final part discusses the concepts of economy, efficiency and effectiveness.

THE NATURE OF THE PUBLIC SECTOR

There is a range of meanings given to the phrase 'public sector'. At one extreme, the government provides measures of the accumulated 'public sector debt' and of the 'public sector borrowing requirement' for the year; at the other extreme, the phrase becomes a slogan, often used pejoratively, to summon up threats of 'taxation' or 'bureaucracy' or 'big government'. A variation of its antonym, 'privatization', is commonly used now to allude to lower taxation or less bureaucracy or greater freedom.

This is significantly more than a matter of semantics because different disciplines, reflecting different world-views, define the public sector differently (see Kaufmann *et al.*, 1986). Politics, public administration, sociology, law and economics offer different, though sometimes overlapping, perspectives using a range of concepts including ownership, control, taxation, accountability, entitlement, rights. And if there is no agreement on what the public sector is, it is no surprise that there is disagreement about what it ought to be.

The etymology of the word 'public' is of little help because it has even more shades of meaning. A common source of difficulty in accounting is with the phrase 'public accountants': from the Anglo-American perspective this is understood as private accountants in public practice, but in Continental Europe, in English translation, it often means accountants in a governmental organization. Indeed, in the UK, there is no natural phrase for the latter: we use the somewhat awkward phrase 'public finance accountants'. One way of portraying the difficulties with the phrase 'public sector' is to state that it is relatively easy to obtain some agreement on the two ends of the spectrum, namely the purely governmental and the purely personal. Defining the money that is purely governmental, in the UK, involves defining an important element of the constitution, involving the relationship between the executive and the legislature, and the Consolidated Fund and National Loans Fund are the concomitant accounting devices. But there are profound complications in the spheres between these funds and the monies of each individual to dispose of at will. We commonly describe institutions of government to aid our understanding: sovereign government, state government, local government, nationalized industries (state-owned enterprises, public corporations, public enterprises). But of course, these are not precise words: 'sovereign government' becomes controversially debatable in the context of the European Union (or Community, or Economic Community) but, more than that, these words beg the questions that what they relate to is definable.

Probably the best modern example of our confusion is adoption of the acronym 'quango' (now standing for quasi-autonomous non-governmental organization) to try to describe those organizations that have proliferated in the West and that are somehow thought of as different from government. But for much longer there has been difficulty characterizing 'charity'. The essence of charity is private individuals contributing to the public good, leading to relief from taxation. Consequently, charities are both public and private – but the extents vary. Phrases such as 'voluntary sector' and 'third sector' similarly imply definition that is not actually there.

As we discuss later, the accounting discipline is not much help in these definitional problems. Accountants have had the ability to provide relevant services to individuals and organizations of any kind but it is not a natural part of accounting practice to consider macro-perspectives. Nevertheless, the discipline did lend its name to a definitive amalgam of economics and statistics: national income accounting. This was developed, as a systematic measurement by government, during the Second World War. In essence, the situation was that government had the responsibility of deciding which resources should be applied to the overriding military needs (and export need) and which to the civilian population. But to do this systematically and rationally required knowledge of the resources available. The subsequent national income accounting was developed and refined after the war and its aggregates have increasingly become a part of (some) daily discourse. Moreover, the management of the war merged with profound changes that were already taking place in the way that the UK (among many others) was being managed, and indeed, thought of. Macro-economic management dating from the 1930s was bolstered by these measurement techniques and the surge in nationalization further reinforced this national economic perspective.

In 1952, the phrase 'public sector' was first used (*Oxford English Dictionary*, 2nd edn, 1989, p. 779). An economist, Surányi-Unger, who had spent most of his life in Hungary but who was writing in the US, offered comparisons of economic systems and synthesized them into three groups: countries like the US that emphasized economic freedom; countries like the Soviet Union that had adopted central planning; and countries like the UK and France that had traditionally emphasized 'Western economic freedom' but in the previous two decades had shifted to a compromise between 'freedom and planning': 'Concerning the public sector of the economy, compromising countries definitely differ from the countries of Eastern planning. The public sector of the former countries is not only much smaller but also qualitatively different. Most of these countries employ governmental economic planning for the purpose of aiding and encouraging their remaining private sectors' (Surányi-Unger, 1952, pp. 59–60).

Whatever one's views of his thesis may be, the sense of the 'public sector' as part of the macro-economic management of a Western economy has had significant influence. If the foregoing provides an overview of the problems of defining the public sector, perhaps it is also useful simply to take a context, the UK, and describe some of the characteristics of some of the organizations that are generally understood to be a part of the public sector: *Public Bodies* (Cabinet Office, 1994) provides a useful reference. And what is immediately clear is that public sector organizations exhibit a variety of social, economic, political and legal characteristics. They have different powers and responsibilities and display different patterns of accountability. They have different objectives, are financed in different ways and have different organizational structures. These differences reflect how public sector development has responded to changing pressures over time and also to historical backgrounds and sources.

One persistent development of recent years has been the exposure of large parts of the public sector to competition and market mechanisms. The most obvious example has been the privatization of major utilities such as gas, electricity and water out of public ownership and into private (but publicly regulated) ownership. In addition, an increasing range of activities are now required to be awarded on the basis of competitive tendering, with private sector contractors competing with public sector organizations for the provision of the whole range of services, from preparing budgets to cleaning offices.

Even at the very heart of the public sector, where open competition may not be possible or desirable, we have seen the introduction of 'managed competition' and internal markets, with the provision of a service being separated from the consumption of that service. A major example is in the National Health Service, where providers (hospitals) supply health care to purchasers (district health authorities and general practitioners) at a negotiated contract price.

These 'market force' pressures have not only led to a change in public sector ownership but have also had a significant impact on the way in which those services that remain in the public sector are managed and accounted for.

A further development in recent years, having a profound impact on the management of public services, is that of 'devolved management'. The principle being followed here is that of identifying self-contained operational activities, and then making a manager responsible not only for these but also for the related financial management and budgetary control aspects. A prime example is the local management of schools, whereby the head and governors of a school are given an operating costs budget that is based largely on the number of students enrolled, and are then required to operate the school and control their costs against the budget. Similarly in central government, many of the executive functions of the government have been devolved to separately identified units known as 'Executive Agencies', which are responsible for performing a defined set of functions and operating within a predetermined budget.

As far as powers and responsibilities are concerned all public sector bodies have one feature in common. Their specific powers are derived ultimately from Parliament, their responsibilities are ultimately to Parliament. However, below this ultimate authority there is a variety of formal and informal networks which have an impact on the way public sector organizations operate. Included in these networks might be central government ministers, civil servants, elected local councils, appointed boards, consultative councils and other pressure groups. In pluralistic societies this is a complex and dynamic structure, and organizations have always had to be aware of these different influences and be prepared to change in response to them.

The way in which public sector bodies are accountable to Parliament takes a variety of forms. For example, the heads of central government departments are directly accountable. A range of nationalized industries, public corporations and other non-departmental public bodies (or quangos), including the authorities and trusts of the National Health Service, are accountable through the sponsoring government departments responsible for their fundamental objectives. Local authorities offer a uniquely different example because, although they are partially accountable to Parliament, through the relevant Secretary of State, they are also more immediately accountable to a local electorate. This dual accountability to electors is still within the context of a unitary state where Parliament is sovereign.

An important effect of the different forms of overall accountability to Parliament is in the setting of objectives for public sector organizations. The objectives of central government departments are determined directly by Parliament. The broad objectives of other public bodies are set by Parliament, but the more detailed operational objectives are often the responsibility of an appointed board. Moreover, although the specific Acts bestow the broad objectives, amplification of these may result from statutory instruments, ministerial directions, discussions of House of Commons select committees, committees of enquiry, consumer councils, and so on.

The way in which local authority objectives are determined is even more complex. For certain services, such as education and social services, the duty to provide at least some minimum standard is imposed by Parliament. An objective to go beyond this minimum standard is the responsibility of the locally elected council. Local authorities can also provide discretionary services, for the objectives of which they are obviously responsible. However, ministers and government departments have considerable influence in determining the objectives of local authorities. Local pressure groups, such as trade unions, community action groups, chambers of trade, and so on also have a definite effect on the direction of local affairs. A consequence of this is that local authorities have to respond to pressures from a variety of sources. The pressures are ever changing, as are the relative strengths and weaknesses of the sources of pressure, and there is, therefore, a constant shifting in the emphasis applied to particular objectives.

Another fundamental way of distinguishing between public sector organizations is the way in which they are financed. The different methods reflect the different objectives. The basic alternatives for revenue purposes are either to finance by taxation or to finance by charges. Which of these alternatives is used depends on the economic nature of the goods and services provided, and also on the political and social attitudes concerning these. For example, the provision of a largely public good could only sensibly be financed by taxation. A public good is often thought of as one where the enjoyment of its benefits cannot be withheld for non-payment – for example, clean air zones.

In such a situation what is known as 'market failure' has occurred. For a free market system to work, the supplier of a service must be able to enter into a contractual relationship to charge consumers for the service provided. Clearly, in the case of clean air zones this is not possible and so financing through taxation is the only answer. A related example of market failure occurs where the *private* benefits that some individuals feel they receive from, say, a refuse collection and disposal service are lower than the costs they would be charged if the service were provided under a market system. In this situation those individuals might decide not to purchase the service, and simply dump their refuse in their garden or in the street. What the market transaction has not taken into account are the benefits to others in the community such as neighbours or visitors to the town. These will suffer if some individuals decide not to contract to have their refuse collected and disposed of. These wider societal benefits are known by economists as 'externalities', and if the market approach fails to take these into account then there will be under-provision of the service.

In addition to public goods there are services which could be withheld for non-payment, but the social pressures of the day might be expected to prevent this happening. Health care offers a possible example of this, and as a result is currently financed primarily by taxation. Clearly, for services which bestow substantial private benefits, charges can be, and are, made. The public sector characteristic of these is that they are not wholly market determined. Even where the public sector organization appears to pursue fully commercial activities, the charges may not completely reflect consumer preferences. Where prices are lower than market values this effectively means that a policy of financing by a mixture of taxes and charges is being adopted. In reality there are very few examples of services that are *totally* tax financed or *totally* charges financed. There are of course services that are very close to the tax-financed end of the continuum, such as defence, or very close to the charges-financed end, such as the InterCity business of British Rail. However, the vast bulk of public sector services lies somewhere between these two extremes, with the proportions that are tax- or charges-financed frequently changing in response to changes in social and political attitudes.

Capital financing is also affected by different and changing objectives. For example, the few remaining nationalized industries are subject to external financing limits which effectively limit their ability to borrow to finance capital expenditure requirements. These external financing limits have often changed quickly and significantly to reflect changes in public concern about standards of service or safety issues.

The control over the external borrowings of public bodies is just one example of the role played by central government in macro-economic management. For those areas of the public sector that are effectively part of central government (including the National Health Service) a close control over resources and spending might be expected. The control over local authorities is more complex. The amount of capital expenditure is regulated by provisions which apply to the various sources of finance for capital spending. A substantial amount of local authority revenue expenditure is financed by central government grants and this provides an obvious means of control.

The proper control of public money is of course a fundamental requirement of any public sector organization. As far as central government's own activities are concerned, the framework of control has been developed over many years and has made use of four important accounting techniques which emphasize central financial control (Pendlebury *et al.*, 1992). These are:

1   *The use of vote accounting*. All revenues and payments go into and out of one central fund, and spending can only take place if specifically authorized, or voted, by Parliament.
2   *The gross budget principle*. All revenues are paid in gross without deducting expenditure. Conversely, expenditure is authorized at the gross cost, and any

revenues earned cannot be used to offset that expenditure but must be paid in full into the central fund.

3 *Annuality.* All spending is authorized (voted) on an annual basis, and unspent balances at the end of the year are returned to the central fund.

4 *Specification.* Spending is authorized (voted) for specific purposes and virement (see p. 37) must be approved by Parliament.

Devolved management has meant the relaxation of these techniques, to a greater or lesser degree depending on the context. But the devolution has taken place within a regime of *cash limits*, which now covers all government budgeting in the UK (Thain and Wright, 1989 and 1990). In essence, cash limits relate to the treatment of price change. All line-items in a budget are price × quantity, where the quantity is a quantity of inputs: government budgets are traditionally statements of what the government intends to buy with the money it raises. One important question that is especially important in the negotiated, static budgets of government is this: What happens between the setting of a budget (one, two, three years in advance of spending) and the spending of the budget, if prices change in the meantime? When double-digit inflation emerged in the early 1970s, the response was 'volume budgeting'. This meant that when a budget was fixed there was an implicit (sometimes explicit) level of quantity in each line-item. The logical consequence was that when prices changed between the setting and spending of the budget, by more than was allowed in the original budget, the budget had to change to maintain the implicit quantity to be bought. This indexation should, in theory, have related to changes in specific prices (rather than in general prices) since it is specific prices that budget-holders have to pay. But in practice, and not least because of the size of governments, volume budgeting tended to become general price level indexation: the institutionalization of inflation. If for no other reason, this meant that the principle behind volume budgeting was obscured because, in the absence of synchronized inflation (all specific prices increasing by the same percentage), the quantities agreed in the original budget were not maintained. We were also in the realms of 'funny money' because, in order to keep the adjustments to the budget under control while prices were changing rapidly, the budgets were anchored in prices of a particular point of time (say, November prices) rather than the prices actually to be paid during the fiscal year. In contrast to volume budgeting, the system of cash limits denies quantity: budgets are set as amounts of cash, with no explicit or implicit quantity of goods or services to be bought. There might be a general price level assumption (often deliberately used by governments to dampen inflationary expectations) but once the budget has been set it is assumed that the budget will not change before it is spent. Some line-items are not cash-limited on the ground that they are 'demand-led' budgets, which usually means that the law other than the budget has established entitlement to government money when certain criteria have to be met (as with unemployment benefit), thus putting budgetary control at the mercy of claimants.

It is always a temptation for accountants to overstate the impact of accounting technique when what really matters is the behaviour of the people involved. However, there can be no doubt that budget-holders throughout the public sector, and in private sector organizations that depend on public money, do now take the system of cash limits for granted. And the most striking effect is the centralization of power and decentralization of responsibility. Because however implausible the general price level assumptions made in the budgetary process are, it is the budget-holder a number of stages removed from the centre of government who has to resolve any contradictions. This effect is further exacerbated by the use of formula-funding, especially using formulas that are deliberately crude and often based on head-counts. Under 'devolved management', the manager then has the responsi-bility to manage and to be accountable against a wide range of financial and non-financial targets.

But however the overall impact is judged, there can be little doubt that the myriad theories and practices which are captured by the phrases 'devolved management' and 'accountable management', and which have been extended to everyone involved in spending public money, have made important changes in the nature of the public sector. They have, not surprisingly therefore, also affected public sector accounting.

PUBLIC SECTOR ACCOUNTING

We know that the practice of accounting, in written form, is ancient, and indeed we think of it as part of human nature (Parker and Yamey, 1994). The accounting discipline, on the other hand, dates from the nineteenth century in the UK. It was, and is, inextricably bound up with what we understand as the accounting profes-sion. The discipline did not begin, and it did not develop, in universities. It undoubt-edly grew from practice (Whittington, 1986), although the causal factors are not well understood.

This accounting profession and the associated accounting discipline, which we now think of as Anglo-American, have grown in influence around the world. Important countries did remain largely immune, most noticeably those in the former Soviet and East European bloc, but since the revolutions of the late 1980s this has already changed. But that is not to say that accounting is without its critics: the past 30 years have witnessed increasing controversy in industry and commerce, and for longer than that economic theorists have produced important criticisms of accounting. More recently, theorists using sociological perspectives have offered radical critiques.

In accounting's great strength lies its main weakness. It is important whenever money, as a medium of exchange and thereby as a source of wealth, is important: people will then pay accountants to make the most of their money. Societies in which money (in this sense) plays a central role will value the accounting discipline; societies in which money does not play this role (such as the former Soviet Union) will not. Moreover, as long as money retains its importance, theoretical critiques of accounting's measurement of income or of the role of accountants in society will easily be answered.

But money as a medium of exchange bestows obvious weaknesses on accounting: the nominal value of money changes between countries; the 'real' value of money changes over time; the interpretation put on the results of money transactions depends on the circumstances in each of the 'markets'. Put another way, at its core, accounting is specific to time and place: its numbers cannot be used to compare organizations over time nor to compare organizations through space. In the core practice of accounting, accountants are paid to offer a view of an organization at a particular time. Accountants are urged to try to be consistent over time and to produce comparable numbers through space but the reason they are so urged is that, while consistency and comparability are desirable from other perspectives, they do not come naturally to accounting.

One consequence is that, while we may legitimately continue an older debate about whether accounting is an art or a science, we must recognize that accounting, by its nature, cannot be used to generalize: its numbers relate to specific cases.

None of this is to say that accounting cannot become something different. Since it is not independent of each of us, we can make it what we want it to be. Indeed, there has been dramatic growth in some parts of the accounting profession in recent years as accountants have successfully competed with management consultants for consultancy work. This appears, among other influences, to be broadening our views of what the boundaries of the profession of accounting are, but it does not change, or at least has not yet changed, the nature of the core of the discipline. Moreover, academics have increasingly called on accountants to measure and report on many more phenomena (Owen, 1992; Gray, 1993; Hopwood and Miller, 1994).

Since accounting has been so closely linked with money, it is not surprising that accountants have been found in all kinds of organizations. A seminal feature of the profession in the UK has been the competition among accountants. The Institute of Chartered Accountants (in England and Wales) was founded in 1880; and The Corporate Treasurers and Accountants Institute in 1885. The latter ostensibly represented accountants in local government, although *de facto* it represented accountants in the powerful municipal corporations, and is the origin of today's Chartered Institute of Public Finance and Accountancy (Sowerby, 1985). Moreover, out of this branch of the profession came the sub-discipline of public sector accounting.

The municipal corporations, at the end of the nineteenth century, provided an enormous range of services to their inhabitants, to such an extent that they were 'accused' of being municipal socialists (Jones, 1992b). These services were what we would consider to be the bulk of the public sector, beyond national defence (and war). Local government accounting, at least in these municipalities, was 'public sector accounting'. But as services were lost by local government, especially to the nationalized industries and the national health service in the middle of the twentieth century, this branch of the accounting discipline tended to divide. The first charter (dated 1926) of the seminal 'nationalized industry', the British Broadcasting Corporation, required an audit by chartered accountants appointed by the government; and subsequently, the government has exercised its power to appoint the auditors of nationalized industries by appointing chartered accountants. And, however much the gas industry may have had in common with local government, there were surely enough differences to make the link between them in syllabuses and examination papers, if nowhere else, increasingly uneasy.

Following the failure of integration of the accounting profession in the early 1970s, the Institute of Municipal Treasurers and Accountants was transformed into the Chartered Institute of Public Finance and Accountancy, and it began to use the phrase 'the public sector' in preference to 'the public services' as part of the body's new objective of representing all professional accountants outside the private sector. Accounting and auditing in the public sector became part of its syllabus (though it has since been taken out).

The main point to be made from this overview is that the creation of the sub-discipline of public sector accounting followed, first, from the ways in which we then thought about our economy (and society), and secondly, and more immediately, from the changed objectives of a professional accounting body. It was, and still is, possible that such impulses would not lead to a sub-discipline of accounting, not least because, as we discussed earlier, the 'public sector' is very heterogeneous. But this criticism would strike at the heart of the accounting discipline, since the 'private sector' is also heterogeneous (incorporated/unincorporated, public/private companies, service/manufacturing, very large/very small, businesses/charities).

Our proposition is that there is enough commonality in the accounting problems of public bodies for these to be worth discussing separately from business accounting, the techniques of which are of most use in the context of physically identifiable units of output for sale to customers. These techniques include cost-volume-profit analysis, standard costing, profit and loss, return on capital employed. And while these can be, and are, used in the public sector, it is when 'units of output' are not identifiable that public sector accounting comes into its own.

To focus our attention on this circumstance, we now turn to a discussion of three fundamental concepts: economy, efficiency and effectiveness.

ECONOMY, EFFICIENCY AND EFFECTIVENESS

Efficiency

This is the most important and all-embracing of the three. It is measured by the ratio:

$$\frac{\text{OUTPUT}}{\text{INPUT}}$$

The greater the ratio, the more output for input, the more efficient the organization. The ratio is not used in an absolute sense but in a relative sense: Unit A is more efficient than Unit B; or Unit A is more efficient this year than last year. Also, because efficiency is measured by a ratio, it can be improved in four ways:

1   by increasing output for the same input;
2   by increasing output by a greater proportion than the proportionate increase in input;
3   by decreasing input for the same output;
4   by decreasing input by a greater proportion than the proportionate decrease in output.

The denominator, namely input, is often measured in units of currency. The numerator, namely output, can be measured in either monetary amounts or physical units when considering public sector organizations. (*Note*: the efficiency ratio is sometimes expressed as input/output, which would be interpreted as, for example, cost per unit of output.)

Effectiveness

This refers to the success or otherwise in achieving objectives. Therefore, it is concerned only with outputs. So, if an organization has the objective of building a 250-bed hospital with four operating units, an accident and emergency department, and an out-patients department, and it subsequently builds such a hospital, then it has achieved its objective and it has been effective. If the hospital is built and fire regulations limit the number of beds to 150, then the organization will of course have been less effective. In practice, the objectives would be specified in more detail so that the measure of effectiveness is more useful. For example, the dimensions of the wards and other facilities would be specified. But however detailed the specifications are, there will always be capacity for interpretation; as with efficiency, effectiveness is rarely an absolute measure. The most important thing to note, however, is that the degree of effectiveness says nothing about how much was spent to achieve it: the hospital may have cost what was budgeted, or twice what was budgeted, or three times what it should have cost, or whatever. Effectiveness is about outputs.

Economy

Where effectiveness concerns only outputs, economy concerns only inputs. Extending the above example, the question would be, did the organization exercise due economy in building the hospital? This means, did the hospital cost more than it needed to?

Economy is also a relative measure and, in practice, questions of economy will become:

1   Did the hospital cost more than the organization said it would cost?
2   Did the hospital cost more than comparable hospitals?

The three Es are clearly related. Economy is about inputs; efficiency is about inputs and outputs; effectiveness is about outputs. Economy is of limited use on its own: it is not much use to know that something was as cheap as possible if it does not satisfy the organization's objectives. This is why, for example, the local authority which appears at the bottom of a league table of education costs is not necessarily the best: it may be that it is providing substandard facilities. Similarly, effectiveness is of limited use on its own; knowing that the organization achieved its objectives, without knowing how much the achievement had cost is of little value since most objectives can be achieved with unlimited resources; the praiseworthy achievement is to satisfy the objectives at the minimum cost.

In contrast, efficiency does capture both inputs and outputs, and does therefore stand on its own. If an organization was efficient it means that it achieved its objectives at a satisfactory cost. Why then do we need the complications of economy and effectiveness? In theory there is no need: efficiency captures all that is required. It is this that underpins the belief in the private sector that a measure of efficiency provides the basis for performance evaluation – the amount by which output exceeds inputs is called *profit*. Whatever limitations this has as a performance measure in the private sector there are two additional and fundamental difficulties in applying it to the public sector:

1   When outputs are measured in money terms the quality of the ratio depends upon the quality of the output measures in capturing consumer preferences. Market failure is a typical problem facing public sector service provision.
2   When outputs are not capable of being measured in monetary terms, then it is necessary to resort to efficiency ratios in which outputs are measured in physical units. The basic problem with this is that the ratio can no longer be a universal standard because the physical output measure is only a surrogate for the ultimate output.

The classic case of the first of these difficulties is that of a public sector organization occupying an effective monopoly position and supplying a service for which there is no immediate alternative. The monopolist supplier can improve the efficiency ratio by increasing charges so that any operating inefficiencies are passed on to consumers, who would have no choice but to pay the higher prices. Even though checks and safeguards in the form of governmental and consumer pressure groups may exist as an attempt to prevent this happening, the output measures can never be market determined in the same sense as in the private sector.

However, the second of these difficulties is even more significant. Non-monetary outputs are hierarchical. There are high-level outputs which reflect the extent to which an activity is successful in meeting some fundamental objective. There are subordinate outputs, often referred to as 'intermediate' outputs, which measure the level of the activity. In the example of building the hospital the output was defined as 'the hospital'. But hospitals are not built for the sake of building them. There are higher-level objectives which we are trying to achieve. Ultimately, the objective is to improve the health of the population. The building of the hospital might have been efficient in the sense that it has been produced to specifications and for the least cost. But if the hospital is not wanted, then it will have no effect on the health of the population and this sense of efficiency is of no use.

In order to resolve the problem, we could specify that the measure of output in the efficiency ratio must be the highest level of output, reflecting the ultimate objective. But this would be impractical, not least because ultimate objectives are very difficult, if not impossible, to measure. In fact, this problem of measurement applies to objectives which are often of a much lower order than 'improving the health of the population'. It is because of this that outputs for efficiency measures are often of a very low order indeed so that, although the conclusion might be that the activity is 'efficient', it is only that it achieves a very limited objective cheaply. Therefore in making meaningful judgements about wider issues we need to test the activity's effectiveness as well (i.e. its effectiveness in terms of the higher-order objective).

A further disadvantage of using intermediate outputs in efficiency ratios is that they can only be used comparatively, and even then they can only be used when comparing like goods and services. Take the following example. A secondary school cost £925,000 to run in the financial year. It educated 500 pupils and this was used as the measure of output. The cost per pupil, a measure of efficiency, is £1,850.

There is no sense in which this single statistic can be used to measure absolute performance. It cannot in itself be considered good or bad. It must be used comparatively: how much better or how much worse is the performance? But even so the comparison must be with another secondary school. We could not compare the cost per pupil in this school with the cost per pupil in a primary school from the same authority to judge which performed better. The output of the two is not the same. It is measured in both cases by 'pupils' but they are different kinds of pupils, requiring different teaching, using different methods and expecting different results. All that could be said about a difference in cost per pupil is that the difference exists and is a result of the different costs incurred in educating the pupils of these two schools. Which, of course, is saying little.

Therefore, the cost per pupil for the secondary school needs to be compared with cost per pupil in other secondary schools, although even here with great caution. And what would such a comparison yield? Let us say that a comparable secondary school had a cost per pupil of £2,100. The implication of the measure of efficiency is that the first school is more efficient. But this ignores important considerations about the objectives of schools. Cost per pupil ratios can be improved by putting more children into the same number of classes. Or by using the same number of staff to teach more classes. Or by teaching the same number of pupils with less members of staff; or less equipment and materials; or less facilities. Or by using less-experienced and therefore less-expensive teachers. In other words, by providing a lower quality of service. In these cases, the question to ask is whether the improved efficiency ratio has produced a more efficient school. The strict answer is that we do not know. If we did, then efficiency could be measured; it is because in these circumstances it cannot that we must resort to artificial and potentially misleading proxies.

The necessary condition that like is compared with like, before anything meaningful can be concluded, means that these measures of efficiency cannot be used to make judgements about different sectors within an organization. For accountability this can often be one of the most important aspects of performance because it affects how resources are distributed within. Unfortunately, a cost per pupil cannot be sensibly compared with a cost per kilometre of road.

One way of putting the three issues of economy, efficiency and effectiveness into perspective is to consider how they may be used together. Take the following example: an organization has experimented with three different ways of providing some kind of restaurant facilities for its 100 employees. Its explicit objective is to encourage employees to take their meals on the premises. Initially it was willing to subsidize them to the extent of £20 per day. The output from each is measured in meals provided and the input is measured in terms of the cost of subsidies. These are the relevant figures:

1   Snack bar service:
     Output – 50 meals per day
     Input – £40 per day

2   Contracting-out of restaurant service:
     Output – 100 meals per day
     Input – £60 per day

3   Restaurant operated by the organization:
     Output – 100 meals per day
     Input – £80 per day

Because the organization budgeted for a subsidy of £20 per day, it is attracted to the most economical because it costs only £40 per day. However, it is not the most effective because it does not provide 100 meals; the restaurant services are more effective. But which is most efficient? In terms of the efficiency ratio, the snack bar is 50/40, the contracted-out restaurant 100/60, and the in-house provision 100/80. Thus, using these definitions, the contracted-out restaurant service is the most efficient.

The problem is that the measure of output adopted is a low-level measure: the ultimate output is likely to be 'securing a happy work-force'. And it may be that, although the same number of meals is served in both restaurant services, the employees are much happier with the in-house provision. For example, they might get their meals quicker because there are more staff or they might get a better choice or the meals might be of better quality or whatever. If we could measure this employee contentment, we could measure the 'output' from each of the three modes of provision, compare them with the respective costs, and discover which was really most efficient. In this example, we could see whether the additional employee contentment was enough to outweigh the extra cost and we would not need to resort to the concepts of economy and effectiveness. If the in-house restaurant did prove to be the most efficient, the subsidy would still be higher than was budgeted; it would then be the organization's responsibility to decide whether the greater efficiency was worth paying extra for. However, because employee contentment is difficult to measure, we would in practice have to use the three measures of economy, efficiency, and effectiveness available to us: by balancing the cost against budget, the achievement against the objective (number of meals) and the relative low-level efficiencies.

But the most important thing to realize is that having accepted the second best approach, it would be very dangerous to take any one of these measures on its own or to promote any one of them to primacy: if that was done, the correct decision would only be taken as a matter of luck. In our example, if we assume that the in-house provision is the most efficient in terms of contentment/subsidy, then taking either economy or efficiency (measured in meals/subsidy) as the primary measure will produce an incorrect decision. If effectiveness is used as the primary measure, there is a 50 per cent chance that the wrong decision will be taken. Indeed, if effectiveness was linked with economy, the decision would be incorrect. The three concepts are important analytical tools but they must be used in conjunction with each other, and with caution and common sense.

The phrase 'value for money' is used to refer to economy, efficiency, and effectiveness. Strictly speaking, it relates output (value) to input (money) and is therefore another way of saying 'efficiency'. As was noted above, if outputs could be measured at their highest level, then value for money would capture all that is required. However, outputs can often only be measured at lower levels, and where the gap between the highest level and the lower – but measurable – levels is large, then the lower levels are of limited use in assessing whether value for money has been achieved. At the extreme, value for money is obtained if the organization incurs the least cost to achieve the maximum output in attaining its objectives.

However, what must be added is that, as the phrase was developed and the consequent use of measurement expanded, it became clear (if it had not already been) that in using quantitative targets in the search for value for money, qualitative factors were being treated as a residual. Some would say that this was one of the purposes of value for money initiatives; others would say that the purpose was to squeeze 'inefficiency' out, while maintaining or improving quality. But whatever one's views might be of the accompanying motives, the focus on measurement does tend to be at the expense of quality. Accountants know as well as, if not better than, most that the measured objective takes precedence over the unmeasured.

The response was at once obvious and yet paradoxical: the 'industry' of quality assurance in manufacturing was progressively applied to public services. Every kind of 'quality' initiative has been experimented with, including adoption of the ISA 9000 and its associated standards. The paradox is that it was the massive extension of the use of the quantitative, precisely to reduce the importance of qualitative judgements, that has led to the drive for quality. In other words, quality is still being treated as a residual; it is just that there tend to be formal mechanisms for so treating it.

DISCUSSION TOPICS

1   Discuss the extent to which the environment of public sector accounting is different from the environment of private sector accounting.

2   'In profit-oriented organizations the amount of profit provides a ready-made measure of performance. In many public sector organizations, however, the absence of suitable output measurements makes performance evaluation much more difficult.' Discuss.

3   'Intermediate output measurements are widely used as efficiency indicators but they must be interpreted with care.' Describe what is meant by 'intermediate output measurements' and discuss their limitations.

PART 1

Management accounting

CHAPTER 2

Management accounting and control

All organizations, whether they operate in the private or the public sector, exist in order to achieve one or more objectives. While the exact nature of the objectives may vary considerably, as may the manner in which they are pursued, there is one feature that seldom varies – the resources available are never sufficient to permit the achievement of every desired aim.

It is against this background of limited human resources, or capital, or plant facilities, or raw materials, etc. that objectives as diverse as profit maximization or the provision of housing for homeless families have to be determined. Thus it is not sufficient merely to decide on objectives but it is also necessary to make plans for their achievement. Decisions need to be taken on which strategies to pursue and which to reject, which activities to undertake immediately and which to delay until later, which activities to modify or abandon, and which to reinforce. This is the *planning* process. Just as all organizations have objectives, so all organizations make plans. However, simply planning what, how and when things should be done is not the same as actually doing them. The plans have to be implemented, and systems are needed to ensure that the planned activities are followed and the ultimate objectives achieved. This is the *control* process.

These processes of planning and control are two of the most important tasks undertaken by the managers of an organization and together they form the nucleus of the overall management system. In order to carry out these tasks, managers require information. It is with the provision of such information that *management accounting* is primarily concerned. Management accounting has been defined by the Chartered Institute of Management Accountants (1994, p. 13) as:

> An integral part of management concerned with identifying, presenting and interpreting information used for:
> (a) formulating strategy;
> (b) planning and controlling activities;
> (c) decision taking;
> (d) optimizing the use of resources;
> (e) disclosure to shareholders and others external to the entity;
> (f) disclosure to employees;
> (g) safeguarding assets.

It can be seen from this definition that an important role of management accounting is to present accounting information that is aimed directly at the key elements of the overall management system, i.e. planning, decision making and control.

Accounting information is not limited to financial information only but also incorporates information about manpower levels and usage, output statistics, activity levels, and so on.

If limited resources are to be put to their best use, effective systems of management and management accounting are an essential requirement of any organization. Most of the descriptions of management systems and management accounting tend to assume a business environment, and whilst there are many similarities between private and public sector organizations the special characteristics of the latter do result in some important differences.

The purpose of this chapter is to describe first of all the principal stages of the planning and control processes of public sector organizations, and then to consider the role that management accounting plays in these processes.

PLANNING AND CONTROL

It is necessary at this point to try to distinguish between two types of planning activity. In the first place, there is the type of planning that is essential for the setting of the overall objectives of the organization. This is planning for fundamental aims and objectives. Secondly, there is the type of planning that is essential for implementing the actions needed to achieve the fundamental aims and objectives. This is operational planning. Although these two types of planning are so closely related that at times it is almost impossible to make a precise distinction between them, it is with the latter type that this chapter is primarily concerned. This is because operational planning is part of the regular managerial planning and control cycle with which managers are closely involved, and for which they are clearly responsible. The extent to which managers of public sector organizations are involved in planning for fundamental aims and objectives is somewhat more obscure.

The principal stages of planning and control are as follows:

1   planning of fundamental aims and objectives;
2   operational planning;
3   budgeting;
4   controlling and measuring;
5   reporting, analysing and feedback.

Stages 2 to 5 form the managerial planning and control cycle. The cyclical nature of these stages and their overall relationship with the planning of fundamental aims and objectives are clearly demonstrated in Fig. 2.1.

Fundamental aims and objectives

The starting point for the process of management consists of setting the overall aims and objectives. The precise way in which these are determined depends very much on the nature of the organization. For a typical private sector organization the folklore of economic theory has led to profit maximization or shareholder wealth maximization being frequently suggested as the fundamental objectives to be pursued. In reality the actual objectives are usually much less well defined and the means by which they evolve are quite complex. Nevertheless, whatever the objectives might be they

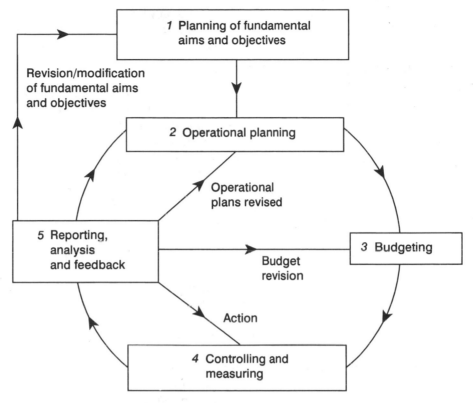

Fig. 2.1   The managerial planning and control processes of public sector organizations.
Source: Adapted from R.N. Anthony and D.W. Young, *Management Control in Nonprofit Organizations*, 5th edn, Irwin, 1994, p. 19. © Richard D. Irwin, Inc. 1975, 1980, 1984, 1988 and 1994.

are essentially determined by management, even though the influence of other groups may be quite significant. However, as we saw in Chapter 1, the responsibility for setting the fundamental objectives of public sector organizations is much more confused. Statutory requirements, central government intervention, and national and local political and domestic processes all have their part to play. Although the managers of a public sector body may at times be closely involved in the initial setting or subsequent modification of the fundamental objectives, it is primarily a political process with ultimate responsibility resting outside the hands of management. Therefore, in Fig. 2.1 the planning of fundamental aims and objectives is shown as being external to the main planning and management control cycle.

Fundamental objectives are often set in fairly broad terms. For example, the objectives of the Forestry Commission are stated in the 1991 Departmental Report of the Ministry of Agriculture, Fisheries and Food (Cm 1503) to be as follows:

To promote the interests of forestry, the establishment and maintenance of adequate reserves of growing trees, the production and supply of timber, the provision of opportunities for recreation, and the development of the potential of forests as a habitat for wildlife.

These are rather broad aims and only by introducing much more detailed managerial plans and controls will it be possible to ensure their achievement.

The management planning and control cycle

Within the context of the imposed, and often broadly stated, fundamental aims and objectives it is necessary first to plan the strategies and techniques required for their implementation. This is the *operational planning* stage. The purpose of operational plans is to break the fundamental objectives down into a series of targets to be aimed for and activities to be pursued. Continuing with the previous example of forestry, operational planning will involve forecasting for several years ahead the future demand for timber and then planning for the forestry development needed to meet this demand. Planning will also be necessary to ensure that all the alternative ways of meeting the objectives are considered; that priorities and time scales are established; and that the capital investment requirements and future annual running costs are known well in advance. Operational plans frequently cover time periods ranging from the immediate future to as many as ten or 20 years ahead and may be expressed in financial or non-financial terms. Thus the operational plans set out the framework within which the organization will operate in order to achieve its fundamental objectives. It is within this framework that the short-term activities that need to be pursued can be identified and expressed in financial terms. This is the *budgeting* stage.

The importance of the budget in public sector organizations stems originally from its use in determining taxation levels or the amounts to be charged for services. Indeed, this basic purpose of the budget can be seen clearly in the way the Budget of the British government is generally thought of as referring to the fiscal policy decisions proposed by the Chancellor of the Exchequer and announced to Parliament on Budget Day. The original meaning of the word budget derives from this British government context, coined from the French word '*bougette*', meaning a small purse (Chan and Jones, 1988).

Whilst the determination of levels of taxation and charges is still an important function, the budget has a much more crucial role to play in the planning and management control cycle. This is because the budget provides the essential link between planning and control. Its planning role is achieved by expressing in monetary terms the inputs needed to achieve the planned activities of the budget period. Many of the inputs will take the form of labour, materials, equipment, heating and lighting, and so on, and the only sensible way that these can be compared or combined is by referring to them in terms of a common denominator, i.e. monetary value. Its control role is achieved by preparing the budget in such a way that it shows clearly the inputs and resources that have been allocated to individuals or to departments to permit them to undertake the tasks for which they are responsible. In other words, the responsibility for fulfilling a task such as providing care for the elderly by a local authority will be reflected by an amount in the budget.

As was pointed out in Chapter 1, public sector organizations are frequently faced with a lack of suitable output measurements and therefore inputs consumed are often used as a measure of effectiveness. Thus the expenditure allocated in the budget for care of the elderly is crucially important because not only does it place a limit on the costs that can be incurred on this service but also the costs themselves reflect the planned level of service. Control can then be exercised by comparing budgeted results with actual results to ensure that expenditure levels are not exceeded and that planned activity levels are achieved. This is the *control and measurement* stage. Measurement consists of recording the expenses actually incurred, and where possible the outputs achieved, and control involves detecting departures from the budgeted position and taking action to correct the deviation. This of course means that the individuals or departments responsible for the budget have to be notified of the deviations as they occur and this is the feedback function of the *reporting, analysing and feedback* stage.

Variances between budget and actual represent a divergence from what was planned to happen, and unless the reasons for the variances are analysed and steps taken to bring the budget and the actual back into line, the whole system will rapidly become out of control. Thus relevant, accurate and timely reports of actual and budgeted positions need to be provided to all levels of management to enable performance to be monitored against the budget. The reasons for variances may be within the control of individuals or departments responsible for the budget, i.e. they may be due to inefficiency or bad management and corrective action can be taken, or they may be due to unexpected changes in the level of service required, or to unexpected changes in the costs of inputs. If these are the reasons, the budget will need to be reviewed and adjusted, and the operational plans may also need revising. Thus the planning and management control cycle can be seen to be a continuous process, as illustrated in Fig. 2.1, with each stage in the cycle affecting or being affected by each of the other stages.

THE ROLE OF MANAGEMENT ACCOUNTING

The basic role of management accounting in public sector organizations is to provide managers with the accounting information they need to carry out the planning and control functions. The information requirement will, of course, depend to some extent on the nature of the organization. It was pointed out in Chapter 1 that the expression 'public sector' can include organizations ranging from those that are quite definitely 'commercial' in outlook to those for whom 'commercial' characteristics would be unthinkable. Public sector organizations may be involved in activities such as catering, construction, retailing, mining, transportation, and so on, where outputs are clearly measurable and costs can be recovered from consumers. Whether the recovered costs should be full costs, market costs, or subsidized costs depends on political attitudes. Nevertheless, costs have to be determined, and the management accounting system must be structured accordingly.

In connection with this the whole kitbag of management accounting tools found in private sector organizations is equally applicable to the public sector. Thus costing practices such as activity-based costing, job costing, batch costing, and product, joint product, and by-product costing may be used. Similarly, marginal costing and standard costing techniques have important roles to play in decision making and control. However, as the basic principles underlying the various techniques are essentially the same for both private and public sector organizations, and as the principles are adequately described in numerous management accounting textbooks, they will not be discussed further here.

Attention is instead turned to the role of management accounting in terms of activities that are more characteristic of public sector organizations, i.e. services for which the outputs are not normally measurable, and for which the costs are, for the most part, recovered by levying a tax on the whole community rather than by charging individual users. It is here that the managerial planning and control cycle is particularly important. This is because a large part of the costs of private sector organizations tend to be engineered costs which vary directly with output, whereas the costs of most public sector organizations are discretionary costs which are fixed at the beginning of the budget period and often have no obvious relationship with level of activity. For example, the costs of the fire service of a local authority will tend to vary only slightly even though the use of the service may be extensive or minimal. Secondly, the planned level of activity of private sector organizations can vary quite dramatically over time as variations in demand are responded to. The ability to react quickly to changes in market forces is an essential requirement for such organizations and so plans and budgets are rather tentative documents. For many public sector organizations the level of activity is usually more predictable. For example, the number of university students enrolled at the beginning of the academic year is unlikely to vary much throughout the year. Moreover, the level of taxation or charges for the services of public sector organizations is often fixed for a twelve-month budget period, and therefore the planned level of activity and associated costs have to be estimated quite accurately and deviations from estimates detected quickly. Local authority taxes, for example, are not normally revised during the budget year. Private sector organizations can alter their charges almost daily if need be.

An effective managerial planning and control system is therefore an essential requirement of public sector organizations. Management accounting has a crucial part to play in providing the information needed to operate such a system. Information is needed at the planning stage to decide which activities to undertake and the resources that will be required. Information is needed at the control stage to measure how effective the organization was in achieving its objective and how efficient it was in the use of resources.

The role that management accounting has to play in the provision of such information is considered in the following sections.

MANAGEMENT ACCOUNTING AND PLANNING

The fundamental aims and objectives of public sector organizations are usually of a long-term nature. The provision of passenger transport or health care or public protection are not required for just this year or next year, but for every year into the future. Moreover, the fundamental aims and objectives often involve bringing about changes in the quality of a particular service by some future date. Even if quality is to remain constant over time, it is unlikely that demand will. Also, changes in technology will introduce new means of satisfying demand. All of this means that operational plans need to be concerned not just with the immediate future but also with the longer term. The lead time needed to adjust for changes in the demand for a service, or the quality of a service, may often be quite long. The planning, designing and building of motorways or nuclear power generating plants are obvious examples of this. Even the building of a new school or health service clinic requires time for design, land acquisition, planning permission, and so on.

It is, of course, notoriously difficult to plan very far into the future and the longer the planning period involved, the more tentative the plans become. It is helpful, therefore, to distinguish between different planning time scales in some way, and the following categories are frequently adopted:

1 long-term planning – usually five years or more ahead;
2 medium-term planning – usually one to five years ahead;
3 short-term planning – up to one year ahead.

Investment appraisal

A key requirement in terms of meeting future demand, whether it be one year, five years, or 20 years from now, is to ensure that the right capital assets will be available. Even if there is no expected change in the level of demand or quality of service, assets will be required, either now or in the future. The cost of investing in new assets is, of course, not only the capital cost of the asset itself, but also the running costs that will be incurred when the asset is brought into use. There will frequently be several alternative possibilities to choose from, and there are a variety of techniques that can be used to calculate and compare the total capital and revenue costs of different proposals and also to evaluate the benefits. This process is known as *investment appraisal*. As far as planning is concerned, particularly long- and medium-term planning, the investment decision is of fundamental importance. The technique of investment appraisal, and the issues surrounding its use, are considered in some detail in Chapter 6.

Financial planning and budgeting

Apart from the investment decision the other aspects of planning with which management accounting is closely involved can be conveniently categorized as follows:

1 financial planning;
2 capital budgeting;
3 revenue budgeting.

The relationship that exists between each of these aspects is very close and at times they merge together in such a way as to be almost indistinguishable. What differences there are tend to be in terms of the planning time scales to which they relate. Thus financial planning is primarily thought of in connection with long- or medium-term planning. Capital budgeting tends to cover medium- and short-term planning. The revenue budget is usually concerned with short-term planning matters, i.e. the current year and the following year, although longer-term revenue budgets covering periods of up to five years ahead are not uncommon.

Financial planning is also intimately related to the process of investment appraisal. This is because a basic purpose of financial planning is to ensure that the financial consequences of fulfilling the fundamental aims and objectives of public sector organizations, and also meeting forecasted demands for services, are considered at the earliest possible stage. It is argued that only by taking into account the estimated costs and benefits of alternative actions can priorities that are consistent with the fundamental aims and objectives be established. For example, population surveys and surveys of demographic trends may indicate an increase in the need for primary and secondary education places over the next ten or 15 years in a particular local authority area. A sound system of long-term financial planning would ensure that the financial implications of the increased demand are assessed now. The consideration of costs and benefits may result in the demand not being fulfilled, for example, heart transplant operations, or being controlled by pricing policy, e.g. public transport charges.

At the heart of public sector financial planning in the UK are the government's public expenditure publications and in recent years these have been subject to several changes. Until 1990 the government produced in January of each year an annual Public Expenditure White Paper, which contained details of the projections for public spending for three years ahead. From 1991 much of the key aggregate information in the White Paper was provided in the November Autumn Statement, with detailed information on the spending plans of individual departments presented in separate Departmental Reports which were published in early February each year. This meant that expenditure proposals were presented to Parliament in November, with the taxation proposals needed to finance the expenditure being presented in the following March, on Budget Day. This separation of tax and spending announcements by the UK government had often been criticized for failing to bring together for public debate and scrutiny the closely related issues of public expenditure, tax and borrowing, and in his 1992 Budget Speech the Chancellor of the Exchequer announced that a 'unified budget' would operate from December 1993 onwards. The Autumn Statement and the March Budget have now been combined into an Autumn Budget presented in late November or early December, which contains tax proposals for the year ahead and spending plans for three years ahead. Further details of the spending plans will continue to be provided in the annual Departmental Reports, which are now published in late February, just before the beginning, on 1 April, of the first of the three financial years covered by the plans.

Although the form of presentation has changed, the underlying financial planning process involved and the information provided are very similar. The process starts in the spring of each year with government departments estimating their spending requirements and submitting bids to the Treasury. The bids are checked and analysed by the Treasury and then submitted to the Cabinet in July. The Cabinet then decides on an overall total for public expenditure, and negotiations take place between the Treasury and the individual departments to ensure that their spending requirements are consistent with this overall total. After agreement this then leads to the Autumn Budget Statement, containing proposals for spending for the next three years, with further publication of more detailed information for each department in the Departmental Reports. The annual survey of public spending affects the whole of the public sector. It is concerned with the planned expenditure of central government departments and local government, and the external financing requirements of nationalized industries.

The annual Departmental Reports provide a vast amount of information on public expenditure. Details are given of spending over a nine-year period, i.e. the actual for the past five years, the estimate for the current year and the estimates for the next three years. Expenditure is analysed by the major programmes of each department, by type of spending authority and by economic category. The Departmental Reports also provide information on the aims and objectives of each service and give some examples of performance targets and output measures.

Because the impact of the survey of public spending is felt throughout the whole of the public sector, it is clearly important for each individual public sector organization to undertake its own medium-term financial planning exercise – if only to ensure that this fits in with the spending plans of the government. It is also likely that some of the information needed by government departments when putting together their spending requirements will have to be obtained from other public sector organizations in the first place. Thus, for example, the Department of Transport includes within its Departmental Report details of the expenditure by local authorities on road maintenance, car parks, concessionary fares, support for rail and bus services, etc., which means that individual local authorities are required to provide details of their estimated revenue and capital expenditure on these activities for at least the three years covered by the Departmental Report.

Capital budgets contain details of the estimated receipts from the sale of assets, such as council houses, and the estimated payments for the acquisition of new assets. The payments normally exceed the receipts and the difference is the amount that has to be found, either by borrowing or from a surplus on revenue account. Capital budgets can be prepared for just one year, but as many of the assets of public sector organizations require long periods of construction, several years may elapse from initial design to completion. Thus the advantage of preparing capital budgets for at least the medium-term planning period is obvious. One important requirement for preparing capital budgets is a schedule of capital works showing the various stages of completion of the individual capital projects and the amount that is expected to be completed, and therefore paid for, in each of the next five years. Capital budgets are considered in more detail in Chapter 3.

The items included in the capital budget are therefore the planned capital asset acquisitions and disposals for the medium-term planning period. The long-term and medium-term financial plans will have provided information on the assets that need replacing and the assets required for new activities, and these are expressed in financial terms. By providing details of the amount and timing of capital receipts and payments, consideration can be given at an early stage to the best ways of providing the necessary finance. Obviously, if it is the intention to finance by contribution from revenue account surpluses then the medium-term financial plan will have to incorporate the need to budget for a surplus in the appropriate year. If loans are to be raised then this will incur loan repayment and interest charges in subsequent years and these, together with the running costs of new schools, hospitals, nuclear power stations, etc. will have to be included in the medium-term financial plans. The link between capital budgeting and medium-term financial planning is therefore very close, and between them they also provide the basis for preparing the annual revenue budget.

The annual revenue budget covers the first year of the medium-term financial plan and is one of the most important planning documents in all public sector organizations. Medium- and long-term planning are rather tentative attempts at planning, but the annual budget is a firm short-term plan of action. It is the annual budget that determines that part of the fundamental aims and objectives which will be achieved in the budget year. It is the annual budget that determines the tax levy or level of charges for services. It is the annual budget that provides a standard against which performance can be evaluated. It is the annual budget that provides the crucial link between planning and control.

A useful illustration of the relationship between medium-term financial plans and the annual budget can be obtained by examining once again the survey of public spending outlined above to see how this links in to the annual supply estimates of the government. The annual Departmental Reports are published in February and contain details of a department's planned expenditure for three years ahead as announced in the Autumn Budget. Most, but not all, of the public expenditure will be expenditure by central government and the detailed estimates for the first of the three years, commencing on the 1 April, will be contained in the Supply Estimates published in March. The basis adopted in the Departmental Reports for analysing expenditure by the major programmes is followed very closely by the analysis adopted in the supply estimates to facilitate comparison between the two. Such a comparison is seen as essential because of the need to ensure that supply estimates are consistent with the framework and ceiling created by the survey of public spending.

Because of the importance of the budget in planning and control, much attention has been focused on the way it is prepared. At one extreme the budget could be prepared by analysing the nature of the income or expenditure, such as wages or materials or running costs (known in local authorities as a 'subjective' analysis). At the other extreme the budget will be analysed in terms of the *objectives* of the service. For example, for the police service of a local authority the budget could be broken down into police salaries, vehicle costs, premises costs, heating, lighting, and so on. Alternatively, an objective of the police service, such as 'counteracting criminal activities' could be identified and this could be broken down into a series of 'programmes', such as crime prevention, crime detection, apprehending criminals, trial, custody, and so on. If these programmes and objectives form the basis of budget preparation a system of planned programmed budgeting is said to exist.

In practice, budget preparation tends to be a combination of analysis by objective and analysis by nature of the expense. This approach to budgeting is discussed in Chapter 3. Chapter 4 considers the issues and controversies surrounding the less widely used but more conceptually sound planning, programming and budgeting approach. In Chapter 5 attention is turned to a system of budget preparation known as 'zero base' budgeting. This system effectively requires that all activities, even those that are going to operate more or less the same as in previous years, have to be justified from a zero base.

Financial modelling

There is obviously inherent uncertainty in any planning activity. Planning involves the future and the future is uncertain. Whether the planning period is the short-term annual budget or the long-term financial plan, there will be many variables that can affect the plan and many of these will be interrelated. For example, when plans for the housing service of a local authority are considered, variables such as population movements, housing construction costs, council house sales, private sector housing provision, slum clearance programmes, rent levels, interest rates, and so on are going to affect the service. One way in which management accounting can help in assessing the effect of each of these variables is through the use of financial models. The purpose of any model is to enable some representation of a real-life situation to be examined and experimented with. Financial modelling involves assigning a numerical value to each variable and then expressing the relationship between the variables in a mathematical form. This information is then incorporated into a computer program. The 'value' attached to each variable is, of course, only an estimate and from time to time the estimate will need revision. The impact of such revisions on the overall activity can be quickly assessed. Also policy decisions can be improved by the use of 'what if' questions. Thus if the values of variables X and Y are revised upwards by 5 per cent but variable Z is revised downwards what will be the effect on the costs of the housing service?

Targets in planning and budgeting

It was pointed out in Chapter 1 how the problem of performance measurement pervades all aspects of the management of public sector organizations. The common yardstick of profit is generally missing. Even for those organizations that have a saleable output the 'quality' of the profit measure depends on how well the price charged captures market preferences. Nevertheless, in spite of its possible imperfections, profit can be used to assess the overall performance of organizations such as nationalized industries, government trading funds, and the direct labour and direct service sections of local authorities. Target rates of return for these activities are either imposed by, or determined by agreement with, the government and the targets are then incorporated into the financial planning and budgeting process. For example, the Royal Mint operates as a trading fund and under the Trading Funds Act 1973, the Minister responsible for this fund (the Chancellor of the Exchequer) agrees with the Treasury on what the Royal Mint's financial objectives are to be. For the three-year period 1 April 1993 to 31 March 1996 the Royal Mint has a financial objective of achieving an average annual rate of return of at least 14 per cent. The annual rate of return for each of the three years is calculated using modified historical cost operating profit as a percentage of the average net assets at modified historical cost.

At the operational level budgets can also incorporate measures which reflect the planned level of activity, such as length of road to be repaired or number of council houses to be painted. Therefore the budget can provide a target of operational efficiency by detailing the inputs deemed necessary to produce the specified output. Even for the less 'commercial' public sector organizations measures that partially reflect outputs could be included in the budget. Examples of such 'intermediate' outputs are frequency of refuse collections, time taken to respond to emergency fire service calls, proportion of crimes that are solved, and so on. These measures attempt to show what a service is doing for its clients rather than the effect it has on them. In other words they measure the level of activity. Activity measures of this type have to be used with care because the measure itself may affect the behaviour of the providers of the service.

Perhaps the most widely used means of relating input costs to the level of service provision is through the use of unit costs. For example, a local authority may calculate the cost per dustbin emptied, or the cost per mile of road cleaned, or the cost of keeping a child in a council home, and so on.

Targets of some form are important in planning and budgeting because rational resource allocation can only be made if there is some specific amount of profit, or quantity of output, or level of activity in mind. Targets are also important in control and performance evaluations and in 'value for money' reviews. All of these will be made easier if there is a planned level of output or activity against which actual achievement can be compared. A key role of management accounting, therefore, is to search for new output and activity level measures, and to refine existing measures.

Unfortunately there are certain services for which not only is the financial output non-measurable, but there are also difficulties in adequately measuring the level of activity. However, even for these services there is presumably some intention that the financial resources allocated in the budget should relate to some specific level of activity. It is generally assumed that the costs incurred are the only way of measuring output. Thus a 5 per cent increase in real terms in the budget allocation indicates a 5 per cent increase in the level of service. The inputs allocated in the budget are the only targets to be met and therefore performance is measured by how closely the budget is achieved. This simple relationship between money spent and level of service provided is, of course, not accepted by everyone. The present government has consistently argued that the route to improved services is through improved efficiency rather than increased spending. This has led to the development of several initiatives aimed at improving efficiency, and a key element of many of these has been the need to set performance targets for all public sector services.

A widely reported example of developments in this area has been the Financial Management Initiative (FMI), which was introduced in 1982 for use in central government departments. The FMI identified the need for each department to produce a system in which managers at all levels have:

(a) a clear view of their objectives, and means to assess, and wherever possible measure, outputs or performance in relation to those objectives;
(b) well defined responsibility for making the best use of their resources, including a critical scrutiny of output and value for money; and
(c) the information (particularly about costs), the training and the access to expert advice which they need to exercise their responsibilities effectively.   (Her Majesty's Government, 1982)

In its original form, therefore, the FMI set much emphasis on the need for clear objectives and output measures so that targets could be set and performance evaluated. Although reports on the implementation of the FMI revealed that some progress was being made, it was clear that this was not uniform across all departments, and a 1988 report by the Efficiency Unit of the Prime Minister's Office (Efficiency Unit, 1988) identified substantial obstacles to further improvement. This report pointed out that even though the vast majority of civil servants are involved in service delivery or executive functions (such as licensing vehicles, paying benefits, issuing passports, collecting taxes, etc.), the top management of many departments is dominated by policy and ministerial support. In addition, it was noted that there was insufficient emphasis on results and improving performance and that the

Civil Service was too big and diverse to be managed as a single entity. The report therefore recommended that the executive functions of government, as distinct from policy advice, should be carried out by clearly identified Executive Agencies which would operate within existing departments. This recommendation, which is generally referred to as the *Next Steps Initiative*, was accepted by the government in February 1988, and by December 1994 a total of 102 Executive Agencies had been established employing over 268,000 civil servants. In addition, HM Customs and Excise has established 30 Executive Units operating on Next Steps lines, and the Inland Revenue has 29 Executive Offices. This meant that by December 1994 over 353,000 civil servants, or 62 per cent of the total, were working on Next Steps lines.

A key feature of the Next Steps Initiative was that strategies, objectives, budgets and targets would be set for each Agency, and then the manager of an Agency should be given as much freedom as possible in its management and in meeting the strategies, objectives, budgets and targets. One consequence of the Next Steps Initiative, therefore, has been to bring about a much more widespread use of targets and performance indicators in many areas of government activity. The key targets that are set for each Agency are published annually and performance against targets is reported in the Agency's annual report and accounts. A Treasury Guide (HM Treasury, 1992) is now available to assist departments in the setting of targets for Agencies and measuring performance against target. A target is defined as 'a quantified objective set by management to be attained at a specified future date'. Using a hypothetical hospital orthopaedic unit as an example, the Guide provides the following illustration of the different types of targets that might be set (HM Treasury, 1992, pp. 34–5):

Output target – The average number of total hip replacement operations per week next year to be 10.5 or more.

Performance target – efficiency – The cost of each operation (unit cost of output) to rise next year by no more than X per cent.

Performance target – quality of service – Waiting time for a first appointment next year to be no more than 2 weeks.

Performance target – financial performance – The hospital to keep within its budget for the forthcoming year.

Pendlebury *et al.* (1994) surveyed the annual reports of 53 of the 59 Executive Agencies that had been established by 31 March 1992. They found that the vast majority of Agencies provided information on performance against targets, with the most widespread types of target and performance indicators being cost-reduction types and procedural-efficiency types. Cost-reduction targets might be to achieve a saving in overall running costs of X per cent (for example, the Information Technology Service Agency's 1992/93 target of achieving an overall saving of 4.5 per cent in running costs), or to achieve reductions in the cost of specific items (for example, HMSO had the target of achieving a reduction in the price paid for paper and stationery).

Procedural efficiency targets generally relate to such things as the speed of response to a request for a particular service, or the time taken to deal with enquiries. Examples include the Patent Office's target of issuing at least 90 per cent of patent search reports within 12 weeks, or Companies House having a target of answering 90 per cent of the 2.25 million telephone calls received each year within 20 seconds.

MANAGEMENT ACCOUNTING AND CONTROL

In Fig. 2.1 the control stages of the management planning and control cycle began with the budget and also included controlling and measuring and reporting, analysing and feedback. These stages are often referred to collectively as *budgetary control*. Budgetary control is concerned with ensuring that actual expenditure is in line with budgeted amounts and that the objectives and levels of activity envisaged in the budget are achieved. A crucial role of management accounting is that of introducing and maintaining a sound system of budgetary control. Closely connected with budgetary control is the question of cost allocation, and an obvious function of management accounting is to devise adequate costing systems. Finally, it is often suggested that the evaluation of managerial performance in public sector organizations could be greatly improved if more services were sold rather than provided at no charge. Although the income received might not always measure accurately the real value of services provided, it might offer an approximate indicator of output. Management accounting can help not only in determining the prices to be charged, but also in putting the issues surrounding charging for services into perspective.

Budgetary control

The first requirement of a good system of budgetary control is to set up accounts for collecting data on inputs and outputs at the lowest distinct level of activity. These accounts are called 'cost centres'. Individual managers will be responsible for one or more of these cost centres and together such cost centres form a *responsibility centre*. The responsibility centres are aggregated to form further responsibility centres at the programme or service level, and an aggregation of such programme or service responsibility centres makes up the individual departments of the organization.

It is the responsibility centres that provide the basis for budgetary control by clearly defining the area of responsibility of individual managers. These individual managers are often referred to as 'budget holders' and are made responsible for achieving their budgets. A responsibility centre receives inputs in the form of labour, materials, etc., and with these inputs is expected to produce output in the form of goods or services. The budget reflects the monetary values of the inputs allocated to each responsibility centre, and, where possible, shows the expected output or level of activity. An example of the use of responsibility centres can be found in the Local Management of Schools (LMS) initiative that has been introduced into the education service. Under the Education Reform Act 1988, every local education authority is required to allocate the bulk of the total budget for schools to each of its secondary and large primary schools. Responsibility for the spending of the budget allocated to a particular school is also required to be delegated to the head and governors of that school. This means that the head and governors of a school will have responsibility for all aspects of managing a school, including appointments and dismissals, and controlling the running of the school within the delegated budget. Budgetary control involves the continuous measuring of actual expenditure and outputs and comparing these with the budgeted position. The differences, or variances, are analysed and the reasons ascertained. Individual managers are then notified so that corrective action can be taken to bring about a correspondence between the actual position and the planned position. The variances may, of course, be due partially or entirely to unforeseen circumstances or to factors outside the control of the individual manager and in these cases the budget should be reconsidered and, where the budget is not cash-limited, adjusted. This is the essence of the control mechanism and in a private sector organization there would be nothing remarkable about a budgetary control system based on the notion of responsibility centres and containing the features outlined above.

For many parts of the public sector such systems are now becoming more evident. In central government, for example, the FMI has led to many line managers now having budget responsibility, and the rapid move to Executive Agencies for much of the activities of government has introduced the need for clear definitions of budget and operational responsibilities. The LMS initiative took effect in April 1990, with a requirement for full implementation by 1993. In higher education, although a 1985 report on the efficiency of universities (Jarratt Report, 1985) noted that budget responsibility was not always clearly defined and that financial information for budget centres was often inadequate, there is now evidence that management accounting in universities has developed significantly since then (see, for example, several of the papers in Berry, 1994).

Given that these developments are occurring, it might be appropriate at this stage to identify the different types of responsibility centre and to consider the essential qualities of a good system of budgetary control. Responsibility centres can be conveniently categorized into expense centres, profit centres, and investment centres.

Expense centres

An expense centre occurs when the expenses of a responsibility centre are measured but not the monetary value of outputs. This is typically the case for public sector organizations where outputs obviously exist but are either not measurable at all, or are measurable in physical but not monetary terms.

Profit centres

If outputs in the form of goods or services are charged for in such a way that the fees are meant to relate to the value of the goods or services, then both inputs (income) and outputs (expenses) can be expressed in monetary values. The difference between the two is profit. Even if there is no intention to make a profit, or even to break even, a profit centre might still exist. A municipal swimming pool could still be thought of as a profit centre even if the admission fees are subsidized so that costs are not intended to be covered.

Investment centres

If not only the profits but also the capital employed in a responsibility centre are measured then an investment centre exists. With an investment centre the profit can be related to the capital employed to produce a rate of return. Nationalized industries have regularly been set target rates of return by the central government. A more recent development has been a *requirement* for the direct labour and direct service organizations of local authorities to produce a rate of return of 5 per cent on the current cost of assets employed.

Ideally the responsibility centre structure for budgetary control will also correspond to the programme or activity structure of the organization. In other words, each responsibility centre will work on a specific programme or activity, and these combined programmes will coincide with the overall programmes of the department or division of service. Such a correspondence does not always exist, however, and in Chapter 4 the programme structure of budget preparation and control is considered in more detail.

Whatever type of responsibility centre exists it is through these that the data on actual expenditure and actual output throughout the budget year are collected and measured. From these data reports are prepared and sent regularly to all levels of management, comparing the actual position with the budgeted position. If the budgetary control system is to work properly, then the information sent to managers must be relevant and timely. For information to be relevant it must be up to date and accurate; it must clearly distinguish between expenses that are directly controllable by the individual manager concerned and those that are only partially controllable; it must include a budget figure not only for the whole year but also for the appropriate proportion of the year; and it must be understandable and contain the right amount of detail.

Accuracy and timeliness

Failure to report quickly to budget holders on their performance will seriously weaken the budgetary control system. Absolute accuracy can be sacrificed in favour of timely reports, and the increasing use of computers means that it should be possible to send out budget reports only a few days after the end of the monthly or four-weekly budgetary control period. A basic problem affecting budgetary control in government departments and in many local authorities is the adherence to a receipts and payments system of accounting. Under this system only the actual cash payments made throughout the year are recorded, although in the case of local government it is usual to 'convert' the payments to expenses at the end of the year by including year-end creditors. The effect of this is that there will appear to be a consistent underspending against the budget during the year, and only at the year end will it be possible to assess the overall position. Ideally, of course, the periodic budgetary control reports should include information about accrued expenditure and also committed items (for example, where contracts have been entered into), so that the financial consequences of every activity to date are captured, rather than merely those activities that have been paid for.

Controllable/non-controllable expenses

An essential requirement of the control aspect of budgetary control is that budget holders can be held responsible for their performance to date. This means that when allocating costs to responsibility centres a distinction should be made between the direct labour, materials, and overhead costs that the budget holder is clearly responsible for incurring, and also those costs which, although indirect, may be capable of being influenced by the actions of the budget holder, and the allocated or apportioned overhead over which the budget holder has no control.

In reality, very few expenses are totally controllable by an individual manager. Even direct labour is not completely controllable because wage rates and hiring and firing decisions are normally outside the manager's discretion. The distinction is therefore one of the degree of control and the degree of responsibility. It is essential, however, that the responsibility/control concept exists to some extent, otherwise the system of budgetary control would be seriously weakened and may break down altogether. For example, in the past one of the frequently cited weaknesses of budgetary control in the National Health Service stemmed from the fact that the budget of a health authority was normally organized on a functional basis. This meant that the responsibility centres followed the functions of direct patient care services such as nursing, medical, pathology, pharmacy, physiotherapy, etc., or support services such as catering, cleaning, and portering. However, the actual responsibility for incurring expenditure on these functions did not rest with the budget holder but with the clinicians. It is the clinicians who admit patients and it is the clinicians who decide on the appropriate treatment. Therefore although pharmacists may be nominally responsible for the budget for drugs, in reality they have no control over the level of spending, because the quantity and type of drugs are prescribed by the clinicians. This lack of control over costs resulted in lack of responsibility for budgetary performance and therefore lack of budgetary control. One possible solution would have been to involve clinicians directly in the budgetary control process by preparing budgets for medical specialties rather than functions. If responsibility centres could be set up for specialties such as general medicine, ophthalmology, paediatric, orthopaedic, geriatric, and so on, then the clinicians would become budget holders, and responsibility would be restored. One of the main recommendations of the Griffiths Report (Department of Health and Social Security, 1983) was that clinicians, as the 'production managers' of the NHS, should be responsible for the costs they incur in the treatment of patients and much work has been undertaken on attempts to develop clinical management budgets. One of the basic difficulties affecting a widespread acceptance of clinical budgeting has been stated to be that of reconciling the conflicting requirements of 'clinical freedom' on the one hand, with those of budgetary control on the other. The doctrine of clinical freedom contends that clinicians should be free to treat patients according to their professional judgement of needs and without having to worry about the cost; whereas budgetary control would require clinicians to accept the financial constraints imposed upon them by a budget. It is largely for these reasons that many of the attempts to involve clinicians in financial management had relatively little success.

However, the implementation through the National Health Service and Community Care Act 1990 of the proposals contained in the 1989 White Paper *Working for Patients* (Department of Health, 1989) have begun to change all this. An internal market system is now in place, with a distinction being made between the purchasers of health care and the providers of health care. The White Paper makes it clear that the government's intention is to involve all medical staff in decisions on resource commitment and on making the best use of available resources and in particular to 'ensure that hospital consultants – whose decisions effectively commit substantial sums of money – are involved in the management of hospitals; are given responsibility for the use of resources; and are encouraged to use those resources more effectively' (Department of Health, 1989, p. 8).

Budgetary position throughout the budget year

The budget, by expressing the planned position, sets a standard against which actual outcomes can be measured. Obviously, the budget for the whole year is of little use for this purpose if only the first month of the year has elapsed. Dividing the budget by twelve might be a solution in this case, but this of course assumes that income and expenditure is incurred evenly throughout the year. A more sophisticated approach is to determine the proportion of the budget that might be expected to have been used up for each four-weekly or monthly or quarterly budgetary control period throughout the year. This is known as a budgetary profile and will involve making assumptions about income and expenditure patterns, possibly by analysing past data. Known factors that might affect the patterns should be adjusted for. For example, pay awards are often finalized long after the effective date of the award. The budget for periods before the finalization date should be based on old rates of pay, and after the finalization date based on the new. Other external factors are less easy to predict. For example, the effect of the weather on heating and lighting costs or the demand for services. A task of this nature with many variables that may affect the outcome lends itself to financial modelling as described earlier.

Budgetary profiles form an important part of the procedures adopted for the in-year monitoring of expenditure by government departments. Shortly before the beginning of the financial year each department is required to forecast the quarterly pattern of expenditure throughout the year. The forecast is based partly on seasonal effects, which might be expected to follow the pattern of previous years, and partly on discussions with line-managers about the likely spending behaviour. The profiles are then compared by the Treasury with the actual spending pattern of earlier years and, after discussions about the reasons for any differences, an agreed budgetary profile is established.

Amount of detail

The budgetary control reports must provide sufficient information to enable budget holders to isolate the nature of variances from the budget but must not contain so much information that the recipient is overwhelmed. At the lowest level of responsibility centre the individual manager will require information on either each programme element or detailed activity that makes up the overall programme or service provided, or on the precise nature of the expenditure, such as wages, materials, and so on. Which of these is used will depend on how the budget for the responsibility centre is built up. At a higher level there may be, say, a regional manager, responsible for several responsibility centres. At this level a summary of the position in each responsibility centre might be sufficient. The level of aggregation of budgetary control information will normally be greater the higher the level of managerial responsibility.

An example of how a budgetary control report might be presented is given in Fig. 2.2. The report is for a street cleaning division of a local authority and shows the position for the first quarter of the budget year. The proportion of the annual

Revenue Budget Report First Quarter		Budgetary Control System Street Cleaning Division				
Narrative- subjective analysis (1)	Code (2)	Budget provision		Actual to date (5)	Over-under- spending (6)	Balance of budget (7)
		Annual (3)	To date (4)			
		£	£	£	£	£
Salaries and on-costs	10	248,904	62,226	63,021	795	185,883
Wages and on-costs	20	967,752	172,097	169,820	2,277CR	797,932
Fuel, light and cleaning	30	41,349	12,224	12,581	357	28,768
Power	31	82,905	25,763	21,071	4,692CR	61,834
Rents	33	575	96	93	3CR	482
Rates	34	258,127	257,800	256,508	1,292CR	1,619
Equipment and tools	40	6,162	1,023	765	258CR	5,397
Materials	42	133,697	22,280	22,824	544	110,873
Other supplies	46	1,540	—	—	—	1,540
Hired and contracted services	48	47,488	7,914	7,012	902CR	40,476
Fuel and lubricants	50	6,196	988	884	104CR	5,312
Transport	53	204,638	30,274	25,866	4,408CR	178,772
Responsible Officer Total		1,999,333	592,685	580,445	12,240CR	1,418,888

Fig. 2.2   Example of a budgetary control report.

budget allocation for the first quarter of the year (as shown in column 4) reflects the expected profile of the budget. For example, although the expected salaries for the first three months are exactly one-quarter of the annual budget provision, other items, such as Power, Rates, Materials show a proportion that is significantly different from one-quarter and this therefore reflects an attempt to profile the likely pattern of usage of the annual allocation by the end of the first three months of the year.

The expected amounts of budgetary usage shown in column 4 can then be compared with the actual amount spent at the end of the first quarter (column 5) to reveal the resultant over- or under-spending (column 6).

The qualities outlined above of accuracy and timeliness, distinction between controllable and non-controllable, budgetary profiles, and appropriate detail are the basic requirements of a sound system of budgetary control and yet the procedures adopted in many public sector organizations have often been criticized for failing to meet these requirements. For example, in 1985 the Jarratt Report (p. 45) on efficiency studies in universities, having pointed out that 'presently most management accounting systems are inadequate', went on to recommend an integrated system of management accounting to provide budgetary control information that would report actual payments and commitments to date against budgets. Presumably such basic requirements were missing in many universities at that time.

It has already been pointed out how the government adopts a receipts and payments system of accounting with the result that the basic budgetary control reports also follow this system. Although many of the recently created Executive Agencies will move towards a system of accrual accounting for financial reporting and budgetary control purposes, much of government spending will continue to be controlled through the receipts and payments based APEX (analysis of public expenditure) reports provided by the Paymaster General's Office. This means that the data lack the basic quality of timeliness and this must affect their relevance for the purpose of budgetary control. Similarly, for local authorities, research undertaken by Pendlebury (1985, p. 42) revealed that:

> The budgetary control statements provided by the finance department frequently suffer from very obvious defects: they lack timeliness, the absence of profiling prevents variance analysis; they fail to distinguish between controllable/non-controllable items; they ignore non-financial output measures. The budgetary process is dominated by financial stewardship requirements with the finance department's statements aimed primarily at disclosing the budgetary compliance position rather than controlling the economy, efficiency and effectiveness of operations.

In 1988 Skousen (1990) replicated the 1983 research by Pendlebury and found that although there had been some encouraging improvements between the two surveys, many of the defects that were identified in 1983 still remained in 1988. In similar vein, the Audit Commission (1989) noted, in a management paper on local government financial management, that although total council spending was usually well controlled, irregularities were infrequent and standards of honesty high, there were still some problem areas. These were identified as follows:

1 responsibility for financial control often fails to match management responsibility;
2 the existence of restrictive, complicated and confusing financial procedures;
3 financial information is often poorly presented and out of date; and
4 financial expertise is too remote.

Behavioural considerations

A further aspect of the whole system of budgeting and budgetary control that should be taken into consideration concerns the vast amount of evidence about its behavioural effects (see Otley, 1977). One of the principal reasons for preparing budgets is to provide a means for ensuring that the behaviour of an organization is consistent with meeting its ultimate objectives. However, the behaviour of an organization is dependent on the actions of the individuals who make up the organization and only if the objectives of the individuals coincide with the objectives of the organization will the latter be achieved. This has important implications for the budgetary process. Ideally, resources should be allocated to programmes in such a way as to ensure the greatest beneficial impact on overall organizational objectives. Because such impacts are not readily measurable, particularly in the more 'non-commercial' parts of the public sector, the allocation of resources to individual departments is often the outcome of subjective evaluations and a complex process of political bargaining and negotiations. This can lead to the existence of 'departmentalism', whereby departments compete with each other for resources, with the aim of the managers or political leaders of each department being to secure as much as possible, with little regard being paid to the optimal allocation needed to achieve overall organizational objectives.

A further behavioural problem that can arise is where the quest for budgetary control involves evaluating the performance of individual managers in terms of budgetary achievement. In this situation it is obviously a useful strategy for managers to ensure that as much slack as possible is built into their budget. This is achieved by 'padding' the budget so that more is included than might reasonably be required. Although padding the budget in this way might be justified because of the need to provide a 'cushion' for dealing with the unexpected, it can also be used to hide inefficiencies and extravagance. Similarly, the manipulation of data or undesirable decision behaviour during the budget control period will obviously affect the control and organizational effectiveness. Manipulation of data may occur as a result of deliberate miscoding of the items to ensure that the actual out-turn appears to be in line with the budget. Undesirable decision behaviour can occur due to actions being taken which produce a favourable impression in terms of performance against budget but are in fact dysfunctional when related to organizational goals. For example, if the performance of the police force of a local authority is measured in terms of cost per prosecution, then resources might be diverted to 'easy' prosecutions for petty offences rather than towards the more serious, but more costly to prove, offences. Thus the budget might be achieved and performance might be judged to be satisfactory, but in reality the police force would be making a very inadequate contribution to accomplishing its fundamental objectives.

The rigidity of the budgets of many public sector bodies can also produce undesirable effects. It is often suggested that the budget restricts flexibility and acts as a strait-jacket on managerial action. This may result in expenditure being incurred merely because it is included in the budget, even though it is no longer required, whereas other activities, which may be much more beneficial in terms of the objectives of the organization, are ignored because of the absence of budgetary provision.

It is apparent that the budget and budgetary control system can have an enormous impact on managerial behaviour. The use of budgets in the planning and control processes of an organization clearly requires an awareness of the ways in which budgets influence the behaviour of individuals and also the ways in which such behaviour is related to the needs of the organization as a whole.

Virement

In the previous section the rigid nature of the budgets of many public sector organizations was mentioned. Such rigidity is a requirement of budgetary control, which involves ensuring that only those items and amounts of expenditure authorized in the budget should be incurred. However, it has long been recognized that some degree of flexibility will be required to deal with changes in circumstances or unexpected events. An increase in the demand for a particular service may result in increased costs, the rate of inflation may be higher than expected, essential equipment may fail, income from fees and charges may be lower than anticipated, and so on. One approach to this problem will be to vary the budget by making a supplementary allocation of resources. Alternatively, it may be possible to meet the overspending by transferring an amount of budgetary provision that is likely to be underspent from elsewhere in the budget. This process of meeting overspending in one area by underspending from another is known as *virement*. Obviously, the widespread use of virement could lead to a breakdown in budgetary control because any overspending, for whatever reason, could be made up by underspending on other items. Individual managers or departments might therefore be encouraged to build hidden reserves, in the form of items that are likely to be underspent, into their budget requests. Because of this it is usual to impose some checks on the use of virement. In central government, for example, virement is not permitted between one vote and another because the total expenditure on any vote may not exceed that granted by Parliament. However, each vote is made up of several subheads and virement between the subheads within a particular vote is permissible but Treasury approval is required. It is clear from the Treasury manual on government accounting (HM Treasury, 1989 – amended 1994) that virement is welcomed because it is seen as leading to economy in the estimates. If spending departments were not given the opportunity to vire it is suggested that this would lead to additional amounts being sought for each subhead. Even so, the Treasury may decide to refuse virement if it feels that the expenditure would:

1   be on a new service of which Parliament should be aware;
2   be novel or contentious;
3   arise from a major change of policy;
4   be large in relation to the original provision in the subhead;
5   although relatively small, be likely to involve heavy liabilities in later years; or
6   involve expenditure on running costs in excess of the department's running cost limit.

Moreover, in an attempt to increase a spending department's discretion over virement, the Treasury will define in advance the conditions under which it expects to agree virement, which means that the efficiency of resource management is not restricted by departments having to seek prior approval every time they wish to vire.

In local authorities it is also usual for virement to have to be formally approved, either by council or finance committee or by the treasurer. In general, the traditional attitude has been to permit virement if the reasons for underspending are due to the increased efficiency or cost saving actions of a particular department but to recognize that if the reasons for underspending are entirely fortuitous, then the savings should accrue to the organization as a whole rather than to the individual department in which the budget item was included. The close involvement of the treasurer in the approval of virement has often been challenged, and in a management paper the Audit Commission (1989, p. 9) argue that 'rules governing virement between different departmental budgets should primarily be the responsibility of departmental management rather than the treasurer'. The Audit Commission point out that, although detailed rules about virement are unnecessary, there are situations where clear rules about approval are needed. The examples they give are:

1 where projects are financed by grants or contributions from outsiders, especially joint finance;
2 where projects have a high political priority;
3 where significant new projects are involved so that there are not incentives for managers to delay new plans and use the savings to finance overspending on existing projects;
4 where virements lead to long-term commitments (e.g. the employment of staff) without these being matched by long-term savings.

Control through cost accounting

The Chartered Institute of Management Accountants (1994, pp. 9–10) define cost accounting as

> The establishment of budgets, standard costs and actual costs of operations, processes, activities or products; and the analysis of variances, profitability or the social use of funds.

All public sector organizations are involved in some form of cost accounting, although this may range from the very rudimentary to the very sophisticated. Similarly, all of the various cost accounting techniques that are described so well in many textbooks are probably capable of being used in some form or other in the public sector. It is not our intention to describe these techniques here. What is discussed in this section are some specific examples of cost accounting in the public sector. The importance of cost accounting varies considerably, depending on the uses to which the information will be put, and so it might be helpful to distinguish between cost accounting for expense centre activities and cost accounting for profit or investment centre activities.

Expense centre activities and cost accounting

Very often the only reason for collecting costs is for the purposes of budgetary control. In this situation, 'cost accounting' will consist of nothing more than ensuring that costs are correctly allocated to the appropriate expense centres. A further stage might be to calculate unit costs but this is usually achieved by simply dividing total costs by some suitable measure of service provision, such as number of library books issued or number of patients treated. For many public sector activities this represents the full extent of any systematic form of cost accounting and for the purposes of day-to-day control might well be sufficient. Nevertheless, even for these activities, an awareness of cost behaviour would often improve decision making and control. Running an extra course at a university, or admitting an extra student on to a course, or treating an extra patient in a hospital are examples of activity level changes that might occur and that will obviously have an effect on costs. However, the additional costs will normally be only the marginal costs. Without a knowledge of the relationship between level of activity and costs it is difficult to exercise proper budgetary control. Ideally, therefore, there should be some attempt to distinguish between the marginal costs and the fixed costs of a service. Taking up the example of the extra patient admitted into a hospital this will clearly produce additional costs on food, drugs, sterile packs, and so on. These are the marginal costs. The labour costs for nursing and medical care, and for cleaning and portering are unlikely to vary. Similarly, the heating costs of the hospital are unlikely to vary. These are the fixed, or semi-fixed, costs. It seems evident that a cost accounting system that could isolate the financial consequences of changes in the level of service provision would greatly improve planning decisions and control. However, the costs of providing such information would not be insignificant and the benefits would have to be weighed very carefully against the costs. Knowing the marginal cost of issuing a library book might not be all that important. Knowing the marginal cost of a heart transplant operation might.

Where expense centre activities have some identifiable and measurable output, such as number of dustbins emptied, or miles of road cleaned, then ideally the budget should include not only the financial resources allocated to the services but also the planned level of activity. If this is done and if costs have been identified as fixed or variable then there is a sufficient data base to introduce techniques such as flexible budgeting, standard costing and variance analysis to assist in managerial control.

A further situation where a proper use of cost accounting is essential occurs when the question of contracting out services is being considered. In local government, for example, it has been recognized that there are many activities that could be contracted out to private sector organizations rather than provided in-house by the local authority. This does not necessarily mean that the private sector could carry out the activity in a more cost-effective manner but it does offer the opportunity to test this by putting the activity out to competitive tender and requiring the in-house department to tender against private sector contractors.

Compulsory competitive tendering is now a requirement for many local authority activities. The Local Government Planning and Land Act 1980 required the direct labour activities of maintenance and construction of buildings and roads to be exposed to competition through competitive tendering. Under the Local Government Act 1988, this requirement was extended to other activities known as 'defined activities'. By September 1994 there were eight defined activities as follows:

1 *Refuse collection* – covers the collection of household and commercial waste.
2 *Building cleaning* – includes the cleaning of the interior of any building (except dwellings, residential homes and police establishments), and the cleaning of windows both inside and out.
3 *Other cleaning* – covers street cleaning and the removal of litter, the emptying of litter bins, and the cleaning of traffic signs and street-name plates.
4 *Catering* – covers schools and welfare.
5 *Other catering* – includes all catering except schools and welfare.
6 *Maintenance of grounds* – includes grass cutting, the control of weeds, the planting and tending of trees, flowers, plants, hedges, etc.
7 *Vehicle repair and maintenance* – covers all motor vehicles except police and fire services.
8 *Leisure management* – includes leisure and sports facilities, leisure centres, tennis courts, bowling greens, etc.

Where these activities are provided in-house, they are required to be organized as separately accountable Direct Service Organizations (DSOs). Similar opportunities also exist in central government and in the health service, and in a circular issued by the DHSS in 1983 (HC (1983) 18) all health authorities were asked to develop competitive tendering programmes for the provision of domestic, catering and laundry services.

When considering the costs of in-house service provision it is important to isolate the avoidable costs of the service. These are the relevant costs to be used in any cost comparison exercise. The Chartered Institute of Public Finance and Accountancy (1984, p. 14) point out that:

> It is important when preparing the in-house tender not to be misled by any existing accounts and budgets relating to the service in question . . . What the in-house team must do is to estimate as accurately as possible what costs would be avoided by the authority if the in-house service were abandoned. The in-house tender must not include arbitrary allocations of overhead costs which would continue to be incurred with or without in-house provision.

The most easily identifiable avoidable costs are the direct operating costs. These would include the employees of the service and the variable costs such as heating, lighting, consumables, etc. The identification of avoidable capital costs requires more thought. The relevant costs are the market values of assets that could be disposed of or transferred to an alternative use and the costs that would have to be incurred on future capital equipment if the service remained in-house. However, it is the indirect costs that create most difficulties. In local authorities, for example, the service departments are charged for part of the functions that are handled centrally, such as payroll preparation and other accounting and finance requirements, or legal and technical matters. These are known as central administration expenses. Just how much of these would be avoided is difficult to identify. In the short term, for example, it may not be possible to make valuable use of redundant office space or reduce the number of finance department staff. Nevertheless, it would be wrong to accept completely the argument that savings in the cost of central administration functions are not possible. What is needed is a careful examination of how much work of this sort, and at what cost, is actually provided for the service in question.

In addition to calculating the avoidable costs of a service there is a further need to ascertain any new costs which will be incurred if the service is contracted out. The most obvious example is the redundancy payments that may have to be made to the existing workforce. A local authority is permitted to take into account the potential redundancy costs when deciding on whether to award a contract in-house or to a private contractor. However, contracts normally run for a period of between three and seven years and if the redundancy argument was used on the first round of tendering, it cannot be used again when the contract ends and the activity is put out to tender the next time. It will also be necessary to incur costs on monitoring the quality of the service provided by outside contractors and on providing a system for handling and responding to any complaints or queries about the service.

Finally, there is the need to recognize the importance of non-financial criteria in contracting out decisions. The most obvious of these is the possibility of default by the private sector contractor. Default may be due to bankruptcy of the contractor or due to an inability or unwillingness to continue to provide a service of the required quality. If a service is contracted out the health or local authority concerned still has the responsibility for its provision and so, whatever the reason for default, this will require some form of emergency and probably high cost cover.

Even so, in spite of the potential problems of contracting out, the introduction of the requirement for competitive tendering in health and local government has brought about major changes in the provision of services, and is also reported to have resulted in cost savings. For example, the Institute of Public Finance (McGuirk, 1993) reports that out of a total of 994 building cleaning contracts awarded under CCT by 1992, 620 had been won by in-house DSOs, 12 by external DSOs, and 362 had been awarded to private sector contractors (six of these were operated by local authority management buy-outs). This means that the private sector has secured a market share of 36 per cent.

Profit and investment centre activities and cost accounting

The prices that are charged for a particular service can be determined either from the estimated costs incurred or by market force pressures. Which approach is used depends on the competition that affects the provision of the service. The increasingly widespread use of compulsory competitive tendering for local government activities is just one example of attempts to expose public services to competition. However, whether prices are market determined or cost determined, the cost accounting system has a crucial role to play in providing information for price-fixing purposes and for the regular monitoring and control of actual results against budgeted costs to ensure that target rates of return or profit levels will be met. Similarly, an awareness of cost behaviour is essential. For example, with passenger transport, knowledge of the influence of peak and off-peak periods on costs, and the need to allocate fares to these periods, are important requirements if pricing policy and control are to be effective. Such cost and revenue allocations are notoriously difficult, particularly the latter, due to the widespread use of season tickets and concessionary passes.

The role of cost accounting in local authority direct service organizations is even more essential because the penalty for not achieving the target rate of return could be the closure of the service. Direct service organizations exist where a local authority uses its own employees to carry out certain activities in-house, rather than contract them out to private sector organizations. As was discussed above, when such activities are carried out in-house, then these have to be exposed to competition in the form of competitive tendering. Thus, under normal circumstances, the price for the activity is determined by market forces. The activities also have to be separately accounted for and are required to earn a specific rate of return on capital employed. The rate of return is calculated as the current cost surplus for the year divided by the current value of the assets employed. For all but one of the 'defined activities' under the Local Government Act 1988, and for the housing and highways construction and maintenance activities identified in the Local Government Planning and Land Act 1980, the required rate of return is 5 per cent. The one exception to this is the cleaning of buildings where the requirement is to break even.

In a situation like this it is essential that a sound system of tendering for jobs is introduced and that proper job costing procedures are used to record the actual costs and to monitor performance against the tender price. The Chartered Institute of Public Finance and Accountancy (1993) identifies three principal methods that could be used for tendering and charging for different types of work. These are:

1   lump sum estimates supported by bills of quantities;
2   schedules of rates;
3   lump sums supported by specifications.

Lump sum estimates are suitable for large construction jobs, but for smaller jobs and for maintenance work, schedules of rates would be used. *Schedules of rates* are based on standard schedules of work for the various activities that make up a job. The rewiring of council houses or the painting of council houses are examples of jobs for which standard schedules would be suitable. In effect, the procedures followed in the preparation of standard schedules are similar to those for the preparation of standard costs. If this method of tendering is used, then the data required for a standard costing system will be available, and standard costing and variance analysis could be introduced for control purposes. *Lump sums supported by specifications* are suitable for activities such as catering or cleaning or grounds maintenance, where detailed specifications of the tasks to be carried out and the frequency of the tasks is possible.

One obvious advantage of the use of profit or investment centres for control purposes is that the existence of a measurable and saleable output means that a whole range of cost accounting techniques are available. Many of these techniques were developed in a private sector environment and yet it has become fashionable in recent years to turn to private sector solutions for public sector problems. Profit or investment centres also provide many more opportunities to expose public sector activities to the disciplines of market forces. A more widespread use of profit or investment centres might therefore be expected to contribute to improved control of public sector activities. However, before this could be done, it would be necessary to extend the scope of charging for services to include those services that are traditionally financed through taxation. This is considered in the next section.

CHARGING FOR SERVICES

Ever since public services were first provided there has been a debate over how they should be financed. The alternatives available are: (a) to finance by taxes, (b) to finance by charges, or (c) to finance by a mixture of both. If taxes are used, the community as a whole pays; if charges are used, the individual consumers pay. In the final analysis the emphasis that prevails in a society at any particular time is a reflection of political choice.

It is not our intention to become involved in this debate but it might be helpful to consider very briefly the issues that surround the question of charging for services. There are in fact two questions that arise:

1   Should a particular service be charged for at all?
2   Should the charge cover full cost, or something less or more than full cost?

As far as the first question is concerned, there are certain services that are clearly provided for the public in general, rather than for individual consumers, and therefore should not be charged for but should be financed by taxes. Such services are called 'public goods' and one way of testing for the existence of a public good is to see whether the service could be withheld from any individual who chose not to pay. The provision of national defence by the armed forces is an obvious example. Even if a service could be withheld for non-payment it might be infeasible to do so, and so it would still be treated as a public good. For example, country parks are frequently crossed by many public roads and paths, and it may be impractical to restrict access to those who pay. Also the withholding of a service might be contrary to public policy. If it is generally agreed that education is something that every child should be entitled to, irrespective of whether or not individual parents are able to pay, then education would be treated as a public good. Some services are thought of as public goods and financed through taxation for historical or cultural reasons. For example, domestic refuse collection is generally a taxation-financed service in the UK, whereas in parts of Germany it is charged for on the basis of number of refuse containers collected. Similarly, street cleaning could perhaps be charged for on the basis of length of street frontage of individual houses or shops or factories. Strictly speaking, in this last example, street cleaning would be being financed not by charges, but by a form of taxation based on street frontages. For a service to be capable of being charged for, consumers should be able to vary their charges by varying their consumption. Demolishing part of a house to reduce street cleaning charges is a somewhat drastic way of doing this.

There are of course many services provided by public sector organizations that are definitely not public goods, and that can definitely be charged for. Rail travel is an obvious example. The question that then arises is: what proportion of the costs of a service should be recovered? A useful strategy to adopt might be to require that all non-public good services should be charged at full cost unless there are good reasons to the contrary. Good reasons to the contrary might include the following:

1 Market price different from cost price. For example, British Coal is competing in a world market for coal products and market prices will not necessarily coincide with costs.
2 A requirement to make a surplus. An increasing number of public sector activities are now required to meet a target rate of return and must therefore charge prices in excess of full cost.
3 A need to conserve scarce resources by discouraging extravagant or frivolous consumption.
4 To encourage the use of a service. For example, adult evening classes.
5 To reflect the 'public benefit' elements of a service. For example, planning permission confers benefits on the individuals who wish to build or extend property and also on society by preventing visually offensive construction. Similarly the subsidization of passenger transport services in rural areas reflects a social need.
6 To utilize unused capacity. For example, the use of 'off-peak' fares for public transport.
7 To support the local economy. For example, local authority enterprise zones.
8 Social justice. If services are charged at full cost, users on low incomes may suffer hardship.

These reasons might be sufficient justification for the actual prices charged to differ from full cost, but before such decisions are taken it might be helpful to appreciate what is meant by the expression 'full cost', because this can vary considerably throughout the public sector. In general, for organizations financed primarily by charges, the major issue is whether depreciation charges should be based on historic cost or current costs. The tendency nowadays is for 'full cost' to reflect the fact that the cost of replacing assets will normally be greater than their historic cost and so the principles of current cost accounting are increasingly used.

As far as organizations financed primarily by taxation are concerned the issues are less clear-cut. As well as the question of depreciation charges there is the problem of the allocation of central administration expenses and overhead. For example, local authorities provide a whole range of services for which charges are made. Activities such as recreation centres, sports halls, swimming baths, allotments, markets, crematoria, and so on are clearly in this category. This is similar to the problem encountered earlier when discussing the contracting out decision. The key question here is concerned with whether the charges for the service should reflect the direct costs of the service only, or should include some contribution to the central administration costs of the local authority. After all the service, if run on its own, would incur administration costs, and yet if the service was withdrawn the administrative departments and premises would still exist and incur costs. The debate over the allocation to service departments of central administration costs has run for many years in local government. In 1981, a report on pricing in local government (Coopers and Lybrand, 1981, p. 52) contained the following criticism:

> There is a widespread failure to charge out central administration and overhead to particular services. Unless this is done, it is impossible to see what charges mean or to delegate to managers proper responsibility for the resources consumed by their services/facilities. Economic pricing remains undefined and the degree of subsidy unknown.

The debate has intensified in recent years with the increased requirement for compulsory competitive tendering for many activities. It was pointed out above that the 'defined activities' under the Local Government Act 1988, and the activities of highways and buildings construction and maintenance under the Local Government Planning and Land Act 1980, require Direct Service Organizations (DSOs) to be separately accountable units which 'charge' client departments for the service provided. In other words, an internal market has been created whereby a service department such as education will purchase activities such as cleaning or school-meals provision from either separately managed in-house providers or from private contractors. Thus, for example, the Environmental Health Department of a local authority will be responsible for providing refuse collection and street-cleaning services. Before the requirements of the Local Government Act 1988, the activities of refuse collection and street cleaning would usually have been managed as an integral part of the Environmental Health Department. Now, if the activities are undertaken in-house, then the in-house units are required to be separately accountable DSOs which 'sell' refuse collection and/or street-cleaning work to the Environmental Health Department at an agreed contract price.

Because the DSOs have to compete on price with private contractors and because, if they win the contract, they then have to achieve a target rate of return, the question of central overhead allocations becomes crucial. Many of the central administration costs incurred by a local authority have nothing to do with providing support for a particular service or activity but are simply the inevitable costs of a multi-functional, democratically elected organization. It is argued that these costs should be separately identified and not charged to DSOs or to service departments. In other words, the price charged to members of the public for a local authority service or the price charged by a DSO to its 'client' departments, should not be expected to cover central administration costs of this type. However, where the central administration costs are incurred on activities which provide definite support for service departments and DSOs, such as financial or legal advice, then these should be charged for.

The recommendation of the Chartered Institute of Public Finance and Accountancy (CIPFA, Financial Information Service, Vol. 4) is for the different elements of overhead to be distinguished as follows:

1 *Support services* – these are the whole range of services which support the provision of services to the public by DSOs and service departments. Examples will include the normal functions of accountants, lawyers, personnel officers, architects, etc.
2 *Service management* – these are the costs of *managing* specific services to the public and support services.
3 *Regulation* – this relates to the costs of ensuring that the statutory minimum standard of service is provided to the public, either by a local authority's own employees or by third parties.
4 *Corporate management* – this includes the cost of all activities arising from the democratically elected, multi-purpose nature of local authorities. Such activities will include the costs of local elections, members' allowances, council meetings, expenses of mayors and chairmen of authorities, preparation of financial accounts and budgets, negotiations over grants, receipts and community charges.

It is recommended that the costs of corporate management should be identified as a separate cost heading which is not allocated to services. Regulation costs should be shown as a separate cost of the relevant service and service management costs and support services costs should be charged to the DSOs or specific services that make use of them. Obviously the impact of competition on the provision of DSO activities meant that DSO managers were reluctant to accept arbitrary allocations of central support service costs. The response to this has been the widespread adoption of service level agreements (SLAs) whereby a support service such as internal audit or payroll preparation is provided to a DSO at a negotiated price for an agreed level of service. The use of SLAs is not restricted to DSOs and they can be applied to other areas. For example, the support services provided to social services functions or schools operating under LMS are increasingly subject to SLAs.

An SLA is a contract to provide a specific service at an agreed quality, frequency and volume. The contract will also specify the basis for charging for the service and procedures for dealing with complaints and disputes. Having established SLAs, the obvious next development would be to apply the principles of competition to the underlying support activity in the form of competitive tendering. The government signalled its intentions in this respect in its *Competing for Quality* consultation paper (Department of the Environment, 1991). This identified a wide range of 'white-collar' support services to which the principles of compulsory competitive tendering might be extended and, under the provisions of the Local Government Act 1992, local authorities can now be required to submit a proportion of their support services to competitive tender.

In central government the philosophy of the *Competing for Quality* consultation paper is reflected in an annual Competing for Quality programme, which requires departments and agencies to review their activities to identify those that may be abolished or privatized or contracted out or awarded to an in-house team following a competition. In the December 1994 *Next Steps Briefing Note* (Next Steps Team, 1994, para. 74), it is reported that by May 1994 an estimated £1.3 billion of activities for 1992–93 and 1993–94 had been examined under the Competing for Quality programme, and this had led to annual savings of at least £150 million in costs.

From the point of view of managerial control, charging for services can produce very definite benefits. In the first place, profit centres rather than expense centres can be used as responsibility centres for costing and budgetary control. The manager of the profit centre is responsible for not only the expenses but also the quantity and quality of services provided to ensure that the budgeted relationship between income and expenses is achieved.

As can be seen from the above discussion of SLAs, charges for services and the use of profit centres do not have to be restricted to situations where a service is provided to external users. Internal markets can be used to provide a mechanism for charging for activities provided within an organization. Under SLAs the managers of support services will be motivated to identify ways of providing additional services and to identify ways of controlling and reducing costs so that they increasingly resemble the managers of profit-oriented companies.

The principle of internal markets is now firmly established in large parts of the public sector and a widely debated example is that of the National Health Service. It was pointed out earlier how the proposals contained in the 1989 White Paper *Working for Patients* (Department of Health, 1989) have led to the introduction of a system whereby providers of hospital services now 'sell' health care to 'buyers'. The 'sellers' or 'providers' are hospitals within the NHS and independent hospitals. Hospitals within the NHS consist of those that have become self-governing NHS Trusts and those that still remain as directly managed units of district health authorities. The 'buyers' or 'purchasers' will be mainly district health authorities but general-practice fundholders are becoming increasingly important. Under this system, the role of district health authorities is that of commissioning or purchasing agents. They are responsible for assessing the health care needs of their local population and then arranging contracts with providers of hospital services to ensure that those needs are met within the resources available. This separation between purchasers and providers of hospital services has permitted an internal market to be created, whereby purchasers and providers enter into contracts based on agreed quantities and prices. There are three types of contract:

1   *block contracts* under which a defined block of service is provided in return for a specific fee. Block contracts are not based on volume of activity and are appropriate for services such as Accident and Emergency;
2   *cost and volume contracts* under which the volume of service to be provided is specified and a fee for this agreed, with additional payments being made if

the volume is exceeded. For example, a contract might be drawn up for a hospital to take a specified number of orthopaedic treatments for a specified fee;

3 *cost-per-care contracts* based on a set fee for a specific type of treatment.

In addition there will be extra contractual referrals (ECRs) which occur either as an emergency, when patients need treatment outside their home locality, or where patients are referred by their GP or consultant to a different locality for specialist treatment. ECRs are paid for by the patient's 'home' district health authority or general-practice fundholders.

The cost accounting systems needed to underpin the information needs of managers running what are effectively NHS profit centres are rapidly being developed (see, for example, Mellett *et al.*, 1993), and, as with the move towards competition in local government, the treatment of overhead costs is under close scrutiny. When discussing the factors that affect the pricing of contracts, Mellett *et al.* point out (p. 187):

> If a particular contract price looks high, it does not automatically mean that the provider is less efficient. It may, for example, simply be that indirect costs and overheads are apportioned in a different way, a way that could be less correct, or more correct. Where such costs form a large part of total costs, even small changes in the apportionment basis can cause major swings in price.

One widely publicized development in the debate about overhead allocation has been the emergence of activity-based costing (ABC). Rather than allocating overhead costs to products on the basis of some measure of volume, such as machine hours or direct labour hours, ABC recognizes that the causes or 'drivers' of overhead are not necessarily volume-related but are related to other variables which can be identified and measured. The potential of ABC to improve the basis of overhead allocation in the NHS has been the subject of several studies. For example, King *et al.* (1994) report on the use of ABC to determine more accurate costings for the support service of radiology. They also report the results of four case studies that they undertook on the applicability of ABC in four different hospitals. They found that although ABC was not widely used it did have the potential to improve and supplement existing cost determination practices.

APPENDIX

It was pointed out earlier in this chapter that an increasing range of public sector activities are now required to be exposed to competition. Typical of these is the laundry service of a hospital, and in the example that follows the issues that need to be considered when deciding whether to continue with in-house provision or contract out to the private sector are examined.

Example

The laundry service of a major teaching hospital is currently carried out partly in-house and partly by a private sector laundry company. The total volume of laundry work that is generated each week averages 210,000 items and, of these, 140,000 items are laundered by the in-house service, with the balance being laundered by the private sector company. The total volume of laundry is not expected to change much over the next few years. The private sector company currently charges 9p per article for the 70,000 items that it undertakes each week, but has recently submitted a written quotation stating that if it were given a contract to undertake *all* of the laundry work, then the economies of scale that this would produce would enable it to reduce its charges to 7.75p per article.

An examination of the revenue budget for the in-house team for the current year reveals the following:

In-house service

		£
Salaries – Managerial staff		92,400
– Laundry employees		272,600
– Casual workers		111,200
Materials and supplies		44,500
Heat, light and water		147,200
Maintenance of equipment		39,300
		707,200

	£
Contracted-out laundry work	327,600
TOTAL COST	£1,034,800

An analysis of the budget reveals that the amounts shown for 'Heat, light and water' and 'Maintenance of equipment' are made up of fixed and variable costs as follows:

	Fixed costs	*Variable costs*
	£	£
Heat, light and water	41,700	105,500
Maintenance of equipment	9,300	30,000

The casual workers are hired as needed to work weekends and evenings and to cover for absences of the permanent employees.

Materials and supplies are assumed to vary directly with the level of activity and there is sufficient capacity to undertake all of the laundry work in-house.

The manager of the hospital has to decide whether to allow the private sector company to undertake all of the laundry work, or to ask the in-house team to undertake all of the laundry work, or to continue with the existing arrangements.

Appraisal of alternatives

The calculations that the manager produces are as follows:

	Complete private sector company provision	*Complete in-house provision*	*Existing arrangement*
Volume of activity (articles per week)	210,000	210,000	210,000
Costs	£	£	£
Private sector provision:			
Contract price			
(210,000×7.75p×52 weeks)	846,300		

	Complete private sector company provision	Complete in-house provision	Existing arrangement
Costs	£	£	£
In-house provision:			
Fixed costs		416,000	
Variable costs			
(210,000×4p×52 weeks)		436,800	
Existing arrangement:			
Current budget			1,034,800
	846,300	852,800	1,034,800

Note: The fixed and variable costs for the in-house provision are calculated as follows:

	Fixed costs £	Variable costs £
Salaries – Managerial staff	92,400	
– Laundry employees	272,600	
– Casual workers		111,200
Materials and supplies		44,500
Heat, light and water	41,700	105,500
Maintenance of equipment	9,300	30,000
	416,000	291,200

Therefore the variable cost per article = £291,200/140,000 articles × 52 weeks = 4p per article.

Discussion

On the basis of the above calculations, the lowest cost alternative would be to award the complete laundry activity to the private sector company. However, the crucial issue in this case is that of *avoidability*. For example, not all of the managerial staff costs would be avoided because there would presumably still be a need for quality control, for checking that work is undertaken in accordance with the terms of the contract and for authorizing payment. Also it might take time to redeploy employees, and therefore short-run avoidability might not be possible. The controversial issue that then emerges is whether short-term avoidability should determine the outcome or whether long-term avoidability should prevail.

If the employees are not to be redeployed but made redundant, then redundancy payments would be incurred. In such a situation a short-term perspective would lead to the rejection of the private sector company offer, but again if a longer-term view is taken a different decision might emerge.

This particular example avoids the issue of capital costs. The equipment used by the in-house laundry service could perhaps be sold if the contract were awarded to the private sector company and the premises might be capable of being used for other hospital activities. Alternatively, a depressed market for laundry services might mean that the equipment has only scrap value, and the costs of dismantling it and clearing the premises could well exceed this scrap value.

Finally, there are intangible factors to take into account such as the quality of service, the continuity of the service, the possibility of the private sector company having to cease operations, or being able to force up prices once the in-house capability has been disbanded, and so on.

DISCUSSION TOPICS

1   Describe the principal stages in the managerial planning and control cycle of any public sector organization with which you are familiar.

2   'A view of the long-term future is necessary in order to determine the strategies to which subsequent medium- and short-term policies and programmes shall conform.'

    Describe the planning and budgeting sequences of a public sector organization and discuss the contribution that management accounting can make in these sequences.

3   'Budgetary control is a continuous process which reviews and adjusts budgetary targets during the financial year and produces a control mechanism to hold budget holders to account.'

    Discuss the importance of budgetary control and describe the essential features of a sound system of budgetary control.

4   The introduction of competitive forces and internal markets into large areas of the public sector will bring about significant changes in management and in the demand for management accounting information.

    Give examples of 'the introduction of competitive forces and internal markets', and discuss the changes in management accounting that are likely to occur.

CHAPTER 3

Budget preparation

In the previous chapter the role of the budget in the managerial planning and control cycle of public sector organizations was examined. Planning is important. Controls to ensure the achievement of plans are important. The budget provides the essential link between the two processes. Although any statement which expresses future plans in financial terms can be thought of as a budget, it is on its role in the regular annual planning cycle that attention is usually focused. Long-term and medium-term plans are obviously important in any well-run organization, but no matter how sophisticated and comprehensive these are they only express intentions. It is only when these intentions are incorporated into the annual budget that they become firm commitments, with funds being allocated to enable their achievement. The annual budget, therefore, clearly expresses what is to be undertaken during the next year and authorizes the financial resources that will be needed. Budgets are invariably expressed in financial terms, although other measures should ideally also be incorporated. Apart from the central government most public sector bodies make a clear distinction between capital income and expenditure, and revenue income and expenditure. This results in the need to prepare separate annual revenue budgets and annual capital budgets.

THE ANNUAL REVENUE BUDGET

For most public sector bodies income and expenditure of a revenue nature is usually much greater than the capital income and outlays in any given year. It is therefore appropriate to begin with an examination of the annual revenue budget.

The origins of the annual budget can be traced back to the attempts of Parliament to exercise control over the activities of the central government. It is now established practice that the total government expenditure and the 'appropriations' of expenditure for particular purposes have to be approved for each financial year by Parliament. A further role of the central government's annual budget developed from the 1930s, when the possibility of using the budget to regulate the economy and control the levels of employment or inflation or economic activity was realized. Similarly, for local authorities, the preparation of annual budgets is a long-established process, originating from the need to determine the level of taxes to be raised from local inhabitants. Whilst these functions of budgeting are still important the budget has nowadays developed into an indispensable management aid for directing, co-ordinating and controlling the activities of public sector organizations. Much of this latter dimension of budgeting arose originally from its adoption by private firms, and most modern textbooks on the topic concentrate on the preparation and use of sales budgets, production budgets, cost of goods sold budgets, and so on. The more commercially oriented public sector organizations are obviously able to make use of such techniques and there seems little point in repeating here what is adequately described elsewhere. Attention is instead focused primarily on the use of budgets in the more traditional areas of the public sector.

Reasons for preparing a revenue budget

When an attempt is made to ascertain the precise reasons for preparing budgets it becomes immediately apparent why the budget has such an important role to play in the management of any organization. The main functions that have been suggested for the annual budget include:

1   determining income and expenditure;
2   assisting in policy making and planning;
3   authorizing future expenditure;
4   providing the basis for controlling income and expenditure;
5   setting a standard for evaluating performance;
6   motivating managers and employees;
7   co-ordinating the activities of multi-purpose organizations.

Many of these roles are of course closely related, but even so the extent to which each of the functions can be fulfilled simultaneously and without conflict with one another is a matter of some conjecture.

The uses of the budget in policy making and planning, in providing the basis for controlling income and expenditure, and in setting standards against which performance can be evaluated have already been discussed in the previous chapter. Of the remaining functions, the most immediately compelling reason for a revenue budget is to determine levels of income and expenditure. For taxation-financed services it is necessary to fix the level of taxation. For charges-financed services it is necessary to fix the level of charges. This process is of course inextricably bound up with the planning function. Either the planned activities are decided on, and this is then translated into a tax or charges requirement, or the overall tax or charges level is first fixed and activities are then planned under this ceiling. In practice, there are many variations between these alternatives. Whether or not an upper ceiling on charges and taxes is imposed before budgets are prepared, limitations on funding will come into the picture sooner or later. Many public sector organizations are responsible for a variety of different services and often these have to be financed from one common pool of revenue. Thus the Cabinet or the Treasury for the central government, or the finance committee for a local authority, will have to decide on the allocations of financial resources to different services, having regard to the upper limit of taxation that will be politically acceptable. It is unlikely that each service will receive sufficient funds to undertake every desired programme. Because everyone knows the rules of the game, requests for funds are kept to what might be thought to be acceptable amounts. It is at this stage that a whole range of strategies for ensuring a reasonable budgetary allocation come into play and these are well described by Wildavsky (1974) in *The Politics of the Budgetary Process*.

Once amounts have been allocated in the budget, then this provides the authorization to incur expenditure or to levy the charges that have been agreed. However, this is not quite so straightforward as it might at first seem. If it is the case that the amount authorized is not needed, then underspending ought to occur, but this might result in cuts in future allocations on the ground that as previous requests were too high then the current request is probably too high. Exactly achieving the budget might suggest that this was the result of spending up to the limit even though this was not necessary. Overspending might result in accusations of bad management. There is a strong connection here with the motivational aspect of budgeting. Only if managers see the budget allocation as reasonable in the first place will they be motivated to achieve it. Only if they perceive the politics and strategies of budgetary allocations to be fair and the assessment of budget achievements as consistent will they avoid dysfunctional behaviour.

Nevertheless, whatever the limitations of the budget, it is clearly important. As far as local and central government are concerned it is probably the single most important financial exercise that they undertake.

LINE-ITEM BUDGETING AND PROGRAMME BUDGETING

The way in which the annual revenue budget is prepared depends on whether the emphasis is on the *nature* of the income and expenditure (e.g. income from grants, fees, sales, or expenditure on salaries, materials, travelling, etc.) or on the *purpose* of the expenditure (e.g. crime prevention, mental health care, refuse disposal, and so on. The first of these methods is often referred to as 'line-item budgeting'. At its most extreme, line-item budgeting for, say, a local authority, would consist of a statement as shown in Fig. 3.1.

Although information may be given in this manner, such a statement by itself would clearly fail to identify the amounts allocated to individual services and would therefore fail to indicate the planned level of activity for each service. Moreover,

Local Authority Budget, 19X1–19X2		
Expenses	£000	£000
Employees	XXX	
Running expenses	XXX	
Debt charges	XXX	
Revenue contributions to capital expenditure	XXX	
Total expenses		XXX
Income		
Government grants	XXX	
Sales	XXX	
Fees and charges	XXX	
Rents	XXX	
Interest	XXX	
Miscellaneous income	XXX	
Total income		XXX
Balance to be met from rates		XXX

Fig. 3.1 Example of a summarized line-item budget.

for budgetary control purposes it is necessary to establish a responsibility centre structure or a programme structure showing clearly the resources provided to individual managers. In reality, most local authorities adopt a basic budget format under which the budget is first broken down into the various services provided by the authority such as police, fire, education, and so on, and then within each service there will be a further breakdown into divisions of service such as nursery education, primary education, etc. For each of the services or divisions of service, line-item budgets will be prepared similar to the one shown in Fig. 3.1. In practice, much more detail is provided. For example, 'Employees' would be broken down into salaries and wages, national insurance, superannuation charges, training expenses, and so on. This means that at the service or division of service level of aggregation, there is what appears to be a mixture of line-item budgeting and programme budgeting in use. The expenditure intended for the *purpose* of the provision of education, or the provision of primary education is clearly shown. However, the emphasis is still firmly on line-item budgeting and even though the expenditure on overall programmes is shown this is not the same as the system of programme budgeting (PPBS) that will be considered in the next chapter. At this stage a simple example may serve to illustrate the difference. The budget for the police service of a local authority might be prepared as shown in Fig. 3.1. There may be more detail within the subject headings, for example 'Employees' may distinguish between civilian employee costs and the costs of members of the police force, but in general the analysis will concentrate on the nature of the income and expenditure. Figure 3.2 shows how the budget might be prepared if a programme budgeting approach were adopted. The total expenditure for the overall objective of 'providing a police service' would be built up from the various sub-objectives or programme elements.

It is argued that the programme budgeting approach as illustrated in Fig. 3.2 should lead to better managerial planning and control because resources could be allocated more precisely to specific activities, and actual achievements could be

Police Authority Annual Budget, 19X1–19X2	
	£
Crime control and detection	XXX
Crime prevention advice	XXX
Traffic control	XXX
Crowd control	XXX
Police training	XXX
Court work	XXX
Prison duties	XXX
Rehabilitation of offenders	XXX
Administration	XXX
Research and planning	XXX
Total	XXX

Fig. 3.2 Possible programme budget structure for the police service of a local authority.

monitored more effectively. One of the arguments against such a programme structure is that it would be difficult to operate. During the course of a typical day, a police officer might be involved on several programmes and so it would be necessary to introduce a method for allocating direct, as well as indirect, costs to specific programmes. The administrative effort in doing this might well result in the costs exceeding any benefits. The recommended format (CIPFA, *Financial Information Service*, Vol. 24) is for police service expenditure to be analysed over the following divisions of service: police general; police pensions; police transport and moveable plant; police canteens; and police training. This represents something of a move towards a programme structure, but information is still lacking on the specific

Recreation and Amenities Committee
Revenue Budget

Item no. (1)	Code (2)	Item (3)	Current year Original estimate (4)		Revised estimate (5)		Next year Original estimate (6)	
			£'000	£'000	£'000	£'000	£'000	£'000
	04 02	WOODSIDE SWIMMING POOL						
	04 02 0	**Employees**						
256	04 02 01	Salaries	344		350		392	
257	04 02 02	Wages	720		823		762	
258	04 02 03	National Insurance	106		130		128	
260	04 02 05	Superannuation	121		142		140	
262				1,291		1,445		1,422
	04 02 1	**Premises and fixed plant**						
263	04 02 10	Repairs, alterations and maintenance	62		50		52	
264	04 02 12	Fuel, light, cleaning materials and water	292		235		331	
265	04 02 13	Furniture and fittings	1		1		1	
266	04 02 14	Rent and rates	98		136		136	
267				453		422		520
	04 02 2	**Supplies and services**						
268	04 02 21	Equipment, tools and materials – direct	40		41		33	
269	04 02 23	Provisions	13		17		23	
270	04 02 24	Clothing and uniforms	4		4		5	
271				57		62		61
	04 02 4	**Establishment expenses**						
272	04 02 40	Printing, stationery, adverts and postage, etc.	–		5		6	
	04 02 6	**Miscellaneous expenses**						
273	04 02 62	Other expenses	–		2		2	
274				1,801		1,936		2,011
	04 02 9	**Less income**						
275	04 02 91	Sales	76		78		84	
276	04 02 92	Fees and charges	936		984		1,036	
277	04 02 93	Rents	47		47		52	
278				1,059		1,109		1,172
279		Net deficit		742		827		839

Fig. 3.3 Example of a revenue budget for an individual cost centre.

activities that a police force is intended to pursue. Nevertheless, whether programme budgeting is used or not, an awareness of the need to achieve programmes and objectives is obviously fundamental to any method of budget preparation, and Schick (1982, p. 46) suggests that:

> Budgeting always has been conceived as a process of systematically relating expenditures of funds to the accomplishments of planned objectives. In this important sense there is a bit of PPB in every budget system.

In some cases the individual services may be broken down into subdivisions of services or cost centres. For example, the recreation and amenities service of a local authority will be responsible for the provision of parks and open spaces, leisure centres, swimming pools, and the like. Figure 3.3 shows how the budget for an individual swimming pool might appear. This example shows how the annual revenue budget can also provide the basis for proper budgetary control. The responsibility centre has been clearly established and the manager of the swimming pool can be held accountable for performance against the budget. Expenditure and income is broken down under standard headings, and the original and revised estimates for the current year and the estimates for the next budget year are shown. The revised current year estimates are the expected out-turn figures based on the information available at the time the next year's budget is being finalized. This is usually in January or February, and so with ten or eleven months of the current year already gone the revised estimates should be a fairly accurate prediction of the final outcome. It is obviously important that the most up-to-date figures for the current year are known when determining the budget for the next year, and so the incorporation of revised current year estimates is standard procedure for budget preparation.

INCREMENTAL BUDGETING

The use of the revised current year estimates of income and expenditure as the starting point for determining the budget for next year is frequently claimed to be one of the most fundamental weaknesses of the budgetary process. It is argued that such an approach fails to consider whether a particular item is still required or whether the amount currently incurred is reasonable. Once an item appears in the budget its inclusion in future budgets is taken for granted and only incremental changes in the item are considered. Attention is therefore focused on the marginal or incremental differences between this year's budget and last year's budget rather than on the whole of the budget, and it is this that gives rise to the term *incremental budgeting*. It is suggested that a more rational approach to budgeting would be to require every item in the budget to be justified as though the particular activity or programme were starting anew. This approach, which is usually referred to as 'zero-base' budgeting, is dealt with in more detail in Chapter 5. At this stage, however, it might be appropriate to consider briefly the reasons why incremental budgeting is so widely used.

Perhaps the most obvious reason for using incremental budgeting is that many of the activities carried out in previous years are either mandatory, or are so fundamental to meeting organizational goals, that will have to continue year in year out.

It seems sensible, therefore, to concentrate only on the changes from the previous year, because these might be all that are controllable. Wildavsky (1974, p. 13) states that:

> The budget may be conceived of as an iceberg with by far the largest part below the surface, outside the control of anyone. Many items in the budget are standard and are simply re-enacted every year unless there is a special reason to challenge them.

Another widely accepted reason for incremental budgeting concerns the complexity of the budgetary process. To make a thorough analysis of every existing programme and activity level would be impossible, and it is only by limiting discussion to the relatively small changes that are proposed that the budgetary process will work. It is argued that the limits on decision makers' knowledge, information, and cognitive ability mean that aids to calculation such as incremental budgeting are necessary. This is the *bounded rationality* argument. By concentrating only on new programmes, or changes in existing programmes, the information that has to be gathered and analysed can be limited to that which humans can process and evaluate.

Other arguments in favour of incrementalism are that it narrows the area open to disputes, thereby reducing conflicts, and that it is consistent with the principles of conservatism. Obviously, by focusing on incremental changes, arguments over budgetary allocations are confined to relatively small amounts. The vast proportion of the annual budget allocation is undisputed. The question of conservative approaches to budgeting is really a variation on the bounded rationality theme. Because of the inability to foresee the full consequences of change, it is argued that these changes should take place gradually rather than all at once. Proponents of incremental budgeting would therefore defend its usefulness on the grounds of conservatism. The position is well summarized by Schultze (1968, p. 50) who states:

> because our ability to foresee the full social consequence of any program change is so limited, movement towards objectives should proceed by small steps. Radical actions take us beyond the realm of reasonable foresight. We make progress by sequential steps, correcting and adjusting for unforeseen circumstances as we go.

In reality, very few public sector organizations make use of *systematic* reviews of the existing expenditure base by using techniques such as zero-base budgeting. It could be argued that an effective management should be aware anyway of programmes where existing levels of activity are no longer necessary and should act accordingly. For other programmes it should perhaps be the role of political masters to question whether the existing base level is sacrosanct or not.

However, as far as routine budget preparation is concerned, the emphasis is firmly incremental. The awareness that it is the incremental changes that are controllable, leads to budget statement formats that attempt to isolate the various reasons for the changes. Figure 3.4 shows how the budget for a children's hostel of a local authority might distinguish between committed growth and further growth. To the original estimate for the current year (column 3) are added the effect of increased costs and pay awards (column 5), and the amounts for committed growth (columns 6–9), to produce the committed budget figure (column 10). In this case, if the base level of activity implied by the expenses included in column 3 is to be undertaken next year, then this will require the amounts shown in column 10. The only incre-

Budget – XYZ Hostels

		Current year			Committed Growth				Next year	Further Growth		
Last year £	Head of account	Original approved estimate £	Revised estimate £	Increased costs and pay awards £	Increments £	Full year of new staff £	Revenue implications of capital programme £	Other £	Committed budget £	Revenue implications of capital programme £	Other £	Estimate £
(1)	(2)	(3)	(4)	(5)	(6)	(7)	(8)	(9)	(10)	(11)	(12)	(13)
	EMPLOYEES											
60,189	Salaries	66,000	67,800	9,600	1,000	2,000			78,600			
4,776	National Insurance	5,700	5,800	2,400		100			8,200			
5,550	Superannuation	6,100	6,400	1,200					7,300			
28,953	Wages	35,000	34,000	2,500		1,000			38,500			
2,563	National Insurance	3,100	2,900	800		50			3,950			
409	Superannuation	500	500			50			550			
1,305	Allowances											
914	Other	300	500	700					1,000			
104,719	TOTAL EMPLOYEES	116,700	117,900	17,200	1,000	3,200			138,100			
	PREMISES											
4,698	Repairs and maintenance	3,200	3,500	500					4,000			
	Fuel, light and cleaning:											
1,474	Gas	2,600	2,200	600					2,200	500		2,700
1,584	Electricity	1,800	2,000	400				–1,000	2,200	200		2,400
308	Water	600	700	100					700			
780	Cleaning	1,000	1,100	200					1,200	400		1,600
80	Fixtures and fittings	1,500	1,500	500					2,000			
2,668	Rent and rates	2,600	3,800	1,000				200	3,800	400		4,200
	SUPPLIES AND SERVICES											
2,283	Equipment, tools and materials	3,600	3,600	200					3,800			
11,127	Provisions	10,100	11,600	1,900					12,000	1,200		13,200
964	Clothing and uniforms	1,300	1,000	–300					1,000			
459	Laundry	600	700	200					800	100		900
82	Other	100	100						100			
	TRANSPORT AND PLANT											
	Use of transport and plant											
214	Petrol, oil, etc.	300	400	100					400			
	Purchase of vehicles											
203	Repairs and maintenance	200	200	50					250			

Fig. 3.4   Example of a budget format distinguishing between committed amounts and incremental amounts.

mental items are the amounts for further growth in columns 11 and 12. If the existing base is not reviewed then these are the only amounts that can be controlled.

A further way of presenting budget statements is to concentrate on the objective of a particular service or programme and also to isolate the budget for the existing base level of activity from the amounts required for increments above the base. Figure 3.5 shows how the programme for providing sports and recreational facilities might be presented in this way. This format clearly distinguishes between the funding needed to operate at the current level of operations and the controllable amount required for programme development. However, this is still incremental budgeting and should not be confused with the alternative zero-base budgeting approach that is discussed in Chapter 5. The examples of budget statements in Figs 3.3, 3.4 and 3.5 are expressed totally in financial terms. Ideally, of course, if output measurements are available these should be included as well.

Parks and Recreation Committee
Programme Area – Sport and Physical Recreation

Policy Budget, 19X3/X4

Price Base

	November 19X1		November 19X2		
	Original	*Revised*	*Estimate 19X3/X4*		*Total*
	19X2/X3	*19X2/X3*	*Increase in requirement*		
Net requirement	787,455	817,741	*Committed*	*Uncommitted*	
Non-recurring items		11,675			
19X3/X4		829,415			829,415
Additions for inflation 19X2/X3					
Manpower costs			35,685		
Price increase			79,970		
			115,655		
Less: Increased income			48,615 cr.		
Total committed increase because of inflation			67,040		67,040
Unscheduled unavoidable expenditure:					
Additional net revenue consequences of reaffirmed capital programme			27,595	7,455	
					35,050
Total cost of existing policies					931,505
Development of policies					
Preferred new policies					20,000
Total net cost of the programmes					**951,505**

Fig. 3.5 Example of programme format showing committed amounts and incremental amounts.

BUDGET PREPARATION

A characteristic feature of budget preparation for public sector organizations is the long and complex process that is involved. There are many factors that will affect the final allocation, and to enable these to be considered fully it is necessary to start before the beginning of the budget year. The exact procedures followed will reflect the circumstances and background of the different organizations, but in general it is usually possible to identify three distinct stages in budget preparation. The first stage involves the preparation of estimates for each individual part or department of the organization. Secondly, these are combined to enable the overall position to be considered. It is often necessary to revise the individual departmental budgets at this stage before the draft budget for the whole organization can be prepared. Finally, the draft budget is submitted to the governing body of the organization for final approval. The governing body will either be an appointed board or elected council or, in the case of central government, Parliament.

An example of the budget preparation timetable that might be used by a local authority is given in Fig. 3.6. This example shows the process starting in June, with the draft budget manual being discussed in the finance department, and ending in February or March with the approval of the final budget by the Council. Between these dates, the estimates of the individual service departments are prepared and then submitted for approval by the committee of elected members responsible for the particular service. The various service department estimates are then put together by the finance department and considered by the finance committee. The service department estimates will be determined by calculating the cost of carrying on the existing level of services and programmes together with the financial consequences of any planned changes in the level of service provision, i.e. an incremental approach, as described in the previous section. After consideration by the finance committee, the overall requirement in terms of financial resources and tax and charges levies will be known, and in the light of this, reductions in the original estimates have to be made by the service department. An increasingly widely used variation on this approach might be for the council to determine, in advance of the preparation of detailed estimates, an overall limit on spending for the coming budget year. This will then be translated into a financial resources or cash limit for each service department and they will then prepare their estimates to comply with this limit.

Whichever approach is adopted, budgets will also have to be frequently reconsidered and revised because of more up-to-date assumptions on inflation rates, or new building completion dates, or because of changes in central government requirements concerning the extension or curtailment of particular services. A further complication is provided by the fact that information on central government grant levels and overall spending limits is often not finally known until December, and this may result in further last minute revisions and changes during the months of January and February. The whole process has to be completed by about the end of February so that final budget recommendations and required tax and charges levies can be submitted to the council for approval.

Although the precise details may differ, the need for budget proposals to be considered at several distinct levels, and the frequent referring back and revising of original estimates before a satisfactory outcome is reached is a feature of all public sector organizations.

Timetable	Process
June	Draft budget manual to departmental finance officers, discuss draft manual with finance department staff.
1 July	Manpower estimates commence.
5 July	Draft budget manual to management team, guidelines determined.
1 September	Estimates framework to departmental finance officers and the budget manual and sessions timetable finalized.
1 September	Price factors issued, together with detailed budget working papers.
24 September	Manpower commitment estimates completed.
8 October	Approved capital programme returned to finance department.
15 October	Commitment estimates, additional income and expenditure details and unapproved capital programme for holding accounts returned to finance department.
29 October	Commitment estimates, additional income and expenditure details and unapproved capital programme for trading accounts returned to finance department.
12 November	Balance of completed commitment estimates submitted to finance department.
17 November	Balance of additional income, expenditure and unapproved capital programme submitted to finance department.
17 December	Management team consider draft budget report, revenue and capital summaries and resource forecasts.
January	Revised current estimate in financial system. (This may require approval in the round of committees prior to that which considers the new budget.)
5 January	Management team considers budget report.
7 January	Management team joint session – leader, deputy leader, and committee chairpersons.
10–21 January	Subcommittees consider preliminary revenue estimates and capital programmes.
24 January	Committees.
25 January	Committees.
26 January	Committees.
31 January	Special Policy Committee to finalize revenue allocation and capital programme.
31 January	Subcommittees and committees – contingency meetings.
21 February	Special Policy Committee to recommend tax levy.
25 February	Final budget book drafted.
3 March	Council meeting and final budget approval.
6 March	Printed budget book published.

Fig. 3.6 Example of a typical local authority budget preparation timetable.

In view of the lengthy and complicated procedures involved, it is essential for a budget manual or set of budget instructions to be prepared so that every participant in the budgetary process is aware of what is required. However, the informal negotiations and bargaining that are essential if the process is to work at all can never be completely captured by a written code. In recent years, the planned reductions in public sector spending have resulted in the budgetary systems of public sector organizations being subjected to a very severe test. At times of growth the process of bargaining and trade-offs and informal negotiations is made much easier because of the existence of a cushion of slack resources. At times of standstill, or cutback, the question of 'who gets what?' becomes much more crucial and urgent, and previously reliable informal networks may break down. When faced with the prospect of long-term organizational decline, the rational response should be to adopt strategies which will minimize the impact on fundamental aims and objectives, rather than strategies which spread spending cuts evenly. Thus a requirement to reduce overall spending by 5 per cent could be achieved by reducing the current budget of every individual part of the organization by 5 per cent. Although this might be perceived as 'fair', it would ignore the fact that in reality certain services are more important than others and cuts should therefore be made selectively. The basis for selection should of course, reflect the relative significance of different activities in terms of overall organizational aims, and yet to adopt this approach leads to harder choices and more chances of political conflict. Equal across-the-board cuts do at least have the advantage of political expediency.

Other strategies that might have short-term political acceptability are to impose complete 'recruitment freezes', or to adopt a last-in-first-out approach to cost reductions, i.e. the most recently commenced services or programmes would be the first to be cut. However, none of these approaches is 'rational' in the sense that they necessarily minimize the loss of organizational effectiveness. Only by undertaking systematic reviews of existing policies, services and programmes can this be done. Informal analysis, intuitive judgements and snap decisions are unlikely to be sufficient.

Whatever approach to budget preparation is adopted by an organization, it is invariably the case that the central finance department has the most important contribution to make. At one extreme, the finance department may be responsible for the detailed preparation of the estimates of the various service departments or geographical divisions. In this case the only part the service departments or geographical divisions would take in the process would be to provide the necessary information. At the other extreme, the service departments and geographical divisions would do all the detailed work, with the finance department merely summarizing the overall position. However, even with this approach the finance department will normally be responsible for setting timetables, providing a uniform framework, giving guidance on assumptions about economic conditions, price levels, etc., and providing information on debt charges and amounts for central administration and overhead allocations.

CAPITAL BUDGETS

Most public sector organizations attempt to make a clear distinction between items of a revenue or current nature and items of a capital nature. In spite of this, there is no single definition of capital expenditure that is acceptable in every circumstance. In general, the approach that is adopted to isolate capital expenditure from revenue expenditure concerns the period of benefit. The benefits flowing from revenue expenditure tend to be limited to the year in which the expenditure is incurred, whereas the benefits that result from capital expenditure extend beyond the year of payment. The 'period of benefit' principle when applied to such items as the costs of a new school or nuclear power station presents few problems of classification. They will clearly provide benefits for several years into the future and are therefore capital expenditure. However, there are situations where the correct classification is less obvious. For example, the education of school children will, hopefully, provide benefits for many years ahead. Does this mean that expenditure on teachers' salaries is capital expenditure? Similarly, expenditure on repairing and maintaining capital assets might merely ensure that the asset remains at its present state, and should therefore be treated as revenue. On the other hand, the repairs and maintenance might result in improvements to the asset, or even an effective replacement of the asset, and so might properly be thought of as capital. At the margin, therefore, there may be problems of an accurate and consistent distinction between revenue and capital. In the absence of clear definitions, it is likely that a large element of creativity would enter into the making of such a distinction. The reaction of the government has been to prescribe certain types of expenditure as capital and thereby provide an effective definition. The Appendix to this chapter gives an example of the items that are to be regarded as capital under the provisions of the Local Government and Housing Act 1989.

It is because capital and revenue expenditures result in different periods of benefit that financing differences exist. Because capital expenditure confers benefits over several years, it is argued that the costs should be spread over the years that will benefit. Thus if a school is built and paid for in the current year, it would seem harsh to expect the total costs to be financed by the current year's taxpayers, when the school could be expected to provide educational services for say the next 40 years. It would, perhaps, be fairer to borrow the amount required and then repay the loan, plus interest, over the 40-year period, thereby spreading the costs equitably over the future generations of taxpayers who will benefit from the school. Certainly, as far as central and local government capital expenditure is concerned, such a philosophy has long been accepted as a cornerstone of financial policy.

The need for capital budgets

If a public sector organization is to be successful in achieving its fundamental aims and objectives, it is necessary to give careful consideration to the planning of capital expenditure requirements. Limitations on resources mean that not all capital programmes can be undertaken immediately and priorities will have to be established. Taking local government as an example, the Chartered Institute of Public Finance and Accountancy (*Financial Information Services*, vol. 4, chapter 7) identifies the objectives of capital programmes as follows:

A capital programme is a major form of expression of the overall plan for the development of an authority's activities and services. It defines priorities between services, and it is an essential tool in assessing the availability of capital resources such as staff, land and finance. The purpose of preparing capital programmes is to enable an authority to take a corporate view of the need for capital expenditure in each area of service provision, to meet the requirements of the Government's capital control system, to assess the extent to which an authority can meet the revenue consequences of proposed capital projects, and to authorise officers to undertake the action necessary to implement individual capital projects.

CIPFA also go on to point out that large capital schemes will typically take several years to complete and will pass through most of the following stages:

- reports by officers on need and viability – including estimates of capital costs and revenue consequences;
- inclusion in the capital programme of a local authority, with bids submitted to government departments for capital approvals;
- site selection and acquisition, town planning applications, planning and approval sought for road closures, etc.;
- architects' designs, preparation of contract documents, bills of quantities and contract conditions;
- issue of contract tenders and decision on award of contract;
- construction – control of contract costs, payments to contractor;
- completion of contract, audit and settlement of final account.

If capital expenditure is to be financed from revenue contributions, the capital budget will be an essential means of determining the pricing structures that will be needed to ensure sufficient resources are generated to meet the capital requirements. If capital expenditure is to be financed from loans, the long-term effect on future revenue budgets is an important issue. Debt charges and the future running costs of capital projects will have important implications for the revenue budget of an organization, and the capital budget is important in assessing what these will be. The capital budget is also needed to determine the timing of loan requirements. Where capital schemes are financed predominantly by borrowing, the need to comply with government controls becomes an important consideration. Because central government is responsible for controlling the overall level of public sector borrowing, there has been a long history of local government capital expenditure being closely controlled. The methods of control have fluctuated over the years between limits on borrowing and limits on actual spending. Under the Local Government and Housing Act 1989, *sources* of finance are regulated. The Act identifies the four main sources of finance for capital expenditure purposes as: (a) credit approvals; (b) capital grants from central government; (c) capital receipts from the sale of land, houses and other assets; and (d) contributions from revenue. However, 75 per cent of the capital receipts from the sale of council houses and 50 per cent of most other receipts are required to be set aside for the redemption of debt, and therefore it is only the balance that is available to finance new capital expenditure. Where this is insufficient, credit approvals have to be sought from central government.

The form of capital budgets

Although capital budgets may be prepared for one year only, the long-term nature of capital schemes suggests that budgets for several years ahead will usually be more appropriate. The time required for planning and designing capital projects and the fact that several years may elapse between conception and final completion means that capital budgeting is essentially a medium- to long-term exercise.

A useful approach to the problem of planning and controlling capital expenditure is to develop capital programmes which express the overall plan of short-, medium-, and long-term capital schemes, and reveal the allocation of priorities

Education Committee

Columns (4)–(7) fall under the heading *Programme of Capital Expenditure*; columns (9)–(11) fall under the heading *Increase in Revenue Expenditure*.

Item	Total Project Cost (1) £	Project and Details (2)	Places	Site Availability (3)	Current Year (4) £	Year 1 (5) £	Year 2 (6) £	Year 3 (7) £	Estimated Date of Opening (8)	Year 1 additional to current year (9) £	Year 2 additional to year 1 (10) £	Year 3 additional to year 2 (11) £
		SECONDARY										
1		Completion of Projects			1,500,375	528,650	79,225			276,375	54,050	7,900
		Starts in previous year										
2	288,125	Northtown Phase 1	250	Owned	171,000	90,650			Sep Yr 1	28,425	15,050	
3	172,800	West Vale	120	Owned	122,350	32,450	5,725		Apr Yr 1	19,550	3,250	500
4	165,925	Northfield	90	Owned	107,000	48,750			Sep Yr 1	15,025	6,825	
5	153,550	South Vale	90	Owned	97,950	46,250			Sep Yr 1	14,150	6,675	
6	181,725	Central	150	Owned	122,675	49,275			Sep Yr 1	18,925	8,950	
		(including Minor Works contribution)										
7	962,125				620,975	267,375	5,725			96,075	40,750	500
		Starts in current year										
8	348,175	Southtown	230	Owned	96,050	191,675	40,575	2,550	Apr Yr 2	17,600	33,350	4,275
		(including Minor Works contribution)										
9	343,575	Eastfield	150	Owned	23,225	190,850	128,950	550	Sep Yr 2	10,750	28,750	16,275
10	206,450	Northtown Phase 2	140	Owned	26,125	173,075	6,225	1,025	Apr Yr 2	10,525	24,900	600
11	366,200	Westfield	150	Owned	25,000	153,275	158,275	29,650	Apr Yr 3	9,150	21,300	25,375
12	156,325	North Vale	100	Owned	29,100	109,375	17,000	850	Jan Yr 1	9,175	15,450	1,775
13	198,050	Bradley Upper – Remodelling		Owned	48,150	132,025	4,225		Sep Yr 1	24,700	23,250	400
14	323,350	East town	120	Owned	21,425	254,275	48,625		Apr Yr 2	13,550	32,875	5,100
		(including. Minor Works contribution)										
15	15,250	Newdale Caretaker's House		Owned	725	14,150	400		Sep Yr 1	700	1,300	25
16	1,957,375				269,800	1,218,700	404,275	34,625		96,150	181,175	53,825
		Starts in Year 1										
17	1,053,150	North Central Phases 1 & 2	500	Negotiating	40,000	187,300	457,900	357,550*	Sep Yr 3	12,100	37,850	76,225
18	284,025	East Vale	150	Owned	7,000	13,000	140,400	116,350*	Sep Yr 3	1,200	7,475	23,450
19	275,750	Northtown Phase 3	150	Owned	7,625	84,625	172,975	10,525	Apr Yr 3	4,075	14,925	25,575
20	166,000	Northfield	70	Owned	12,000	80,600	69,425	3,975	Sep Yr 2	4,700	13,050	8,650
21	1,778,925				66,625	365,525	840,700	488,400		22,075	73,300	133,900
		Starts in Year 2										
22	182,325	Westfield	90	Owned	1,000	10,000	93,000	74,325*	Sep Yr 3	550	5,100	15,075
23	221,750	South Central	90	Owned	1,000	12,000	116,500	86,775*	Sep Yr 3	650	6,400	17,850
24	149,625	Eastfield	90	Owned		9,750	67,900	66,500*	Sep Yr 3	450	4,300	13,125
25	518,875	North Central Phase 3	250	Negotiating	1,000	26,000	100,000	280,000*	Sep Yr 4	1,275	6,900	21,875
26	1,072,575				3,000	57,750	377,400	507,600		2,925	22,700	67,925
		Starts in Year 3										
27	605,925	East Central	300	Searching		6,000	20,600	104,876*	Sep Yr 5	275	1,475	6,650
28	662,350	Southfield Phase 1	300	Owned		5,000	40,000	95,000*	Sep Yr 5	225	2,250	7,875
29	1,268,275					11,000	60,600	199,875		500	3,725	14,525
30		Total Secondary			2,460,775	2,449,000	1,767,925	1,230,500		494,100	375,700	278,575

Note: Costs are based on November current year price levels or latest known costs in relation to projects already started.
* Payments will not be completed by 31 March, Year 3.

Fig. 3.7 Example of a published capital programme.

A Description of project   Name of scheme _____

B Capital payments	Debt repayment period (yrs)	Financial code	Approved capital cost	Total capital cost	Last year's actual	Estimated payments							
						Current year	Year 1	Year 2	Year 3	Year 4	Year 5	Year 6	
	Total to run		£000	£000	£000	£000	£000	£000	£000	£000	£000	£000	
Site purchase													
Construction													
Furniture/equipment – general													
School meals equipment													
Additional fitted equipment													
Professional fees													
Architect's charges													
Other													
GRAND TOTAL													
TOTAL (exc architect's charges)													

C Progress (tick appropriate boxes) (at 19.10)   In progress or contractually committed ☐   Not committed ☐

    Site – not determined ☐ – determined ☐   Approved by council _____   Date _____

       – in negotiation ☐ – acquired/appropriated ☐   Ministry – not applicable ☐   Amount £ _____

                                 – awaited ☐   £ _____

    Brief to architect ☐ Tender sent out ☐   – received ☐

D Notes

Revenue implications of approved
capital schemes

Name of compiler _____ Tel ext
Name of QS _____ Tel ext

Expenditure heading	Vote	Original provision in current year	Additional current year	Additional year 1	Additional year 2	Additional year 3	Additional year 4	Maximum cost in full year

Fig. 3.8   **Example of format for an individual capital project.**

between different parts of the organization. The capital programme is essential in assessing the availability of resources, the implications for revenue, and the orderly achievement of fundamental aims and objectives.

The Chartered Institute of Public Finance and Accountancy (*Financial Information Service*, vol. 4, para. 55) suggests that the basic information to be included in a capital programme should be the following:

- title of the capital scheme;
- the committee, department and officer responsible;
- a description of the scheme;
- the priority rating;
- for schemes in progress, actual capital expenditure to end of last financial year, revised estimates for current and future years, and revised estimate of total capital cost;
- for new schemes, total estimated capital cost over future years;
- estimated net revenue costs for following financial year and for a full year of operation;
- grant contributions and any revenue expense savings (e.g. energy conservation);
- target dates for progressing scheme through the various stages of approval, site selection, design, planning permission, land acquisition, preparation of contract documents, award of tenders, start on site, and completion.

This information should preferably be shown for each capital scheme as well as in total for each service. Expenditure should also be analysed between land and site works, construction, landscaping, furniture, fees, and so on, as such an analysis will be useful for the subsequent control of actual expenditure against budgeted.

An example of how a capital programme might be presented is shown in Fig. 3.7. Details are provided of the planned capital expenditure for the current year and the three future years on each identified capital project. Information is also given on the likely date of completion of each project and the expected impact there will then be on revenue expenditure. Figure 3.8 shows a detailed breakdown of an individual capital project.

APPENDIX: CAPITAL EXPENDITURE ITEMS

The following categories of expenditure are defined under the Local Government and Housing Act 1989, s. 40 as expenditure for capital purposes:

(a) the acquisition, reclamation, enhancement or laying-out of land, exclusive of roads, buildings or other structures;

(b) the acquisition, construction, preparation, enhancement or replacement of roads, buildings and other structures;

(c) the acquisition, installation or replacement of movable or immovable plant, machinery and apparatus, and vehicles and vessels;

(d) the making of advances, grants or other financial assistance to any person towards expenditure incurred or to be incurred by him on the matters mentioned in paragraphs (a) to (c) above or in the acquisition of investments; and

(e) the acquisition of share capital or loan capital in any body corporate.

The term 'enhancement' in (a) and (b) above is defined as the carrying out of works which are intended:

(a) to lengthen substantially the useful life of the asset; or
(b) to increase substantially the open market value of the asset; or
(c) to increase substantially the extent to which the asset can or will be used for the purposes of or in connection with the functions of the local authority concerned.

In addition, the Act authorizes the appropriate Secretary of State to permit expenditure which does not fall within the definition of capital expenditure, as given above, to be treated as capital expenditure. Circular 11/90 from the Department of the Environment states that the Secretary of State does not expect to give such permission except in situations where an unforeseen catastrophe has occurred or where unbudgeted expenditure (e.g. for redundancy costs) will lead to continuing revenue account savings in future years.

DISCUSSION TOPICS

1 'Budgeting is an important part of the management control process in any organization, but it is even more important in a non-profit organization than in a profit-oriented company.'
   Discuss the reasons for the importance of budgets and explain why the budget is particularly important in public sector organizations.

2 Explain what is meant by 'line-item budgeting' and give an example of the line-item approach to budgeting.

3 Explain what is meant by 'incremental budgeting' and discuss the advantages and disadvantages of this approach to budgeting.

4 Capital budgets are an important requirement for public sector organizations. Explain the purpose of capital budgets and discuss their importance.

CHAPTER 4

Programme budgeting

In Chapter 2 the importance of determining the long-term fundamental aims and objectives of public sector organizations as a framework for the proper management and control of resources was emphasized. In reality, however, there is a wide gap between theory and practice, and many examples still exist of organizations being criticized for pursuing a variety of ill-defined and occasionally contradictory goals. The reasons for this are not hard to find. Many public sector organizations face an environment of changing government attitudes and changing social and economic pressures; senior managers are therefore reluctant to develop long-term policies that might restrict their ability to react quickly to changing circumstances. The need to retain flexibility to deal with future uncertainties leads to short-term decision making and a focusing of attention on the annual budget. Emphasis is on the monetary inputs rather than on the objectives that the inputs might achieve. The result is the so-called 'traditional' approach to budgeting, budgets being prepared on a line-item basis with only the increments over a previously established base being subjected to close scrutiny. Such an approach was described in Chapter 3. Whatever justification there might be in terms of political expediency, it is obvious that traditional budgeting does not provide a sound basis for 'rational' decision making. It is difficult to decide whether requests for more staff or equipment or premises are justified without knowing what they are to be used for, and whether expenditures will lead to the achievement of fundamental objectives, unless the relationship between the two is established. It was in response to the perceived deficiencies of the traditional approach to budgeting that the technique of programme budgeting, or more precisely, a planning, programming and budgeting system (PPBS) was developed.

THE CONCEPT OF PPBS

PPBS is primarily concerned with the needs of decision makers. It is invariably the case that the resources available to public sector organizations are limited in relation to the demands for them. This means that choices have to be made to ensure that the limited resources are allocated in such a way as to produce the greatest beneficial impact on the overall objectives. PPBS provides a framework for making such choices. The starting point is to determine the overall objectives of the organization, or segments of an organization, as precisely as possible. It is then necessary to consider and evaluate the alternative programmes that might be undertaken to achieve these objectives. To do this properly requires some measure of the favourable impact that each programme will have, i.e. its benefits. The next stage involves calculating the costs of each programme so that a cost/benefit relationship can be established. Budgetary allocations can then be made against a background of known cost/benefit relationships.

The Chartered Institute of Public Finance and Accountancy (FIS, vol. 4) provides the following definition:

> Programme budgeting is primarily a system associated with corporate management which identifies alternative policies, presents the implications of their adoption and provides for the efficient control of those policies chosen. It embraces several established concepts and analytical techniques within the framework of a systematic approach to decision making, planning, management and control. The principal features of programme budgeting are that it relates to objectives, it relates to outputs, it emphasizes the future, and it emphasizes choice.

When considering PPBS it is useful to distinguish between the programme structure part of the system, and programme analysis. The *programme structure* provides the framework for linking resources and activities to objectives. The relationship between ends and means has to be established and it may often be the case that the resources required to undertake a particular programme are scattered over several departments. PPBS involves cutting across the normal organizational structure so that the appropriate inputs can be drawn together. For example, an objective of a local authority may be the care of the elderly, and yet more than one department may make a contribution towards this objective. The social services department may provide residential homes and social work visitors. The housing department may provide sheltered housing facilities or specially designed one-bedroom flats. The purpose of the programme structure is to enable the resources provided for these activities in the separate social services budget and housing budget to be grouped together so that they can be related to the single objective of providing care for old people. However, producing a programme structure is only the beginning. It is the next stage of programme analysis that is responsible for providing the information for decision making.

Programme analysis is concerned with the analysis of the costs and benefits of each programme so that choices can be made. When faced with competing demands for scarce resources, decision makers need to know the effect that proposed expenditure might be expected to have on objectives. This means that the output of each programme must be measured in a manner that captures the entire beneficial impacts of the programme. For example, for a programme involving the building of roads and motorways, it is not sufficient to measure output merely in terms of number of miles of road built but in terms of the overall effect on transportation. This would involve measuring a complex range of economic, social and environmental benefits and consequences. These are the benefits that are expected to result from proposed expenditure on a particular programme, and this is the information decision makers need. The relationship between costs and benefits can be established and used as a basis for making choices between alternative programmes.

THE DEVELOPMENT OF PPBS

Dissatisfaction with the traditional subjective, or line-item, form of budgeting is not a recent phenomenon. As far back as 1953, the Seventh Report of the Select Committee on Estimates, 1952–53, suggested that a system of presenting service department estimates 'whereby a clearer exposition of the purpose of the expenditure should be given', would be a desirable innovation. Novick (1973, p. 19) states that in the USA examples of the use of management tools of the programme budgeting type being used in industry can be traced back to the 1920s or earlier. However, it seems to be generally agreed that most of the impetus for the development of PPBS as an operational system capable of being used by public sector bodies stems from its adoption in 1961 by the US Department of Defense. Its use was then extended to all departments of the Federal Government by President Johnson in 1965. For the rest of the 1960s and into the early 1970s PPBS was very fashionable. It was implemented, or at least experimented with, by many state and local governments, both in the USA and the UK. PPBS was seen as a solution to the frustrations and problems caused by traditional approaches to budgeting. Relating resources to ultimate objectives was the obvious way to proceed. Duplication and waste would be eliminated by clearly identifying objectives and gearing resource planning to their achievement, and efficiency and effectiveness would therefore be improved. Unfortunately, by the mid-1970s most of the euphoria surrounding PPBS had disappeared. It had been abandoned by the US Federal Government and also by many of the other organizations that had introduced it. This is not to say that there are no examples of PPBS remaining. In a study of the budgeting practices of municipalities in the state of Victoria in Australia, Bellamy and Kluvers (1995) found that as many as 18 out of a sample of 122 local authorities (14.8 per cent) used PPBS as their sole method of budget preparation. Even so, it is clear that PPBS has failed to find widespread acceptance, and the question of why such a seemingly rational approach to planning and budgeting has been so frequently rejected is considered later in this chapter. But first of all it might be useful to examine how PPBS might be applied.

APPLICATION OF PPBS

When attempts are made to implement PPBS it is first of all necessary to determine the overall objectives of the organization, and also the various sub-objectives that make up the overall objectives. Unless this is done, it is not possible to organize the appropriate programme structure. The programme structure has to be such that the programmes serving the same objective are grouped together into programme categories. Programme categories are then broken down into specific activities known as 'programme elements'. It is then necessary to estimate the costs and benefits of the individual programme elements. These costs and benefits are then aggregated to provide the total costs and benefits of the programme. As the main purpose of PPBS is to provide a basis for decision making, alternative ways of achieving objectives should also be expressed in the form of programme categories and programme elements and the costs and benefits determined. A choice can then be made between alternative programmes. In order to illustrate the relationship between programmes, programme categories, and programme elements, a possible structure for the social services department of a local authority is shown in Fig. 4.1. The process starts with the expression of the overall objective. Specific programmes are then required to achieve this. For each programme there will be programme categories, and for the purpose of this example the programme categories for the

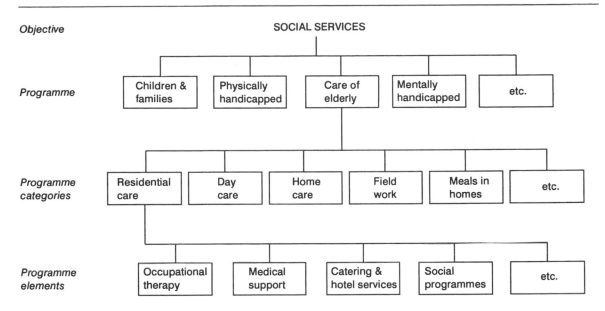

Fig. 4.1 Possible programme structure for social services.

care of the elderly programme are shown. Each programme category will be made up of programme elements. The programme elements for the residential care programme category is shown. The final stage is to determine the estimated costs and benefits of each programme element. The estimated costs could be classified according to their nature, such as salaries, materials, services, and so on. The benefits would be the expected output of each programme element.

Although such a procedure may appear at first glance to be relatively straightforward, in reality there will often be serious problems to be overcome at every stage. Difficulties will be encountered when determining objectives, when isolating programme categories and programme elements, when measuring outputs, and when selecting alternatives. For example, the objectives of a local authority social services department may be generally agreed as being 'to provide services for those in need of care and support'. However, such a requirement is really far too broad to provide a useful framework for setting up a suitable programme structure, and yet attempts to enlarge upon this objective only serve to emphasize the difficulties involved. Social services departments exist to carry out a wide range of direct care, support and practical help activities for the young, the elderly, the handicapped, the mentally ill and others, with the intention of improving the lives of the most vulnerable in the community. At times, these various purposes will not be capable of being clearly and unambiguously defined in such a way that would find general agreement. As Van Gunsteren (1976, p. 61) points out:

> Basic objectives of government are not given, pre-existing in fixed form and waiting to be discovered. They are made and chosen by people. So the programme structure designer has to look for authoritative 'makers' of objectives. The law? The legislature? The President? The agency head? Public opinion?

Assuming that objectives can be found or chosen in some way, the development of a programme structure should pose fewer problems. The existing organizational structure of many public sector bodies is often arranged so that each department is responsible for providing a particular service. To the extent that most of the necessary programmes are already grouped together within one department, the problems of setting up a programme structure will be reduced. For example, in Fig. 4.1 the programmes for social services are shown as 'children and families', 'physically handicapped', 'care of the elderly', 'mentally handicapped', and so on. These programmes are already provided by local authorities and the budget format that most authorities follow will give information on the income and expenditure of each of these programmes or 'divisions of service'. Thus at the programme level there is an apparent similarity between existing budgetary practices and the programme structure of PPBS. However, it is when the budget is broken down into its further stages that the fundamental differences between the two approaches are revealed. For example, if current practice is for the division of service or programme to be broken down into responsibility centres, such as individual nursing homes or individual day care centres, then this would mean that the programme categories and programme elements of Fig. 4.1 would not be revealed in the budget. Even if current practice is for programme categories to be identified before the budget is broken down into the responsibility centres of individual nursing homes, etc., the programme elements would not be revealed. With programme budgeting the emphasis is firmly on the objectives of the overall programme and at each stage the objective becomes more detailed. Thus the programme categories reflect the activities needed to undertake each programme. The programme elements are the activities needed to accomplish each programme category.

It is important that the programme structure should enable the inputs used for each programme category and programme element to be clearly identified, and this really requires a correspondence between programme structure and organization structure. Once again using Fig. 4.1 as an example, the care of the elderly programme will involve a variety of programme categories. These are the distinct groups of activities that support the care of the elderly programme. Providing that the organizational structure is such that staff time and other resources spent on one programme element or category are capable of being distinguished from that spent on another programme element or category, then a programme structure is appropriate.

The expenses of each programme element will either be presented as a total amount or, depending on the amount of detail required, will be classified as salaries, materials, services, etc. The budget of each programme category is the sum of the budgets of its programme elements. The programme structure approach to budgeting is therefore meant to provide a system which relates the expenditure at each stage of the budget to the purposes of the expenditure.

Even though most of the activities required to achieve the objectives of 'providing services for those in need of care and support' will be found in the social services department, it will at times be necessary to recognize that the activities of other departments, such as housing or education, may also be directed at this objective. These will have to be brought together with those of the social services department and therefore there will be a need to cut across departmental lines of responsibility.

Although setting up a programme structure for social services, as illustrated in Fig. 4.1, and bringing the activities of other departments into this structure may be an improvement on existing practices, this is still not PPBS. The programme analysis stage is now required and it is at this point that the most overwhelming difficulties associated with the implementation of PPBS occur. Programme analysis requires not only the costs to be measured, but also the expected beneficial impacts that each programme, programme category, and programme element will have on the objectives. It is therefore necessary to be able to measure in some way the outputs of programme elements such as 'occupational therapy' or 'medical support', or 'social programmes', etc. The ultimate outputs do, of course, depend upon the objectives of social services and, even if these could be agreed upon, they are not capable, as yet, of being expressed in a manner in which they could be objectively measured. Programme structures aimed at broadly stated objectives may offer a useful way of classifying expenditure allocations for budget presentation, but without the cost/benefit analysis stage this is not PPBS.

Attempts to show how the principle of PPBS might be applied therefore require a framework of accepted objectives with measurable targets and programme outputs. The following hypothetical example, based on the flood protection function of a local authority, illustrates how PPBS might be implemented.

PPBS – an example

Coastal local authorities have responsibility for flood protection and, in order to meet this responsibility, might well have programmes aimed at 'sea defences' and 'surface water drainage'. The beneficial impacts of flood protection relate to the avoidance of the loss of agricultural production caused by flooding, and also the avoidance of damage to property. Providing the areas at risk can be adequately estimated it ought to be possible to express the benefits of flood protection in monetary amounts. The benefits would therefore be measured in terms of the economic consequences of avoiding crop spoilage, or livestock losses, or domestic and commercial property damage. Ideally, of course, measures reflecting the benefits of protecting human beings from death or injury, or benefits concerned with the 'quality of life' or 'peace of mind' should also be included. However, the more easily measurable economic benefits offer a starting point.

For each of the basic programmes of 'sea defences' and 'surface water drainage' there will be a variety of programme categories. For example, the *programme categories* for the 'sea defences' programme might include:

1 hard sea defences – concrete and steel defences;
2 soft sea defences – earthbanks, groynes, dunes, etc;
3 dredging of estuaries;
4 tidal barriers.

The programme elements and the related costs and benefits for the 'soft sea defences' programme category could then be expressed as in Fig. 4.2.

A similar procedure would be adopted for each programme element so that the total costs and benefits of each programme category and of each overall programme could be determined. The outputs are measured in terms of the estimated direct financial benefits of protection from flooding. Such a measurement would not be without its problems but providing realistic assumptions about loss of crops, livestock losses, and property damage are made, it should be possible to place a

Programme category 'Soft sea defences'	Costs/benefits Monetary measures (in Year 0 prices) represented by X. Physical measures represented by Y.						
Programme elements	Year 0 = current year						
	−1	0	1	2	3	4	5
1. *Existing soft sea defences*							
1.9 Estimated costs	X	X	X	X	X	X	X
Estimated benefits:							
1.1 Agricultural area offered protection	Y	Y	Y	Y	Y	Y	Y
1.2 Financial benefits of 1.1	X	X	X	X	X	X	X
1.3 Urban area offered protection	Y	Y	Y	Y	Y	Y	Y
1.4 Urban population offered protection	Y	Y	Y	Y	Y	Y	Y
1.5 Financial benefits of 1.3 and 1.4	X	X	X	X	X	X	X
1.0 Total financial benefits	X	X	X	X	X	X	X
2. *Extensions to soft sea defences*							
2.9 Estimated costs	X	X	X	X	X	X	X
Estimated benefits:							
2.1 Agricultural area offered protection	Y	Y	Y	Y	Y	Y	Y
2.2 Financial benefits of 2.1	X	X	X	X	X	X	X
2.3 Urban area offered protection	Y	Y	Y	Y	Y	Y	Y
2.4 Urban population offered protection	Y	Y	Y	Y	Y	Y	Y
2.5 Financial benefits of 2.3 and 2.4	X	X	X	X	X	X	X
2.0 Total financial benefits	X	X	X	X	X	X	X

Fig. 4.2 Example of programme elements presentation, showing the costs and related benefits of each programme element.

monetary value on these benefits. Market values are available to determine the direct financial losses that might be avoided by flood protection. However, the more intangible benefits such as the 'peace of mind' of residents in an area where the threat of flooding has been reduced are much more difficult to express in monetary terms. In this example no attempt has been made to measure these. One approach that could be adopted would be to use surrogate measures. For example, increases in property values might be thought of as capturing to some extent the capitalized value of the benefits. Ideally, such measures should be included but often all that can be done is to note the existence of the benefits in a non-quantified manner. The costs of each programme element could be expressed in a line-item format or simply as a total amount depending on the amount of detail required.

The features of such an approach to budget preparation are that the separate stages of planning, programming, and budgeting are incorporated into one document, and that objectives are clearly expressed with the costs and benefits associated with each programme clearly stated. These are the fundamental requirements of PPBS.

A CRITIQUE OF PPBS

Many of the advantages of PPBS have already been mentioned and these are essentially concerned with its role in providing a framework for rational decision making. The advantages can be summarized as follows:

1 It provides information on the objectives of the organization.
2 It cuts across conventional lines of responsibility and departmental structures by drawing together the activities that are directed towards a particular objective.
3 It exposes programmes that are overlapping or contradictory in terms of achieving objectives.
4 It concentrates on long-term effects.
5 It provides information on the impact that existing and alternative programmes will have on objectives, and the associated programme costs.
6 It enables resource allocation choices to be made on the basis of benefit/cost relationships.

However, when attention is turned to the implementation of PPBS it is apparent that there are serious practical difficulties to be overcome. The information needed for PPBS purposes is far from readily available. The problems of defining the objectives and measuring the output of a service such as social services were discussed in the previous section. Such problems will be typical for many public sector services where the objective is ultimately concerned with meeting the needs of society in some respect. Such needs, even if definable, are rarely measurable, and the effectiveness of particular activities in meeting needs can only be judged in very subjective terms. Hofstede (1981) argues that attempts to implement a system of PPBS under such circumstances would represent a fundamental error in the choice of management control models. He points out that the appropriate control model where objectives are ambiguous and outputs non-measurable is 'political' control. Even the correct determination of costs is not as straightforward as it may at first seem. Many activities are of a multi-purpose nature and it is not always obvious how the costs of such activities should be allocated to particular 'output' categories. For example, the libraries service of a local authority may exist to fulfil both the educational needs and the recreational needs of a community. An allocation of costs between these two aspects would often be extremely difficult to make.

For many public sector organizations PPBS might therefore be thought of as just one more example of a technique that is conceptually sound, and yet, because of practical limitations, difficult to implement. However, such reasoning does not completely explain the widespread rejection of PPBS. After all, if the technique is so sound it might be expected that attention would be focused on overcoming the practical problems. Although perfect output measurements might not be attainable, workable compromises might still be possible. Nevertheless, as Wildavsky (1974, p. 205) points out:

> PPBS has failed everywhere and at all times. Nowhere has PPBS been established and influenced governmental decisions according to its own principles.

This leads to the suggestion that if PPBS has failed it is not because of the absence of sufficient data, or measurement techniques, or lack of adequate training, but because of a more fundamental deficiency. PPBS is meant to introduce a highly formalized and rational approach to long-run decision making and planning, and yet it is argued that such an approach ignores the political and organizational realities of complex human organizations. When faced with loosely defined social objectives and future uncertainties political processes form an important part of decision making. For example, Van Gunsteren (1976, p. 58) when describing the use of PPBS in the US Federal Government, observes that:

> Vested-interest groups see their influence threatened and made more uncertain by the new ways of budgetary decision-making. Many politicians do not like the increase in bureaucratic centralization and power they expect from PPBS. They feel that they are becoming still more exclusively dependent on executive presentation and manipulation of information.

As far as organizational structure is concerned, PPBS requires the existence of a hierarchical pyramid structure, with decision making being centralized and reduced to a relatively small number of alternative choices. In reality, existing power bases are not hierarchical but reflect long-established traditions, and decisions arise as a result of a rich variety of formal and informal negotiations and bargaining at different organizational levels. The decisions that emerge are not necessarily 'rational' in the PPBS sense but are determined by short-term preoccupations and the need to retain flexibility. PPBS would be unlikely to survive in such an environment. This, as Wildavsky (1974, p. 207) points out, is the paradox of PPBS. The system that PPBS is intended to change must first undergo that change before it can accommodate PPBS.

SUMMARY

In this chapter the technique of PPBS has been examined and a possible application illustrated. PPBS is a prime example of the rational-orthodox approach to planning and budgeting. Its potential advantages suggest that it ought to be an indispensable part of decision making and resource allocation. In spite of this, the evidence suggests that it has had only limited success. It is important to try to isolate whether the causes for this lack of success were simply due to practical limitations, or, more importantly, because the environment in which attempts were made to implement it was hostile to its development. Presumably, with sufficient research and effort put into objectives definition and output measurements, a workable, if not perfect, form of PPBS might be possible. The evidence from the Bellamy and Kluvers (1995) study of Australian municipalities confirms that there are examples of PPBS being used in practice, and the flood protection example in Fig. 4.2 offers an illustration of how PPBS might be applied. The practical limitations argument might therefore be no more than an excuse. Alternatively, PPBS might not work because orthodox planning approaches and cybernetic management control models are not always appropriate for public sector activities. Van Gunsteren (1976), Hofstede (1981), and others offer strong support for this line of reasoning.

DISCUSSION TOPICS

1   Explain what is meant by PPBS, and discuss the strengths and limitations of PPBS.

2   'Public sector budgeting can not be reduced to a set of analytical and management techniques and therefore PPBS has only limited relevance.' Discuss.

3   'The pay off from PPBS comes not from the drawing-up of a programme structure but from programme analysis.' Discuss.

4   'Line-item budgeting is about means, programme budgeting is about ends.' Discuss.

5   'Programme budgeting is incompatible with a system of devolved budgeting.' Discuss.

CHAPTER 5

Zero-base budgeting

In Chapter 3 the use of incremental budgeting as an example of the bounded rationality approach to budgeting was described. Chapter 4 explored programme budgeting as an example of an alternative rational decision-making approach, and in this chapter a further example, namely zero-base budgeting, is discussed. The chapter begins by examining the concept of zero-base budgeting and then goes on to discuss its suggested practical application in complex organizations. Finally, the concept of zero-base budgeting and the practical applications are critically evaluated.

THE CONCEPT OF ZERO-BASE BUDGETING

Zero-base budgeting in its pure form is precisely what its name implies, i.e. the preparation of operating budgets from a zero base; even though the organization might be operating more or less as in previous years, the budgetary process assumes that it is starting anew. Resources are not necessarily allocated in accordance with previous patterns and consequently each existing item of expenditure has to be annually rejustified. Thus by focusing on this need to rejustify existing levels of expenditure the apparent weakness of incremental budgeting, i.e. the perpetuation of obsolete expenditure, is avoided. Zero-base budgeting has therefore an obvious appeal to a society which continually demands assurances concerning the most effective allocation of scarce public resources.

The concept of budgeting from a zero base is not new. Obviously, each time an individual or organization begins a totally new venture a budget must be built from zero. However, in terms of budgeting for large complex organizations this is a trivial case. The root of the problem is that on the whole such organizations continue in much the same form for many years, and therefore to build a budget from zero is less obvious.

It is against this background that the concept of zero-base budgeting has developed.

THE DEVELOPMENT OF ZERO-BASE BUDGETING

The first known application of zero-base budgeting was by the US Department of Agriculture in 1962 (Wildavsky and Hammond, 1965). However, the general problem of incremental budgeting that zero-base budgeting attempts to solve has been recognized from a much earlier period. For example, in 1915 E. Hilton Young (1915, pp. 28–9) described the British Treasury requirements for the preparation of annual estimates (budgets) and these included:

A circular letter to the officers responsible for the preparation of the estimates [which included] a particular warning against assuming last year's estimates as the starting point for those of the next.

Hilton Young goes on to say that this is a necessary warning because:

It must always be a temptation to one drawing up an estimate to save himself trouble by taking last year's estimate for granted, adding something to any item for which an increased expenditure is foreseen. Nothing could be easier, or more wasteful and extravagant. It is in that way obsolete expenditure is able to make its appearance year after year long after all reason for it has ceased to be.

A further example can be found in Lewis (1952, p. 52) who stated that:

Budget reviewers are frequently criticised for concentrating on the increases and giving too little attention to items in the base amount. This criticism is justified in part because the amount appropriated last year is not necessarily appropriate for this year and the activities carried on last year are not necessarily appropriate for this year.

However, Lewis tended to reject zero-base budgeting as the solution to the problem when he suggested, 'the sheer mass of work involved in reviewing budget estimates precludes examination of every detail every year'.

The 'sheer mass of work' argument was possibly the main reason for the US Department of Agriculture application being a one-year experiment (Wildavsky and Hammond, 1965).

The next major leap forward occurred with the development at Texas Instruments Inc. of a way of at least beginning to handle the mass of data (Phyrr, 1973). This involved the implementation of a 'decision package' approach to prepare the 1970 budget for the Staff and Research Divisions.

Since then much attention has been focused on zero-base budgeting largely due to the publicity surrounding its most celebrated advocate, Jimmy Carter: initially as Governor of the State of Georgia, where zero-base budgeting was introduced in 1973 (Lauth, 1978), and then as President of the United States of America.

Although there have been relatively few attempts to implement zero-base budgeting in the UK, different versions of it have been tried by many governmental organizations in the USA, for example, the states of New Jersey and Illinois and the city of New Orleans (see Worthley and Ludwin, 1979).

APPLICATIONS OF ZERO-BASE BUDGETING

Most of the practical applications of zero-base budgeting involve the use of the 'decision package' approach. In this section this approach is described and an example is given of its use.

All budgeting procedures involve an identification of organizational objectives. In the context of these objectives, zero-base budgeting involves the following three basic stages:

1 identification of decision units;
2 development of decision packages;
3 review and ranking of decision packages.

Identification of decision units

The existing organization structure identifies the units in the hierarchy for which budgets are prepared. These could be responsibility centres, cost centres, profit centres, investment centres, programme categories or programme elements. This is the starting point for identifying decision units for zero-base budgeting purposes. Ideally, a decision unit should have the following characteristics:

1   a specific manager should be clearly responsible for the operation of the programme;
2   it must have well-defined and measurable impacts;
3   it must have well-defined and measurable objectives.

As with other budgeting techniques, the crucial factor is the appropriate level of aggregation and it is this that will determine the decision units. For example, for a local authority the decision units could be at any of the levels shown in Fig. 5.1. In other words, using the education service as an example, the decision units could be at any of the following levels:

● the service level, with the whole of the education service being one decision unit, the whole of the highways service being one decision unit, and so on;

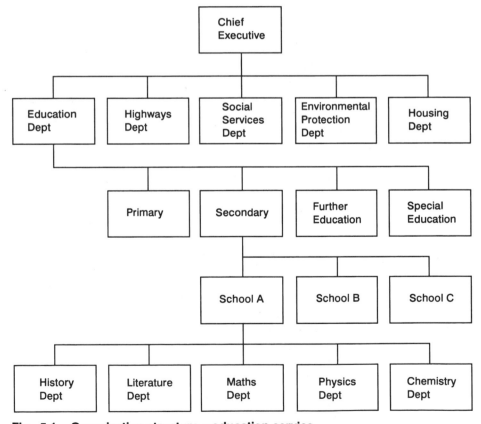

Fig. 5.1   Organization structure – education service.

- the 'division of service' level, which for education would mean the whole of primary education being one decision unit, the whole of secondary education being one decision unit, and so on;
- the subdivision of service level, which would mean that each school would be one decision unit; or
- the school department level, with each department, such as history or physics, being one decision unit.

In connection with this Sarant (1978, p. 31) stresses that:

> Agencies should ensure that the basic decision units selected are not so low in the structure as to result in excessive paperwork and review. On the other hand, the units selected should not be so high as to mask important considerations and prevent meaningful review of the work being performed.

Thus, for example, a local authority with, say, 400 schools, each with five departments, would have a total of 2,000 decision units, and this is only for the education service. On the other hand, if the decision unit was at the level of the individual school, the number of units would be reduced by a factor of 5 but this might prevent an effective review of the needs of a particular department.

In the UK the introduction of local management in schools has resulted in the total budget available for schools being distributed to individual schools on a formula-determined basis, which means that each school receives a cash-limited budget allocation. Under this system, the levels at which decision units can be selected are restricted to either the individual school, or the specific departments within that school.

Having identified appropriate decision units, the next step is to prepare for each of these a document which describes the objectives or purpose of the decision unit and the actions that could be taken to achieve them. Such documents are referred to as *decision packages*. In the next two sections we describe packages and their format, and we will see then how crucial it is to strike the correct balance when determining the level of decision units.

Development of decision packages

There are two types of decision package:

1 *The mutually exclusive decision package.* The purpose of this type is to identify for each decision unit the alternative ways of performing its functions so as to enable management to choose the best alternative. One such alternative will be to abolish the decision unit and not perform its functions at all.

2 *The incremental decision package.* This identifies the different levels of effort (and associated costs) and their effect on the function. For example, there will be a minimum level below which it would be impossible to exercise the function; a base level which reflects the current level of activity; and improvement levels which reflect the effect of increases over the current level. Fig. 5.2 illustrates an incremental decision package.

At the theoretical level, decision packages are intended to identify alternative ways of performing the functions of a decision unit and to determine the effect of

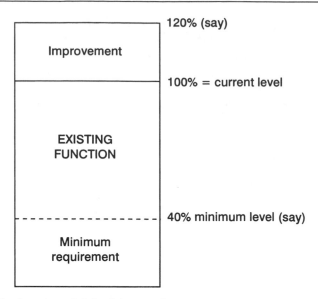

Fig. 5.2 An incremental decision package.

different levels of effort on each alternative. However, Phyrr (1973) and Sarant (1978) suggest that in practice it is adequate first to select the best alternative from among the mutually exclusive decision packages, and then use this as the basis for the incremental decision package analysis. We can perhaps best illustrate the distinction between these two approaches by use of a decision tree as shown in Fig. 5.3.

In this illustration, three alternative ways of performing a function of a decision unit have been identified, i.e. mutually-exclusive decision packages (MEDP) A, B, and C respectively. For each of these MEDPs the effect of many different levels of effort could be determined. However, in our example just three, i.e. a 50 per cent level, a 75 per cent level, and a 100 per cent level, have been considered, and this therefore results in an overall total of nine decision packages. Rather than develop all nine, the practical approach involves choosing first of all between the MEDP at a given level of effort, say 100 per cent, and then only for the one chosen developing further incremental decision packages. For example, if A is selected, then two incremental packages A_{50} and A_{75} are developed representing 50 per cent level of effort and 75 per cent level of effort, respectively. The effect of this is to avoid the burden of analysing B_{50}, B_{75}, C_{50}, and C_{75} when B and C alternatives have been rejected. It is therefore apparent that in a situation involving a large number of mutually exclusive alternatives and incremental levels of effort, the savings in the administrative load will be considerable. On the other hand, this approach sacrifices information needed to trade off B_{75} with A_{75}, or C_{50} with A_{50}, etc., which may lead to sub-optimal decisions being taken.

The format of decision packages

A decision package is merely a document which displays information concerning the effects on a function of alternative courses of action. Its purpose is to provide the basis on which top management can review and rank recommendations

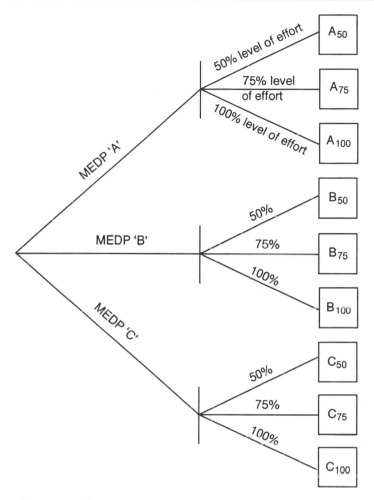

Fig. 5.3 Mutually exclusive and incremental decision packages.

concerning the organization's functions. An example of a possible format is shown in Fig. 5.4.

The decision package document starts off with general information about *package name, department, activity,* and *manager* responsible.

The document then shows details of *statement of purpose,* i.e. the specific objective of the decision unit, and *description of actions,* i.e. the recommended package for fulfilling the objective in terms of the quantity and nature of the resources required. *Achievements from actions* and *quantitative package measures* summarize in a descriptive way and a quantitative way respectively the tangible benefits expected from performance of the package. *Resources required* are the inputs in terms of costs, manpower, etc. needed to implement the package. It is important at this point to determine the correct balance of detail. Obviously, top management would prefer as much information as possible concerning past and projected costs, operating costs, capital costs, and any related income, e.g. government grants. However, the costs of providing such information must be

```
Package Name:                              Rank:

Department:

Activity:                                  Manager:

Statement of purpose:

Description of actions:

Achievements from actions:

Quantitative package measures:

Resources required:

Consequences of not approving package:

Incremental packages:
Different levels of effort (and cost):

Mutually-exclusive packages:
Different ways of performing the same function:
```

Fig. 5.4 Format of a decision package.

borne in mind, particularly given that many decision packages will ultimately be rejected.

It is evident that the *consequences of not approving packages* are that there will be a saving of the resources required, and that the benefits will be forgone. In addition, it must be borne in mind that non-approval may lead to penalty costs being incurred. These could take the form of an increased burden on other packages due to either the internal effect caused by the interrelationships between packages, or the external effects caused by contravention of statutory regulations. *Incremental packages: different levels of effort (and cost)* – there will be a complete decision package document for each level of effort. For example, if just three levels of effort are considered, say a minimum level, a base level, and an improvement level, then a complete decision package document will be prepared for each of these incremental packages and submitted to top management. However, to facilitate the decision-making process it is useful to have a brief description of each decision package document for the other levels of effort proposed. For example, the decision package document for, say, the base level of effort would describe briefly the costs and achievements of the minimum level package and the improvement level package.

In the section *mutually exclusive packages: different ways of performing the same function,* brief details are given of the mutually exclusive alternatives that have previously been considered by the manager of the decision unit and rejected. The purpose is not only to show that the decision unit manager has considered different ways of undertaking the function but also to permit top management to review the alternatives. As we pointed out earlier, this in effect means that the incremental levels of mutually exclusive packages are not being considered.

The final heading in the package is that of *rank*, and this records the number assigned to each package to reflect order of priority.

Example of a decision package

Figure 5.5 shows how a decision package might look in practice. We have developed a hypothetical example for the mathematics department of a secondary school and show in detail the decision package document for the existing (base) level of effort for the next year. This is package 1 of 3. The other two packages are for a reduction and improvement respectively of the existing level of effort and are described briefly in this decision package. This is for memorandum purposes only because a complete decision package would of course be prepared for each of these different levels.

We can now return to the point we made earlier about the importance of striking the correct balance when determining the level of decision units. If in our example of St Margaret's secondary school the decision unit selected was the whole school, then important considerations might be ignored. For example, the quantitative package measures might well be the total number of GCSE examination passes for the whole school so that the incremental packages would merely represent overall changes rather than the changes relating to specific subjects. This is obviously less useful for decision making because the issue would tend to be one of the need for the school rather than the need for a mathematics department within the school. The choice of decision unit must therefore be closely related to the type of decision that needs to be made. For example, the mathematics department might be too high a level of decision unit if the issue under consideration ought to be concerned with trading off elementary, intermediate, and advanced mathematics teaching. Of course, the more basic the issue is perceived to be, the more detailed is the required analysis and therefore the greater the administrative burden.

Review and ranking of decision packages

Once the decision packages have been prepared they are ranked on an ordinal scale (i.e. 1st, 2nd, 3rd, etc.) in order of priority. In a situation where a 'bottom-up' approach to budget determination in the education service existed, there would be a large number of decision packages and therefore the ranking process would take place at a number of levels. In the example illustrated in Fig. 5.5, the decision units are at the level of the various departments (e.g. mathematics, English, science, history, and so on) and therefore the lowest level at which the decision packages from these departments would be ranked would be the whole school. The next stage in the ranking process would involve the consolidation at a higher level of all the lower-level rankings.

Continuing with the example of a school (and following from Fig. 5.1), this would mean consolidating the decision package rankings from every secondary school into one overall ranking for secondary education. A similar process would be undertaken for all primary schools, all special schools, and all colleges of further education. The next consolidation level would be even higher. In our example it would

1. **Package Name**	Mathematics teaching (1 of 3)		2. *Rank:*	
3. **Department**	Education department			
4. **Activity**	School A (St Margaret's Secondary School)			
5. **Manager**	Mr R. Boyson			
6. **Statement of purpose**	To provide mathematics teaching to 750 GCSE pupils.			
7. **Description of actions**	To provide teaching facilities at the pupil/teacher ratio of 20:1 for students preparing for the upper GCSE grades and 30:1 for students preparing for the intermediate grades. This will amount to a total teaching staff requirement of 5. To provide computer facilities for all students and this will require one computer technician and equipment.			
8. **Achievements from actions**	To improve the number and level of GCSE examination passes in mathematics.			

9. **Quantitative package measures**		*Previous year*	*Current year* Revised	*Next year*
		Actual	*budget*	*Budget*
	% of passes GCSE upper	78%	81%	83%
	% of passes GCSE intermediate	63%	64%	65%

10. **Resources required**		*Previous year* £	*Current year* £	*Next year* £
	Operating costs			
	Teaching	78,000	84,000	90,000
	Technicians	13,500	14,500	15,500
	Equipment	10,500	11,500	12,500
	Capital costs	–	–	–
	Income	–	–	–
	Total	102,000	110,000	118,000
	Employees	6	6	6

11. **Consequences of not approving package**	Mathematics taken out of syllabus. Mathematics has traditionally been one of the strengths of St Margaret's School and there is a definite possibility of pupils moving to other schools. Also this may not be possible, given core-subject status of mathematics.
12. **Incremental packages:** *Different levels of effort*	*Mathematics teaching* (2 of 3). Improve pupil/teacher ratio for intermediate grade GCSE teaching to try to bring this up to that for upper grade. This could be achieved by improving pupil/teacher ratios for intermediate grades to 20:1, resulting in the requirement of a further one teacher. Additional annual cost next year – £18,000.
	Mathematics teaching (3 of 3). Intermediate grade GCSE pass rate is considered the level appropriate for all students. Therefore pupil/teacher ratio for upper grade students increased to 30:1 resulting in a reduction of one teacher. Reduction in annual cost for next year – £18,000.
13. **Mutually exclusive packages:** *Different ways of performing the same function*	(i) Abolish mathematics teaching at St Margaret's. *Consequences* as shown in 11 above. (ii) Merge teaching of upper and intermediate grade GCSE students. *Benefits* are that assuming mixed ability students can be taught together the merger should result in economies of scale. *Disadvantages*: (a) Mixed ability teaching is unsuitable for mathematics. Such a merger may adversely affect all examination pass rates. (b) Restrictions on teaching loads and limits on classroom sizes will prevent the economies of scale being realized.

Fig. 5.5   Example of a decision package for the next budget year for the mathematics department of a secondary school.

be at the departmental level so that rankings for primary, secondary, special, and further education would be consolidated into one overall ranking for the whole of the education department. The final ranking would be for the whole organization, combining the individual rankings of departments.

Obviously when faced with many different decision packages the ranking exercise is not straightforward. The process is inherently political and it is usual for the ranking decision at each level of consolidation to be taken by a special committee. Under this approach, the decision packages are considered by the committee and final rankings determined by a system of voting. In order to assist the committee members in assessing the respective merits of each decision package it is useful to introduce criteria for ranking purposes. One method might be to isolate several criteria such as:

1   whether the activity is specifically required by law;
2   whether the organization has the resources and technical skills to implement the activity;
3   whether the package is cost effective;
4   whether the package will be politically acceptable.

Weights can then be attached to each criterion and the result of the weightings will form the basis of the ranking exercise. Alternatively, a single criterion, such as cost/benefit ratio or cost effectiveness, might be selected and used for ranking.

The ranking process is often modified in practice to facilitate the consolidation exercise. As it has been described above, *each* decision package would be considered at every consolidation level and this would involve an enormous administrative burden. One way that has been proposed to reduce the burden is through the use of 'cut-off' points at each level of consolidation. Thus at the first consolidation level a cut-off point of, say, 75 per cent of the total budget request for that level might be applied, so that only those packages falling below this cut-off point would be reviewed and ranked at the next consolidation level.

Referring once again to the example of St Margaret's secondary school featured in Fig. 5.5, the school ranking committee might produce the decision package rankings shown in Fig. 5.6.

Figure 5.6 shows the prioritization of the packages, their costs and cumulative expenses. The procedure has to follow a system of starting with the lowest-level packages of each decision unit and then ordering the incremental packages so that the total budget request is built up from the lowest level. For example, the decision package 3 of 3 of the mathematics department can be seen from Fig. 5.5 to represent the minimum level of activity that was considered for this department. Decision package 1 of 3 brings the budget request for mathematics up to the amount required at the current level of activity (i.e. £118,000). Decision package 2 of 3 shows the amount required for improvements over and above the current level.

If the cut-off point is set at 75 per cent of the total budget request of £692,000, this means that all the decision packages on the ranking sheet above the cumulative cut-off point of £519,000 (75 per cent of £692,000) will be consolidated as a whole, and will be accepted without further consideration at the next level in the ranking process.

In our example, this would be the ranking committee for all secondary schools, and only the six decision packages falling below the cut-off point would be consid-

Organizational Unit: School A – St Margaret's Secondary		Prepared by: Mr R. Boyson and School Ranking Committee		Ref: .... Date: ....

Ranking of Decision Packages			Next Year Proposed Expenses	Next Year Cumulative Expenses	Current Year Budget
Rank	Name	Package No.	£000	£000	£
1	Mathematics	3 of 3	100	100	
2	English	4 of 4	94	194	
3	Science	3 of 3	117	311	
4	Modern Languages	4 of 4	58	369	
5	History	3 of 3	47	416	
6	Mathematics	1 of 3	18	434	
7	Science	1 of 3	18	452	
8	Modern Languages	3 of 4	16	468	
9	History	1 of 3	16	484	
10	Mathematics	2 of 3	18	502	
11	English	3 of 4	17	519	
12	Science	2 of 3		562	
13	History	2 of 3		592	
14	English	1 of 4		631	
15	Modern Languages	1 of 4		660	
16	English	2 of 4		676	
17	Modern Languages	2 of 4		692	
	Total		692	692	

Fig. 5.6 Decision package ranking sheet.

ered at this level. This process would therefore avoid the need for the secondary schools' ranking committee to rank all 17 packages of St Margaret's secondary school, plus an equivalent number from every other secondary school. All that would remain to be determined would be the relative merit of the six packages 12–17 for St Margaret's school, and the similar packages from each of the other secondary schools. At each succeeding consolidation level, the cut-off point would be increased perhaps to 80 per cent, or even 90 per cent, and the same procedure would be followed as above.

In reality, the position in the UK, following the local management of schools initiative, would mean that the school itself would be the only level at which ranking would take place, and there would therefore be no need for consolidation at a higher level. In such a situation, the purpose of the ranking exercise would be to identify which packages should be undertaken and which rejected when faced with a cash-limited budget allocation. If, for example, the budget allocation for next year for

St Margaret's school was fixed at £660,000, then the decision package approach to zero-base budgeting would lead to packages 1–15 being accepted, and packages 16 and 17 rejected.

It might appear advantageous therefore to apply zero-based budgeting to relatively small self-contained units within an organization because this avoids the complexity of ranking decision packages at different levels. However, the basic purpose of zero-based budgeting is to produce the optimal budget allocation for the *whole* organization. In our example, St Margaret's school (see Fig. 5.5) is just one of several secondary schools that make up the secondary education programme of a local authority. Secondary education is just one of several programmes undertaken by the education department. Education is just one of the many services provided by the local authority. The 'bottom-up' approach of zero-base budgeting should, when all the decision packages are ranked at the highest level (i.e. the whole local authority) ensure a rationally determined budget allocation which is made up of only the highest-ranked packages. With formula-funding and local management of schools (LMS), zero-base budgeting could not be used to provide the *overall* picture but would simply help individual schools to determine how best to make use of the cash limited amounts they have been allocated.

A CRITIQUE OF ZERO-BASE BUDGETING

The primary advantage of zero-base budgeting is that, unlike incremental budgeting, it does not assume that last year's allocation of resources is necessarily appropriate for the current year. This assumption is avoided because the mechanics of zero-base budgeting require that, at least conceptually, all the functions of an organization are re-evaluated annually from a zero base. The systematic nature of such a fundamental review imposes a discipline on the organization which has produced in practice secondary advantages. The most obvious example of these is that it produces in a readily accessible form more and better management information. A typical comment of managers in the state of Georgia, reported by Lauth (1978, p. 427), is

> Zero-base is a useful management control device. The forms require people to organize and develop their information. Managers are better able, I think, to make decisions on the basis of an improved reporting system.

Thus the zero-base budgeting process forces managers at all levels to identify their specific objectives, to quantify them, and to evaluate the cost effectiveness of the alternative ways of achieving them. The belief is that this improves the quality of management's decisions.

An advantage that stems from this improved management information is that its production involves the participation of lower-level management in the budgetary process, and the smaller the decision units are, the greater this involvement will become. Apparently such increased participation is beneficial; again from a manager in the state of Georgia (Lauth, 1978, p. 427):

> I like zero-base. We used to make up the budget in this office with very little communication with the operating people. Now the budget format makes us reach to the lowest levels for information – that has advantages for everyone even beyond putting together a budget.

A further advantage is that unexpected events that occur during the financial year can be more readily adjusted for. This is because the basic information for modifying goals has already been generated.

These are some of the advantages that have been claimed for zero-base budgeting. However, although the technique is conceptually sound, its fundamental disadvantage is that it 'vastly overestimates man's ability to calculate' (Wildavsky and Hammond, 1985, p. 343). It is because of this that the decision package approach was developed. However, even with this development the number of decision packages that a complex organization will generate effectively precludes an annual zero-base review for all functions. This has manifested itself in practice by a zero base being replaced by what amounted to a 70, 80 or even 90 per cent base. So much so that advocates of zero-base budgeting have rationalized its definition. Sarant (1978, p. 3) typifies this when he says:

> Some definitions are implying that zero-base budgeting is the act of starting budgets from 'scratch' or requiring each program or activity to be justified from the 'ground up'. This is not true; the acronym ZBB is a misnomer. ZBB refers to the review and justification of selected, not all, current program elements starting somewhere at a point *in* the base area and not necessarily *at* 'zero-base'.

Furthermore, as we pointed out earlier, in practice the effects of different levels of effort on each alternative mutually exclusive decision package are not considered. Thus practical expediency avoids consideration of all alternatives, and this might well lead to a sub-optimal allocation of resources.

Even having introduced this modification of non-examination of all available alternatives, the large number of decision packages may still be unmanageable. As Anthony (1977, p. 9) points out:

> In Georgia, there were 11,000 of them. If the Governor set aside four hours every day for two months he could spend about a minute on each decision package, not enough time to read it, let alone make an analysis of the merits.

The practical response to this volume problem, as we have seen, has been to modify the ranking process by imposing cut-off rates at each level of consolidation. This means that at the highest level top management does not need to rank all the organization's decision packages, but only those falling below a cut-off level of, say, 90 per cent of total budget. This cut-off technique means that we are left with a budgetary process which bears little relation to the concept of zero-base budgeting.

Furthermore, the behavioural consequence resulting from the use of cut-off techniques must not be overlooked. A system which ensures that all decision packages above some cut-off point are accepted without further scrutiny at higher levels in the ranking hierarchy, might well lead to ranking low-priority 'pet' programmes above high-priority and essential programmes. If, as a result of this strategy, the 'pet' programmes fall within the cut-off point their acceptance is assured, whereas if they were subjected to consideration at some higher level of ranking their survival would be doubtful. It is therefore better to let the high-priority programmes fall outside the cut-off point, because if they really are essential their acceptance at higher levels is much more certain. To overcome such undesirable strategies it may be necessary not only to establish well-defined criteria for ranking programmes, but also to introduce some means of monitoring the adherence to such criteria.

A further dysfunctional consequence could be that incremental packages above the current level of activity might be somewhat overenthusiastic in terms of the request for improvement level funds. Excessive improvement level packages, although unlikely to be accepted, would serve to increase the overall budget request. Therefore, if, as in Fig. 5.6, the cut-off point was 75 per cent of the overall budget request, there would be an obvious advantage in making the latter as high as possible, because the cut-off point would then be higher. One way to counteract such a strategy might be to express the cut-off point as a percentage of the total amount required to undertake the current level of activity, rather than as a percentage of the overall budget request.

Although the implementation of zero-based budgeting would undoubtedly present some practical and behavioural difficulties, these are not necessarily insurmountable. Perhaps a more telling reason for the lack of any widespread development of zero-base budgeting in the public sector is because, like PPBS, it attempts to impose a highly formal and economically rational approach to budgeting on to a system that is essentially based on political choice and political control. Nevertheless, there is still a willingness to accept the conceptual soundness of zero-base budgeting. It has been clear for some time that the philosophy of zero-base budgeting, if not the bureaucracy of a full decision-package approach, has been at work in the budgeting practices of many public sector organizations, and it has been increasingly common for base budgets to be challenged and justifications sought for their acceptance. More recently, there is also evidence to suggest that even the more formal approaches to zero-base budgeting have been experimented with and attempts at implementation have begun. For example, Pendlebury (1994) reports on an attempt by a local authority social services department to introduce a zero-base approach to budget preparation for the 1992/93 budget year. The department followed a variant of the decision package system described above, with each budget-holder being required to compile three incremental decision packages as follows:

1   the current budget provision;
2   the budget provision required to provide the statutory minimum level of service;
3   a 90 per cent provision – the purpose of this being to identify amounts within the base that might be capable of being deployed more effectively elsewhere.

The anxieties that the 90 per cent level created amongst the budget-holders and the reassurances that had to be given to them meant that very little redistribution of budgets occurred and disputes over definitions of the quality and volume of service needed to satisfy statutory minimum requirements were difficult to resolve. All this resulted in attempts to rank decision packages to determine overall priorities soon being abandoned. Pendlebury concludes that although a system of zero-base budgeting was not achieved in this case, the project clearly had important benefits in terms of forcing the status quo to be challenged and bringing home to managers the need to evaluate very carefully the relationship between the levels of service provided and costs. In this particular local authority and elsewhere, there is still much support for zero-base budgeting and it would be unwise to dismiss it too readily.

DISCUSSION TOPICS

1 Explain clearly what is meant by the term 'zero-base budgeting'. Describe how zero-base budgeting might be implemented in practice, and discuss its strengths and limitations.

2 Compare and contrast incremental budgeting with zero-base.

3 Imagine you are member of top management. Mr R. Boyson, manager of St Margaret's Secondary School, has presented you with the decision package shown in this chapter. Ruthlessly evaluate this package by challenging all the assumptions upon which it is based.

4 A crucial aspect of zero-base budgeting involves determining the optimal level for decision units. This involves striking a balance between administrative expediency and sensitivity in decision making. Discuss, using your own examples, why this is so crucial.

5 Describe and critically evaluate non-incremental budgeting using a practical example of which you are aware.

6 'Zero-base budgeting can only be implemented properly in an organization that already uses programme budgeting.' Discuss.

7 'Zero-base budgeting is essentially a "bottom-up" approach to budgeting and many of its benefits are therefore lost under a system of devolved budgeting.' Discuss.

CHAPTER 6

Investment appraisal

The distinction between the revenue expenditure and capital expenditure of public sector organizations has already been described in Chapter 3. Revenue expenditure provides benefits for the current year, whereas capital expenditure provides benefits which extend beyond the current year. A careful evaluation of the costs and benefits of both types of expenditure is essential if the organization is to be successful in achieving its objectives. The recognition that programmes should be assessed in terms of cost/benefit relationships was a feature of the PPBS approach outlined in Chapter 4. Such an assessment involves the use of *investment appraisal*. An investment has been defined by Carsberg (1974, pp. 1–2) as 'any activity for which the required outlays and the benefits are not expected to be concurrent', and capital expenditure provides a prime example of such a situation. Because investment in capital projects has an inescapable impact on future revenue expenditure, a sound system of investment appraisal is essential. The capital costs, future running costs, and future benefits of each proposed project need to be calculated as accurately as possible before a decision is taken on the implementation of the project. It is with the techniques of capital investment appraisal that this chapter is primarily concerned.

THE BASIC REQUIREMENTS OF INVESTMENT APPRAISAL

The basic notion of investment appraisal is very simple. It involves defining the objectives of the organization; identifying the capital projects that will achieve the objectives; evaluating the costs and benefits of each project; making a decision on whether to accept or reject the projects. In reality, the actual implementation of investment appraisal is not so straightforward and each stage in the process requires careful consideration.

Defining objectives

The difficulties of deciding on the precise objectives of many public sector organizations have already been described in Chapter 4. Nevertheless, providing realistic assumptions are made, a workable and generally acceptable definition of the goals of the organization can usually be found. It is important that the objectives should not be too broad otherwise they will be of little use in investment appraisal. On the other hand, they must not be defined so narrowly that they effectively conceal the ultimate purpose of the service. Attention will need to be given to the interrelationships of objectives so that situations where some are logically subordinate to others can be recognized and an order of priority established.

Identifying investment possibilities

There will often be a wide range of alternative ways of meeting objectives and it will be necessary to list these in some way. Some may be technically feasible but may have to be ruled out because of legal or political constraints, and there is therefore little point in appraising these in great detail. However, there will always be at least two options, i.e. a 'do nothing' option, and an investment option. For example, when considering the replacement of existing assets this should not be thought of as an unavoidable requirement. The costs and benefits of replacement, and therefore the continuation of the service, should be compared with the costs and benefits of ceasing to operate the service, or providing it at a different level of activity. Proposed investment projects may have an impact on other projects or may be dependent on the acceptance of other projects and the interrelationship of projects will have to be taken into consideration.

Evaluating the costs and benefits of investments

It is on this aspect of investment appraisal that most attention is usually focused. The first requirement is to assess the magnitude of the costs and benefits of each project and also the time when these will be expected to occur. It is then necessary to recognize that costs and benefits that arise at different points in time are not directly comparable and therefore must be discounted in some way. It is on the comparison of discounted costs and benefits that investment decisions should be based. The feasibility of such a procedure is obviously dependent on the ability to make realistic estimates concerning the amount and timing of future costs and benefits, and also the ability to select an appropriate discount rate for use in the discounting process. Nevertheless, the use of discounting techniques in private sector investment appraisals is well established and so presumably these problems can be overcome. However, where there is a commercial output it is clear that costs and benefits can be expressed directly in monetary amounts and so the appraisal can be restricted to the consideration of net cash flows. In the public sector this is not always possible. Similarly, for private sector organizations it is generally agreed that the discount rate should reflect the cost of capital of each firm (although in reality there is less than total agreement on how this should be calculated). In the public sector the choice of discount rate is less obvious.

It is because many of the costs and benefits of public sector organizations are not directly measurable in money terms that the techniques of *cost-benefit analysis* are appropriate. Cost-benefit analysis is concerned with assessing all of the economic and social advantages (benefits) and disadvantages (costs) of a project and then quantifying these in monetary terms. For example, when constructing a new motorway there will be *monetary costs* in the form of construction and maintenance costs, and there will be *social costs* in the form of landscape disfiguration, exhaust pollution, traffic noise, and possible increases in accidents. The *social benefits* will result from reduced traffic congestion, reductions in travelling time, reductions in distribution costs of goods, the advantages of by-passing towns and villages thereby reducing noise, nuisance, and property damage, possible reductions in accidents, etc.

Where the social costs and benefits are very important, then their monetary values need to be included in the evaluation process, and so cost-benefit analysis is called for. There may be times, however, when the social costs and benefits are either non-quantifiable in monetary terms, or the 'costs' of the quantification exercise would exceed the 'benefits' of having this information. For example, a programme to introduce a clean air zone would result in definite benefits, but it would be difficult to place a monetary value on them. In such a situation investment appraisal can still be of use by indicating the cheapest method of implementing the programme. This is known as *cost-effectiveness analysis*. Cost-effectiveness analysis can also be used to show the effect of different levels of service provision on costs. Cost-benefit analysis and cost-effectiveness analysis are considered further in the following sections of this chapter.

Choosing projects

The discounted cost/benefit ratios, or cost-effectiveness profiles do of course offer no more than a starting point for deciding on which projects to accept. It is evident that there are many uncertainties that could affect the calculations. Not all of the social costs and benefits will have been included, and many of those that have, will not have been capable of objective measurement in monetary terms. The analysis indicates those projects that appear to give the best value for money, but political factors and the need to respond to changes in governmental and societal pressures may often cause cost/benefit considerations to be overruled.

COST-BENEFIT ANALYSIS

Nowhere is the distinction between private sector and public sector activities more precise than in the use of cost-benefit analysis. The investment decision in private firms is concerned with assessing whether the owners of the firm will be made better-off by undertaking a particular activity. The investment decision of a public sector organization is concerned with assessing whether society as a whole will be made better-off. Cost-benefit analysis developed as a means of establishing criteria for public sector investment appraisal in terms of the net social benefits accruing from the investment. To determine the net social benefits it is necessary to place a monetary value not only on tangible benefits, but also on such intangibles as freedom from noise, or the peace of mind of living in a safe and secure environment, or savings in travelling time, and so on. These intangible benefits are the 'outputs' of many public sector activities. Even when the outputs appear to be more measurable (e.g. public transport revenues), there are still wider implications, such as the social benefits of providing transport facilities to rural communities, that need to be evaluated.

Similarly, when attention is turned to measuring costs there will be intangible items, such as 'spoiling the environment', and also the more tangible items that might be capable of measurement by reference to market values. The basic distinction for both costs and benefits is therefore between items for which market values do not exist at all and items for which market prices are usually available. However, even when considering costs for which there is a market value the position is not always so straightforward. For example, suppose that a public sector project makes use of workers who would otherwise be unemployed. In this case the costs are not necessarily represented by the market rate for wages but should be based on the value of the lost leisure time that the workers will have forgone. For workers who were involuntarily unemployed this is usually thought to be less than wages costs. A further example concerns the market price of materials produced by a monopolist and sold at a price well above marginal cost. The question that then arises is whether the price of the materials should be the market price or the marginal cost. Furthermore, the price of material resources will often include indirect taxes and, to the extent that the taxes are a form of transfer payment, they should clearly not be thought of as a resource cost. In all of these examples the market price is either distorted, or reflects a market disequilibrium, and therefore does not include the correct social opportunity cost. The correct procedure to adopt in such a situation is to resort to 'shadow prices'. These are surrogate prices that are derived to reflect more accurately the true social opportunity costs of using resources in a particular project. Unfortunately, there is often no obvious practical means of determining shadow prices.

The valuation of intangible costs and benefits

Apart from the problems of determining correct shadow prices to correct for market failure, there is also the need to value in some way those intangible costs and benefits for which no market value exists in the first place. Although there is no completely satisfactory way of doing this, several approaches have been suggested (Mishan, 1988) and these include the following:

1   Surrogate prices can be established by finding out what consumers would be willing to pay if there were a market in the intangible cost or benefit. This involves undertaking a survey of consumers. For example, attempts to value a benefit such as 'savings in travelling time' might be achieved by asking travellers what they would be willing to pay to save an extra 30 minutes in travelling time.

2   Surrogate prices can be implied by observing existing behaviour. Thus a passenger when faced with the choice of travelling by bus or by taxi may choose the faster but more expensive form of transport. It is argued that this implicitly values the time saved as the difference between the costs of the two methods. A similar approach concerns the use of property and land values to reflect the cost of a nuisance such as aircraft noise. It is suggested that the lower market price of a house situated near an airport captures the capitalized value of the nuisance over a reasonable time horizon.

3   A third approach involves tracing the effects of a programme as far as possible and then trying to place a value on the costs and benefits of each effect. A programme to overcome inner city decay might be expected to provide a variety of benefits. Tracing just one benefit, such as a reduction in juvenile delinquency, may in turn reveal several further benefits; for example, a reduction in damage to property, which perhaps could be measured; a reduction in damage to people, which might be measured in terms of reduced medical costs, health care, loss of working time, etc.; a reduction in crime, which might result in reductions in police work, savings in detention costs; and so on. In reality the relationships

are so tenuous and the impact of the programme on each of these benefits so imprecise that any attempt to place monetary values on intangibles of this nature is usually abandoned. Often, all that can be done in such a situation is to develop some non-monetary expression of the likely benefits from a particular programme, or from various levels of spending on a particular programme. In other words, a cost-effectiveness approach is adopted.

The choice of discount rate

Assuming that all the costs and benefits of a project can be adequately valued, the next problem to be considered concerns the appropriate discount rate to be used. It is clear that where costs and benefits occur at different points of time it will be necessary to discount them to some common time period before they can be realistically compared. For cost-benefit analysis purposes the social discount rate is used but there is considerable disagreement over how such a rate should be derived. The discussions surrounding the social discount rate debate are well developed elsewhere and it is not proposed to repeat them here. However, it might be useful to summarize briefly the issues involved.

One possible approach is to attempt to express the social discount rate as a rate which reflects society's preference for present benefits over future benefits, in other words the social time preference rate (STPR). The problem here is that the reasons for preferring present benefits may be because individuals underestimate the pleasure that future consumption might provide. The risk of not being around to benefit from later consumption, or the belief that future generations will be wealthier than present generations, and therefore in less need of benefits provided today, leads to a shortsighted attitude to time preference decisions. This places a question mark over the use of STPR.

A further possibility is to try to determine a social opportunity cost rate (SOCR). The philosophy underlying the use of SOCR is that as resources are limited their use in public sector investments means that they are not available for use elsewhere. It is usually assumed that it is private sector investments that will be forgone and so the rate that could have been earned in the private sector reflects the opportunity cost of public sector investment. Thus if the project forgone in the private sector could have earned 7 per cent, then a public sector investment should not be undertaken unless it will earn 7 per cent or more. The obvious difficulty is that of determining the rate of return in the private sector. Also as privately earned profits are subject to corporation tax, the pre-tax returns in the private sector ought to be higher than returns on public sector investments to satisfy the after-tax returns required by shareholders. Moreover, the rates of return required on private sector investments reflect attitudes to the financial risk and business risk of private firms. This leads to the suggestion that the social discount rate should be based on the rate of return required on government debt, i.e. the rate on gilt-edged securities. Alternatively, for local authority debt, there is an established market rate of return that could be used. However, market rates of this sort reflect many factors that are not relevant to the choice of a social discount rate – for example, the monetary policy of central government.

A further aspect of market rates of interest is that they incorporate expectations about future rates of inflation. This leads to the need to reflect expected price changes in the estimates of future costs and benefits, thereby adding a further complication to an already difficult process. One solution is to isolate the *real* social discount rate, and use this in the discounting process. This means that to the extent that costs and benefits might be expected to change at the same rate as changes in general price levels the need to forecast the latter is avoided. Only where the value of a particular cost or benefit is expected to change faster or slower than the general price level do price changes need to be taken into account. This is the approach adopted in the government's suggestions that the discount rate for use in public sector investment appraisal should be the *test discount rate*. The basic test discount rate for public expenditure is currently assessed at 8 per cent in *real* terms.

In reality, any discount rate that is chosen will suffer from some imperfections. Whether a real discount rate is assessed in some way or market rates are used, they will always be lacking in theoretical foundation. The important thing to remember is that like should always be discounted by like. Thus if a real discount rate is used, the costs and benefits should also be in real terms. If a market-determined discount rate is used, the costs and benefits should also reflect anticipated price changes. Because of difficulties in assessing the correct discount rate, it might be appropriate to discount public sector costs and benefits by a series of discount rates. This also has the advantage of providing a means of dealing with the uncertainty inherent in investment appraisal by showing the sensitivity of a project's outcome to different discount rates. In connection with this Bohm (1977, p. 110) suggests that:

> By estimating the net benefits of projects at different levels of discount rates, it is possible to ascertain the extent to which project outcomes are sensitive to differences in this respect.

Risk and uncertainty

In the above quotation Bohm is supporting the use of different discount rates to take account of the uncertainty surrounding the correct *rate* to use. This should be distinguished from the uncertainty about the *amount* of future costs and benefits. As far as the latter is concerned, it is usual to adopt a 'sensitivity analysis' approach, whereby attention is focused on those assumptions on which the outcome of the appraisal is heavily dependent. The sensitivity of the outcome to changes in the assumptions can then be examined.

The whole question of attitudes to risk and uncertainty in public sector investment decisions offers a further example of a departure from the position in the private sector. It is generally assumed that private investments are not selected simply on the basis of maximizing the present value of expected returns, but that the riskiness of the returns is also an important consideration. For public sector investments the situation is more controversial. First there is the suggestion that public sector organizations should behave as though they were indifferent to risk. This means that projects should be assessed on the basis of their expected present values and that the variability of the outcomes around the expected value should not influence the decision. Thus a project with equally likely net present values of £2,000, £4,000, £6,000, or £8,000, has an *expected* net present value of £5,000. This should be considered neither more nor less attractive than an alternative project with a *certain* net present value of £5,000. The arguments supporting this line of reasoning are that many of the uncertainties that exist in the private sector are not present in the public sector, and also that for the public sector as a whole the benefits of diversification will occur.

A second suggestion is that risk should not be treated differently in the public sector from its treatment in the private sector, because any failure to take risk into account would result in an over-investment in the public sector. In other words, public sector organizations should not be indifferent to risk. The problems with both of these approaches are related to the problems mentioned earlier of selecting a discount rate. With the first possibility the expected costs and benefits should be discounted at the risk free social opportunity cost rate, i.e. the private sector rate appropriate for investments with certain returns. For the second possibility the full social opportunity cost rate could be used. However, imperfections in the capital market provide very little relevant information on what either of these rates should be.

A third suggestion is that government action should be responsible for determining a national policy regarding time and risk preference. This brings us back to the world of *test discount rates*. If national objectives concerning some long-term rate of growth exist, then the test discount rate might be thought of as reflecting, in a very broad way, this growth requirement. Where a test discount rate is used to discount expected costs and benefits the public sector organization should behave as though indifferent to risk, and therefore the criteria for investment selection will be the expected net present values of the projects under consideration.

Cost-benefit analysis in practice

In spite of the practical difficulties involved, there have been several notable attempts in the UK to make use of cost-benefit analysis principles in investment appraisal. Perhaps the best known of these are the M1 motorway project, the Victoria Line on the London underground system, and the siting of the third London Airport.

The results of the Victoria Line study offer an interesting example of the factors that were taken into account to establish likely benefits. On purely financial considerations, based on existing and projected fare structures, the Victoria Line was predicted to incur an annual operating loss of around £2 million. However, when social benefits were taken into consideration the present value of the benefits exceeded the present value of the costs by approximately £31 million, using a 6 per cent discount rate. The estimated benefits of the project were as follows:

1 *Benefits from traffic diverted to Victoria Line.* These reflected the time saved by existing underground passengers switching to the more direct Victoria Line, and also the time saved by previous surface travellers who would use the new line. Also because passengers who had previously used cars or buses or surface rail methods of travel would now use the Victoria Line, the congestion on surface travel would be relieved, resulting in further time savings. Other benefits such as increased comfort and reduced stress were also included.

2 *Benefits from traffic not diverted to Victoria Line.* The easing of traffic on all other underground lines would result in operating cost savings, and increased comfort and convenience for the remaining passengers. Similarly there would be cost savings and time savings for surface transport.

3 *Generated traffic.* In addition to existing travellers benefiting from the new line

it was thought that additional numbers of people would be induced to travel. An estimate of the time savings, fare savings and convenience benefits to be attributed to this generated traffic was also included.

The monetary values attached to the various costs and benefits are illustrated in Fig. 6.1. The present values of the costs and benefits were obtained by using a 6 per cent discount rate and assumed an operating period of 50 years. Using a 4 per cent discount rate the present values of the benefits exceeded the present value of costs by almost £65 million. Using an 8 per cent discount rate the difference amounted to approximately £13 million.

COST-EFFECTIVENESS ANALYSIS

It is because social costs and benefits are not always easily measurable that cost-effectiveness analysis, with its more realistic requirements, is more widely used. Cost-effectiveness analysis involves a careful appraisal of the quantifiable costs and benefits, both now and in the future, of undertaking a project, with the non-quantifiable effects described but not evaluated. In other words, cost-effectiveness analysis concentrates on measuring the measurable.

The steps to be followed are these:

1 Determine the amount and timing of all capital costs. These will include the costs of buildings, equipment and land. It is important that the resources required for a project should be valued at their full opportunity cost. Thus, if an organization already owns land on which a building is to be erected the 'cost' used should be the current market value.
2 Estimate the annual running costs over the expected life of the project.
3 Estimate the measurable outputs over the expected life of the project. For example, revenues from fees and charges.
4 Estimate the effect of costs and revenues on existing activities. For example, building a new swimming pool may divert users, and therefore revenue, from an existing pool.
5 Discount the costs and measurable benefits to enable comparisons to be made. The usual procedure is to calculate present values but where projects with different expected lifetimes are being compared the use of equivalent annual costs may be more appropriate.
6 Describe in as realistic a manner as possible the non-quantifiable costs and benefits that will result from the project.

The practical difficulties associated with cost-effectiveness analysis are nevertheless quite considerable. Although only the measurable costs and benefits are included in the analysis, there are obviously going to be very real problems in forecasting the magnitude and timing of future amounts. Also the difficulties of selecting the correct discount rate or adjusting for risk and uncertainty, as described in the previous section on cost-benefit analysis, are equally applicable to cost-effectiveness analysis. However the actual *mechanics* of discounting are no different from those used in private sector applications and so they are not described further here. The examples that follow show how cost-effectiveness analysis might be applied in public sector investment appraisal. In the first two examples a *real* discount rate of 5 per cent is used. The third example illustrates the use of a market rate of interest.

Cost-Benefit Analysis – Victoria Line

	Annual amount £m	Present value at 6% £m
COSTS		
Capital expenditure	–	38.81
Annual working expenses	1.413	16.16
Total costs	–	54.97
BENEFITS		
1. Traffic diverted to VL		
Underground: time saved	0.378	4.32
Underground: comfort/convenience	0.347	3.96
BR: time savings	0.205	2.93
Buses: time savings	0.573	6.58
Motorists: time savings	0.153	3.25
Motorists: savings in vehicle operating costs	0.377	8.02
Pedestrians: time savings	0.020	0.28
Sub-total (1)	2.055	29.34
2. Traffic not diverted to VL		
Underground: cost savings	0.150	1.72
Underground: comfort/convenience	0.457	5.22
Buses: cost savings	0.645	7.38
Road users: time savings	1.883	21.54
Road users: savings in vehicle operating costs	0.781	8.93
Sub-total (2)	3.916	44.79
3. Generated traffic		
Outer areas: time savings	0.096	1.37
Outer areas: fare savings	0.063	0.90
Outer areas: other benefits	0.375	5.36
Central area: time savings	0.056	0.80
Central area: fare savings	0.029	0.41
Central area: other benefits	0.203	2.90
Sub-total (3)	0.822	11.74
4. Terminal scrap value		0.29
Total benefits (1)+(2)+(3)+(4)	–	86.16
Net benefits		31.19

Fig. 6.1   Example of a cost-benefit analysis survey for the Victoria Line.

EXAMPLES OF INVESTMENT APPRAISAL

Example 1

Description of
investment
project

A public utility is facing difficulties in meeting the demands of its repairs and maintenance divisions on the services of its regional stores depots. A survey of the stores operations reveals that improvements can be achieved in the following ways:

1   taking on extra employees;
2   purchasing stores handling equipment.

Identification of
costs

1   *Increasing work-force.* The additional wages costs for the first year at current wages rates, etc. would be £25,000 and it is estimated that these will increase by one percentage point per year faster than the rate of general inflation.
2   *Purchasing of equipment.* This would require an immediate payment of £80,000. The equipment suppliers guarantee a trade-in price of £16,000 at the end of five years but require the public utility to enter into a service and maintenance agreement. The terms of the agreement require an annual payment in advance. For the first year, this will be £4,000 with increases in subsequent years by an amount equal to the rise in general inflation. Although the equipment will avoid the need to take on additional employees a rescheduling of the duties of the existing work-force will be required and this will result in additional wages payments of £3,000 per year at current wages rates. The use of the equipment will also incur operating costs of £2,000 in the first year at current prices and in subsequent years these are expected to increase at the same rate as increases in general inflation. The predicted rate of general inflation is 6 per cent per year for the next five years.

Discount rate

A discount rate of 5 per cent in *real* terms is to be used. As the increase in the service and maintenance costs and the operating costs of the equipment will be the same as the increase in the rate of general inflation, the current prices at the start of Year 1 can be thought of as *real* values. There is therefore no need to adjust for general inflation because the discount rate of 5 per cent is also in *real* terms. However, as the wages costs increase at a rate of 1 per cent per year faster than the increase in general inflation it is necessary to adjust for this. The most convenient approach to adopt in this situation is to adjust the discount rate and use a rate of $1.05 \div 1.01$, i.e. 1.0396 which, for calculation purposes, approximates to 1.04, or 4 per cent.

In addition it should be noted that the trade-in price of the equipment is fixed at £16,000 and therefore this will have to be adjusted for the effects of general inflation. £16,000 received in five years' time has a real value at the start of Year 1 of $£16,000/(1.06)^5$, (i.e. $£16,000 \times 0.7473$) = £11,956. It is this value that should be used in an appraisal of the alternatives.

It is assumed that wages costs and equipment operating costs will occur evenly throughout the year, and so the annual costs can be considered to be equivalent to a single payment at mid-year. A mid-year discount factor should therefore be used. The approach adopted is to discount to the middle of Year 1, and then convert mid-year 1 present values to the beginning of Year 1 presents values by a factor of $1/(1+r)^{1/2}$, or $1/\sqrt{1+r}$, (where r is the discount rate). Thus with a discount rate of

4 per cent the conversion factor is $1/\sqrt{1.04} = 0.9806$. With a discount rate of 5 per cent the conversion factor is $1/\sqrt{1.05} = 0.9759$.

Appraisal of alternatives

1   *Additional employees.* The additional wages costs amount to £25,000 per year. However, if the equipment is purchased this will involve extra wages costs of £3,000 per year and therefore the net cost of taking on additional employees reduces to £22,000 per year.

	Additional wages costs per year £	Equipment wages costs £	Net wages cost per year £	Discount factor at 4% £	PV at beginning of year 1 £
Year 1 – mid-year	25,000	3,000	22,000	0.9806	21,573
Year 2/5 – mid-year	25,000	3,000	22,000	3.630×0.9806	78,311
				Present value	£99,884

2   *Purchasing stores handling equipment*

	Purchase price £	Maintenance agreement £	Operating costs £	Discount factor at 5% £	PV at beginning of year 1 £
Year 1 – start	80,000	4,000		1	84,000
Year 1 – mid-year			2,000	0.9759	1,952
Years 2/5 – start		4,000		3.546	14,184
Years 2/5 – mid-year			2,000	3.546×0.9759	6,921
Year 5 – end	(11,956)			0.7835	(9,368)
(real value of trade-in price)			Total present value		£97,689

Presentation of results

In present value terms the purchase of stores handling equipment is the most cost-effective way of achieving the required improvements. In reality, it is unlikely that the improvement in service will be identical in both cases and the alternatives were merely seen as different ways of overcoming a particular problem. Other factors would need to be taken into account, such as the reliability of the equipment, or the possibility of the existing work-force being discontented with the rescheduling of duties.

Also there has been no attempt to take account of the benefits of the alternative approaches. For example, the wider social benefits of creating employment opportunities, particularly in an area of high unemployment, might be considerable. Although such benefits cannot be quantified in any precise way, they should not be overlooked when the final decision is taken.

Example 2

Description of investment project

The social services department of a local authority is currently housed in a very old and dilapidated building in a run-down part of the city. If the building is to continue to be occupied it will need to be completely renovated and even then a large amount must be spent each year on heating, lighting, cleaning, and maintenance costs. An alternative option is to build new accommodation on a site in a different part of the town. Although the construction costs would be higher than the costs of renovation, the annual running costs of the new building would be much lower.

Identification of costs

The architects' department estimates the cost of renovating the building at £250,000. The building is owned by the local authority and if the social services department moves out it will eventually be demolished and the land will be included as part of an inner-city parks and open spaces project. It is decided therefore to treat the market value of the property as zero. It is also estimated that the new building would cost £430,000 to construct. The site is already owned by the local authority and a recent professional valuation gave it current market value of £100,000.

The difference in annual running costs is estimated to be £10,000 at current prices, and it is expected that this will increase at the same rate as the increase in general inflation. It is anticipated that all construction or renovation work will be completed within one year of commencement. The renovated building should have a useful life of about 18 years, whereas the new building is expected to last for 25 years

Discount rate

A discount rate of 5 per cent in *real* terms is to be used. Because the alternative options have different expected lives, it will not be correct to compare on the basis of discounted present value. One approach is to assume that the social services department will be required to operate for the indefinite future and that after 18 or 25 years the options available, and their costs in real terms, will be the same as they are today. It is then possible to compare on the basis of 'annuitized values' or 'equivalent annual costs'.

Appraisal of alternatives

1 *Renovating existing building*

Capital costs – renovation	£250,000	
5% annuity factor for 18 years	0.0855	
Equivalent annual cost		£21,375
Additional annual running costs		10,000
Total		£31,375

2 *Constructing new building*

Capital costs – construction	£430,000		
– land	£100,000	£530,000	
5% annuity factor for 25 years		0.0710	
Equivalent annual cost			£37,630

Presentation of results

In annual cost terms the renovation of the existing building is the most cost-effective way of providing proper accommodation for the social services department. However, it must be borne in mind that it is difficult to construct a new building that would provide exactly the same level of facilities as the existing building. In reality, the facilities might well be improved above their present level. Because of this, it is often useful to consider a hypothetical third option of constructing a new building that would provide equivalent facilities to those of the renovated building. For example, the architects' department might estimate that the construction costs of such a building would amount to £340,000. The total cost with land would therefore be £440,000 and the equivalent annual cost of £440,000 × 0.0710, i.e. £31,240, would be slightly less than the cost of renovation. The question that then arises is whether the 'extra' facilities are worth an additional £6,390 per year (£37,630 − £31,240), and this depends on the benefits that might result. The 'benefits' might be improved staff satisfaction, resulting in a better service to the public; greater accessibility to the public; better communications, and so on. Such benefits are obviously intangible and therefore incapable of exact measurement, and the final decision must be largely a matter of judgement.

Example 3

Description of investment project

A local highways authority is responsible for operating a toll bridge on a busy secondary road. The bridge is in urgent need of repair and the highways engineer reports that unless some work is undertaken immediately the bridge will have to be closed. He also points out that during the winter months the volume of traffic using the bridge is quite low relative to the rest of the year, and as it is now December he submits the following alternatives for consideration:

1   To close the bridge completely for twelve weeks and complete the repairs in one operation.
2   To carry out repairs whilst the bridge is in use. This will require undertaking part of the work immediately and spreading the rest over the winter months of the next three years.

Identification of costs

1   *Closing the bridge for twelve weeks.* This will involve immediate repair costs of £48,000 and loss in toll revenues of £18,000.
2   *Spreading the work over future years.* This will involve immediate repair costs of £12,000, plus a further £16,000 one year from now, £18,000 two years from now, and £20,000 three years from now. It is anticipated that the delays to traffic that the repairs will cause will divert users of the bridge to an alternative crossing point. This will result in an estimated loss of revenue from toll charges of £3,000 this year, £3,900 next year, £4,000 two years from now, and £4,600 three years from now.

Discount rate

The local authority can currently borrow at a rate of approximately 10 per cent p.a., and this is the rate to be used for discounting purposes. As this is a market rate of interest it reflects lenders' expectations about interest rates, and is therefore a 'nominal' or 'money' discount rate. This is the appropriate discount rate to use because the costs and revenue losses of each year are also expressed in 'money' terms. In other words, they reflect the anticipated price levels that will prevail at the times they will be incurred.

Appraisal of alternatives

1 *Closing bridge for twelve weeks*

	Present value £
Immediate repair costs	48,000
Loss in toll revenues	18,000
	£66,000

2 *Spreading repairs over future years*

	£	PV factor (10%)	Present value £
Immediate repair costs	12,000	–	12,000
Loss in toll revenues	3,000	–	3,000
First year repair costs	16,000	0.909	14,544
Loss in toll revenues	3,900	0.909	3,545
Second year repair costs	18,000	0.826	14,868
Loss in toll revenues	4,000	0.826	3,304
Third year repair costs	20,000	0.751	15,020
Loss in toll revenues	4,600	0.751	3,455
			£69,736

Presentation of results

On the basis of present values, the complete closure of the bridge for a twelve-week period is the most cost-effective way of undertaking the repairs. Other factors that would have to be taken into consideration would be the inconvenience to regular users, the possible permanent loss of revenue caused by some users being diverted to alternative crossing points and, perhaps most importantly, the effect on the provision of emergency services to communities situated near the bridge. As in many public sector investment appraisals the intangible consequences are often as important as the more tangible, and the relative weighting to be attached to each is very much a matter of judgement.

DISCUSSION TOPICS

1 'It is because the social costs and benefits that are required for cost-benefit analysis are so notoriously difficult to measure that cost-effectiveness analysis, with its more realistic requirements, is more widely used.'

Describe clearly what is meant by the techniques of 'cost-benefit analysis' and 'cost-effectiveness analysis', and critically examine the arguments for and against the use of each technique when evaluating investment proposals in the public sector.

2 Give three examples of public sector programmes or services for which cost-benefit analysis would be appropriate. Describe for each programme how the cost-benefit analysis might be implemented, and discuss the problems that might be encountered.

PART 2
Financial accounting

CHAPTER 7

Financial accounting theory

This chapter is concerned with the published accounts of public sector organizations from a theoretical point of view. We examine different approaches to identifying users and their needs. We also discuss different approaches to defining the reporting unit. We end with a discussion of the accounting policy-making environment in the public sector.

ACCOUNTING THEORY

Accounting theory is conventionally concerned with financial accounting, i.e. with accounting to external providers of finance. It includes all aspects of published financial reports:

1   their purpose;
2   their form;
3   their content;
4   the laws, regulations, and guidelines governing them;
5   the accounting policy-makers who determine them.

The literature on accounting theory is relatively new (the bulk of it has been generated over the last 50 years), and it has, until recently, been almost exclusively concerned with public limited companies (Whittington, 1986). The 1970s saw the beginning of serious and substantial attempts to understand and improve the financial reporting practices of public sector organizations. But in order to understand the problems faced in accounting theory, students must often look to the literature on business organizations and apply it to the public sector context, albeit with great caution and common sense.

The conventional way of defining financial accounting (the convention was established in 1966 by the American Accounting Association's *A Statement of Basic Accounting Theory*) has it that accounting is a purposive activity, i.e. it is directed towards a specified end. Previously, accounting was thought of in much the same way as mathematics, as though it was an abstract but systematic manipulation of numbers. Now accounting must above all be useful. In the UK the most authoritative statement of this position comes from *The Corporate Report* (ASC 1975, pp. 9 and 15):

> Our subject is, in essence, the fundamental aims of published financial reports and the means by which these aims can be achieved. The form of report with which we are dealing we have termed the 'corporate report', by which we mean the comprehensive package of information of all kinds which most completely describes an organization's economic

activity. . . . Our basic approach has been that corporate reports should seek to satisfy, as far as possible, the information needs of users: they should be useful.

If accounting reports are to be useful, therefore, we must define the users of those reports and the uses to which they put them. If we assume that accountants play a passive role in this, namely that they provide only what is expressly requested, then we build our accounting theory on that. However, if we assume that accountants also have an educational role, we might add to our definitions, to include potential users and potential users' needs.

Either way, this approach to accounting introduces a central difficulty: how do we find out who the users are and how do we find out their needs? Some of the problems associated with answering these questions are as follows:

1 The number of users will be huge.
2 Their needs may/will conflict.
3 Users have been conditioned by accountants over many years, so that their expressed needs may simply reflect marginal improvements on what they have already been receiving.
4 Users are not necessarily rational and their needs are likely to change over time.

From the beginning, however, these difficulties have been recognized and although there have been attempts to overcome them – attempts which will no doubt continue – there had to be a way of progressing while these studies were being undertaken. The approach adopted was to say that accounting can be based, not on users and their needs, but on *hypothesized* users and *hypothesized* needs. A further refinement that has often been adopted is to rank the supposed users in order of importance and then to concentrate on the most important. The many theories which concern themselves exclusively with needs of shareholders in public limited companies are typical of this approach.

In the business sector, the users' needs approach to accounting theory has been adopted in a number of authoritative statements. The most notable examples now are the Financial Accounting Standards Board's *Objectives Of Financial Reporting by Business Organizations* (1978) in the US and, in the UK, the Accounting Standards Board's proposed Statement of Principles, *The Objective of Financial Statements and the Qualitative Characteristics of Financial Information* (1991).

ACCOUNTING THEORY AND PUBLIC SECTOR ORGANIZATIONS

Although there are difficulties involved in defining the business sector for accounting purposes, these difficulties have never been considered primary. For example, the question of whether accounting is or should be the same for a public limited company as for a private company has never unduly concerned accounting theorists.

However, when you move away from the narrowly defined business sector there is a more significant problem: which organizations or groups of organizations are you theorizing about? If you discover the users (and their needs) of the accounting reports of a local government, does the resulting theory apply to a central government? Does it indeed apply to a local government in a different country, where the body itself may be of a completely different kind? Does it apply to a public utility which may or may not appear to be similar to a local government?

The main difficulty is that the non-business sector is not a homogeneous group of organizations. It comprises:

1   governments;
2   local governments;
3   state governments;
4   nationalized industries and public corporations;
5   non-departmental public bodies (NDPBs), also known as quasi-autonomous non-governmental organizations (QUANGOs);
6   charities;
7   co-operatives;
8   trade unions, etc.

Even when the discussion is limited to public sector organizations there are still difficulties. Organizationally, British Rail is not the same as Cardiff City Council: they are responsible to different sets of elected members, they provide different services, and they are financed differently. There is, therefore, no reason to assume that their accounting needs are the same.

One approach to the problem has been to list all the various kinds of non-business organizations, pointing out their political, economic, and social differences, and then build the accounting theories from there. However, the number of organizations this produces is unmanageable, and it also tends to emphasize differences rather than similarities. A more realistic alternative is to deduce which characteristics of organizations have the most impact on accounting. This offers the best hope because in the end we are not interested in organizational differences *per se*, but in those differences which affect accounting.

The best example of this latter approach is to be found in Professor R. N. Anthony's *Financial Accounting in Nonbusiness Organizations* (1978). This now standard reference work was commissioned by the Financial Accounting Standards Board (FASB) in the USA. At the time, the Board was primarily concerned with accounting standard-setting for business organizations, but it saw the need to involve itself with non-business organizations as well and this research study was its first move in that direction. The study is not explicitly concerned with providing answers but with putting the relevant questions, along with the arguments pro and con for each. Of primary interest to Anthony was whether, and if so how, a distinction ought to be drawn between accounting theories, standards and practices for business and non-business organizations. He suggested that in order to take the decision, organizations could most usefully be categorized in one of three different ways:

1   *Profit-oriented* – organizations whose primary goal is the pursuit of profit.
2   *Type A non-profit* – non-profit organizations whose financial resources are obtained entirely, or almost entirely, from revenues from the sale of goods and services.
3   *Type B non-profit* – non-profit organizations which obtain a significant amount of financial resources from sources other than the sale of goods and services.

Categories 1 and 3 present relatively few difficulties. An example of a profit-oriented organization is of course a public limited company, while an example of Type B non-profit is a local government, because it receives the bulk of its finance from taxes, grants and borrowings.

Further, the broad experience of published accounting reports warrants the distinction being drawn. For example, the profit-oriented organization would almost invariably produce a Profit and Loss Account, a Balance Sheet, and a Cash Flow Statement. On the other hand, a Type B non-profit might produce a series of Revenue Accounts (which may or may not be on the 'income and expenditure' basis), a series of Balance Sheets, no overall Balance Sheet and no Cash Flow Statement. At the same time, the two categories do cover a wide range of organizations. The profit-oriented group would include the local butcher and BP plc; the Type B non-profits, a local charity and Her Majesty's Government. The biggest difficulty, however, is with the Type A non-profit. Experience tells us that there are organizations which fall between the profit-oriented and the Type B non-profit. In the UK, these are most typically the nationalized industries and public corporations. They are not, by definition, strictly profit-oriented. They also do receive a significant proportion of their *income* from the sale of goods and services rather than from taxes. However, the definition of the Type A non-profit relates to a significant proportion of their 'financial resources', which of course includes capital finance. Strictly, then, it is hard to imagine that such organizations exist. One solution would be to redefine the Type A in terms of *current* financial resources and perhaps also to replace 'entirely or almost entirely' with 'a significant proportion', so that the Type A non-profit organizations become: non-profit organizations which obtain a significant amount of their current financial resources from the sale of goods and services.

The nationalized industries would clearly be Type A non-profit. Further, British Rail, for example, would be distinguished from a Type B non-profit, even though it receives substantial capital and revenue grants from the government.

Indeed, this might suggest that the Type A non-profit might usefully be dichotomized into those nationalized industries which have traditionally been 'profitable' and those which have not. Such a distinction would require fine tuning but an *a priori* case might be made for the financial reports of the two groups being different.

Broadly speaking, the nationalized industries' and public corporations' accounts follow the business model of the Profit and Loss Account, Balance Sheet and Cash Flow Statement whilst including sector profit and loss accounts, echoing the Type B non-profit model.

Anthony's purpose in offering the above categories was to help answer the following question: how, if at all, should business organizations be distinguished from other organizations for the purpose of setting accounting standards? He offered three alternatives:

- profit/non-profit distinction;
- 'sources of finance' distinction;
- no distinction.

Profit/non-profit distinction

1 Profit is the most fundamental measure of performance in the business sector. Accounting reports measure profit and therefore provide direct evidence as to the organization's performance in a year. In contrast, where the profit motive

is absent, services are provided for reasons other than the pursuit of profit; for example, they are provided for the welfare of individuals who cannot afford to pay the economic cost. Profit is an inappropriate measure of performance for these organizations. Accounting for them is therefore different.

2   Organizations where the profit motive is absent typically have not just one alternative goal but many. A local authority, for example, may provide health, education and highway services. Each of these services has different specific goals, and therefore the accounting reports should show the extent to which these differing goals are achieved. Consequently, in contrast to the single set of accounts for a profit-oriented organization, the non-profit organization needs a series of accounts for each service.

3   The profit-oriented organization is usually financed by shareholders' equity. The accounts are largely designed to provide information about the returns achieved on that risk investment. The non-profit organization typically has no risk capital invested in it, and therefore the returns on capital are of little importance.

'Sources of finance' distinction

1   In profit-oriented and Type A non-profit organizations the primary source of current finance is revenues. This usually means that the goods and services provided by these organizations have been tested in the market-place. Therefore, whether the organization is pursuing profit or aiming to break even, the difference between costs and revenues is a measure of performance. In both, the profit and loss account reflects its respective achievements. On the other hand, for the Type B non-profit, the extent to which income from non-revenue sources such as taxation covers cost is only a very narrow measure of performance: it only measures the extent to which the organization spent what it said it would spend, saying nothing about how the market valued its goods and services.

2   In Type B non-profit, because their finance is not provided in direct exchange for goods and services, there are often restrictions placed on what the organization can do with the finance. For example, there may be a grant which is specifically for building a capital asset. In this case it would be wrong to spend the money in any other way. Accounting systems have been developed to handle these kinds of restrictions (fund accounting). But these are irrelevant to an organization which charges for its goods and services because here the revenue gained can be used for any activity deemed appropriate: it can be reinvested, it can be distributed as dividends, it can be used to repay loans, etc.

3   Because of the importance of the profit and loss account in both the profit-oriented and the Type A non-profit organization, the final accounts are the primary instruments of financial accountability. For the Type B non-profit the final accounts are also important in explaining how money was spent. But of considerable, perhaps even equal importance, is the budget, because it is the budget which determines how much will be collected in taxation. This means that the budget is in itself an important part of financial accountability and it also means that the final accounts often include, for comparative purposes, budgetary information. Budgetary information is rarely included in the accounts of a profit-oriented or Type A non-profit organization.

No distinction

1   Double-entry bookkeeping, which is the foundation for financial reporting, is universal. All organizations, of any size and in most countries of the world, use double entry. This reflects the simple truth that whichever kind of organization is being considered, information is required about revenues, expenses, assets, liabilities and cash flows. Different interpretations might be applied to different organizations, but the basic information needs are the same. The Operating Statement, Balance Sheet and Cash Flow Statement provide this basic information.

2   Because so much more work has been done and so much more is known about the business way of accounting, having alternative methods leads to confusion. The business model is generally understood and so should be applied to all organizations.

3   Because accounting reports are used to monitor the allocation of resources in the economy, they should all be on the same basis. By making all financial reports directly comparable, better decisions can be taken about whether resources would not be better spent in different areas or in different amounts. This argument is used particularly in discussions about the relative strengths of providing services through the public sector as against the private sector.

4   The unifying concepts such as 'capital' (all organizations have capital and all need to have a measure of the capital they own) outweigh the differentiating concepts such as 'profit'.

There is no 'correct' answer to how the distinctions should be made. For our immediate purposes, we need only keep in mind that particular public sector organizations can fall in either of the categories of Type A non-profit and Type B non-profit. We shall also see cases where we do not categorize whole organizations in this way but separate out those functions within the organization which could be classed as Type A and those which could be classed as Type B. This can also lead to parts of public sector organizations being classified as 'profit-oriented', a trend that has been particularly marked during the 1980s with the increasing use of Direct Service Organizations in local authorities, Hospital Trusts in the health service, and Executive Agencies in the civil service.

STEWARDSHIP AND ACCOUNTABILITY

There are two basic concepts of financial accounting which it will be useful to define before we discuss users and their needs, particularly because their use in ordinary language is often not helpful in understanding their technical meaning. These are *stewardship* and *accountability*, and they represent the two ends of a spectrum of reporting possibilities.

Stewardship refers to the holding of someone else's assets by a steward. In its narrowly defined sense the responsibility of stewardship is to demonstrate that those assets have not been misappropriated.

Stewardship accounting is, therefore, typically limited to the balance sheet showing the money collected by the stewards, the form in which that money is held, and an audit certificate vouching for the truth and fairness of the statement. The profit and loss account shows the increase or decrease in the money held over the year.

Accountability, in its widest sense, refers to the responsibility for your actions to someone else. It is therefore much more than just accounting, however widely accounting is defined. There are many ways through which public sector organizations are held accountable (through elections, higher-level governments, the media, public inquiries, etc.) and for many different aspects of their performance (see Stewart, 1984). Though not easy to define, accounting is concerned with financial accountability plus some aspects of economic accountability. This kind of accountability goes beyond the narrowly defined stewardship of assets to include responsibility for the performance of those assets.

The simplest example of this is the inclusion of an 'earnings per share' figure in the accounts of a business. That ratio has little to do with stewardship, being concerned with indicating the success or failure of the business during the year.

Financial reports in all organizations have traditionally emphasized the stewardship function. In profit-oriented organizations this emphasis has not been to the exclusion of performance measures for the simple reason that, because of the existence of the profit measure, the stewardship accounts can be analysed to yield pointers to performance. Ratio analysis, which produces such measures as return on capital employed and liquidity measures, is the best example of this.

However, there are broader performance measures which could be included and which go beyond the traditional stewardship accounts. *The Corporate Report* takes the view that published accounts should include additional indicators of performance via additional statements, such as statements of value added, employment reports, statements of money exchanges with governments, etc.

In non-profit organizations, particularly in Type B, the stewardship accounts provide much more limited measures of performance. The typical measure provided is the comparison of what the organizations said they would spend (articulated in their budget) with what they actually spent. Although useful information, this demonstrates nothing about either the quality or quantity of the services they provide. As a consequence, it is often argued that there is a greater need for additional performance measures, and that these measures should be more detailed in non-profit organizations; in other words, that the wider accountability questions are more immediate and important.

OBJECTIVES IN PUBLIC SECTOR ACCOUNTING THEORY

The overall objective of financial reports is to be relevant. In order to define this further, we need to know who the users are and what their needs are. Since we do not currently have this knowledge we hypothesize the user groups and their needs. We could assume that everyone in the population is a user or a potential user of the accounts of public sector organizations. This would accord with basic notions of democracy and indeed with much of the work that has been done in user analysis. The problem is, however, that it is of little help in producing a list of user needs: the temptation would be to say either that everyone requires the same information or that everyone requires different information; the former would make the exercise redundant and the latter would make it impossible to handle.

The practical approach therefore is to group users and potential users so that, first, the members of each group require the same information, and secondly, the number of groups is manageable. This is the approach that has been adopted in the past but, particularly in the non-business area, it has yielded markedly different conclusions. On the one hand, there has been the approach which emphasizes the complexity of financial accounting and thus produces many user groups (which we might call the *differential approach*); alternatively, there has been the approach which emphasizes the commonalities and produces few user groups (which we might call the *integral approach*).

The differential approach to users and their needs

The best example of this approach comes from a research report entitled *Objectives of Accounting and Financial Reporting for Governmental Units* by Drebin *et al.* (1981). This report was commissioned and published by the National Council on Government Accounting (NCGA) in the USA. The NCGA was the main standard-setting body for the financial reports of US local and state governments, before the formation of the Governmental Accounting Standards Board (GASB) in 1984. The report offers a list of ten user groups:

1　taxpayers;
2　grantors;
3　investors;
4　fee-paying service recipients;
5　employees;
6　vendors;
7　legislative bodies;
8　management;
9　voters;
10　oversight bodies.

The rationale for these groups is that taxpayers, grantors, investors, and fee-paying service recipients all provide financial resources; employees and vendors provide labour and material resources; the legislative bodies and management take the resource allocation decision; and they are all under the constraints imposed by voters and oversight bodies (which include higher-level governments). The complexity of these groups and their interrelationships is shown by Fig. 7.1, taken from the report.

Taking this list of users and keeping in mind their relationships with the governmental organization, the report says that the overall goal of accounting and financial reporting for governmental units is:

> To provide (1) financial information useful for making economic, political and social decisions, and demonstrating accountability and stewardship, and (2) information useful for evaluating managerial and organizational performance. (p. 126.)

(Note that this definition separates accountability from performance measurement. This means that the report is taking 'accountability' to be much narrower than our definition.)

The report then offers a series of basic objectives which support the overall goals and are themselves supported by the users' needs which stem from them.

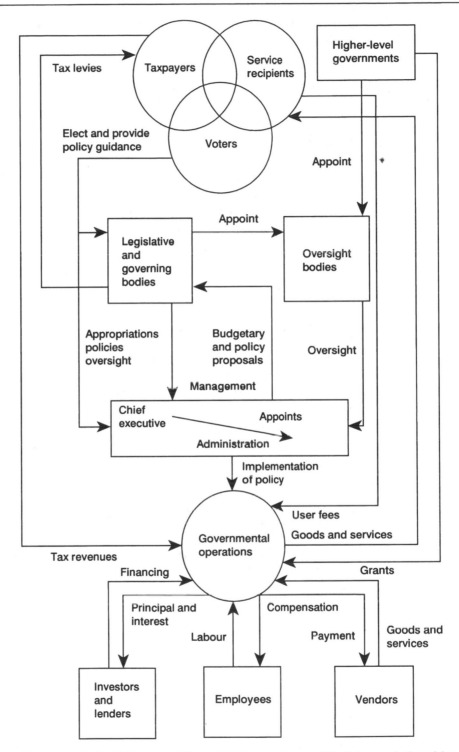

Fig. 7.1   Potential users of financial information and their interrelationships.
Source: A.R. Drebin, J.L. Chan and L.C. Ferguson, *Objectives of Accounting and Financial Reporting for Government Units: A Research Study*, Vol. 1, NCGA, 1981, p.79.

Objective 1 To provide financial information useful for determining and predicting the flows, balances, and requirements of short-term financial resources of the governmental unit.
Users' need:

1 for determining and predicting the balances and availability of short-term financial resources, including cash, for specific uses;
2 for predicting the need to obtain additional short-term finance resources;
3 for predicting the impact on short-term financial resources of specific revenue and other financial sources;
4 for predicting the impact on short-term financial resources of planned programmes and activities;
5 for predicting the ability of the governmental unit to meet its short-term obligations as they come due.

Objective 2 To provide financial information useful for determining and predicting the economic condition of the governmental unit and changes therein.
Users' need:

1 for determining the value and predicting the service potential of resources held by the governmental unit;
2 for determining whether the value and service potential of physical resources have been maintained during a period;
3 for predicting the amounts and timing of future outflows resulting from existing commitments and the ability of the governmental unit to meet these when they come due;
4 for determining and predicting the cost of programmes or services provided by the governmental unit.

Objective 3 To provide financial information useful for monitoring performance under terms of legal, contractual and fiduciary requirements.
Users' need:

1 for determining whether resources were utilized in accordance with legal and contractual requirements;
2 for determining whether resource contributions of taxpayers, grantors, and service recipients intended to support activities of a given time period were sufficient to recover the cost of those activities;
3 for determining whether fees or reimbursements are in accordance with legal, grant, or contractual requirements;
4 for accounting for the use and disposition of resources entrusted to public officials.

Objective 4 To provide information useful for planning and budgeting, and for predicting the impact of the acquisition and allocation of resources on the achievement of operational objectives.
Users' need:

1 for predicting the impact of programme alternatives on short-term financial resources of the governmental unit;
2 for predicting the impact of programme alternatives on the economic condition of the governmental unit;

3   for predicting the amount of resource contributions of taxpayers, grantors, and service recipients needed to support activities of a given time period;
4   for predicting the effectiveness, including the distribution of benefits among groups, of proposed programmes and activities in achieving goals and objectives;
5   for predicting the incidence of the burden of providing resources for governmental operations.

Objective 5   To provide information useful for evaluating managerial and organizational performance.
Users' need:

1   for determining the cost of programmes, functions and activities in a manner which facilitates analysis and valid comparisons with established criteria, among time periods, and with other governmental units;
2   for evaluating the efficiency and economy of operations of organizational units, programmes, activities and functions;
3   for evaluating the results of programmes, activities and functions, and their effectiveness in achieving their goals and objectives;
4   for evaluating the equity with which the burden of providing resources for governmental operations is imposed.

The effect of adopting the differential approach to establishing users' needs can now be seen. For example, a clear distinction is drawn between revenue items (which are the concern of Objective 1) and capital items (which are the concern of Objective 2). Similarly, the distinction between historical financial accounting (Objective 3) and financial information for planning and budgeting (Objective 4) is clearly made. Users' need (3b) implies that a distinction must be made, and must be accounted for, between the resources provided by taxpayers, grantors and service recipients, which shows whether their contributions were sufficient to cover the costs.

In fact, it is fair to say that these distinctions characterize the existing reporting models of governmental organizations, particularly in the USA. And, although it must be said that if the needs suggested by the report were met there would be many changes to existing reporting practices, it is also true that many of the needs rationalize the existing complexities of governmental accounting reports.

The integral approach to users and their needs

Anthony's previously cited study for the FASB is a good example of the integral approach to users' needs. His whole thrust is to produce an easily understood bedrock upon which the specific nuances of particular organizations can be built. Thus, for example, at the outset he excludes consideration of budgetary information, because he feels that to have validity in financial reports it must be produced on the same basis as the financial accounts. Since he cannot conceive of a situation where the financial accounts would be determined by the budgetary information, he suggests that users' needs can be developed in financial accounting terms and then, if budgetary information is required, it should be made consistent with the financial accounts.

His report produces a list of five user groups:

1   governing bodies;
2   investors and creditors;
3   resource providers;
4   oversight bodies;
5   constituents.

Of course, we must remember that Anthony is considering all non-business organizations, not just governmental organizations as Drebin *et al.* were considering. This is another reason for the tendency to take a much broader view. A direct comparison with Drebin *et al.* shows that Anthony puts taxpayers, voters and employees in one group, which he calls *constituents*; he calls grantors and fee-paying service recipients *resource providers*; investors and vendors are also grouped together. In the light of this list of users, Anthony offers the following four users' needs:

1   *Financial viability.* This refers to the ability of the organization to continue in its present form or in its planned form. Typical questions relating to this need would be: Has the education authority enough funds to continue to provide a place for all school-age pupils? Has the railway company enough funds to replace its obsolete assets? Is the government's tax base strong enough to support a planned expansion of services? Anthony suggests this information need is satisfied by:
    (a) tests of solvency and liquidity;
    (b) the relationship between inflows and outflows;
    (c) the degree of resource transferability – which refers to the extent to which resources might be restricted.
    He emphasizes that the information which helps meet this need is useful to those in business organizations as well.
2   *Fiscal compliance.* This refers to the extent to which the organization has complied with the conditions laid down in its authority to spend. These conditions might be imposed internally, by a budget; in which case, fiscal compliance will be demonstrated by a comparison of actual spending with budgeted spending. Or the conditions might be imposed by the law: for example, spending limits fixed as a percentage of last year's spending. This could be demonstrated explicitly or via an audit report which was exception-based, i.e. it reported on any instances where the law was contravened.
3   *Management performance.* This does not refer to measuring effectiveness as we have defined it. We know this because Anthony explicitly excludes information about attainment of the organization's objectives; he believes that not enough is known about measuring effectiveness to include it as a user need. Consequently, management performance is defined as a need to know whether money was spent wisely. In terms of our definitions in Chapter 1, this refers to efficiency measured in terms of low-level outputs.
4   *Cost of services provided.* This is self-explanatory and is needed for comparison purposes both between organizations and between the needs of present and future generations.

Since Anthony is above all concerned with highlighting the issues involved, rather than with providing solutions, he then suggests the kind of specific accounting information which might satisfy the above four needs, and puts the arguments pro and con for each.

However, the integral approach does tend to lead to an emphasis on the similarities of business and non-business financial reporting; this is in contrast to the differential approach which tends to accept the dissimilarities as having equal importance.

For example, in terms of performance measurement, Anthony is explicitly concerned with economy, to the exclusion of efficiency and effectiveness. His rationale is understandable: there is no generally accepted way of defining and reporting the measurement of high-level outputs in non-profit organizations. Efficiency and effectiveness demand the measurement of outputs. Anthony, therefore, chooses to ignore them. Since the business model is a generally accepted way of reporting *measurable* outputs, the tendency is to conclude that the business model can serve as the basis for satisfying Anthony's users' needs. Thus, financial viability and management performance are satisfied with the traditional business model, while fiscal compliance and cost of services demand an expansion of this basic information.

This line of argument is in stark contrast to Drebin *et al*. They are explicit, in Objective 5, that users need information for evaluating efficiency and effectiveness. If they accept Anthony's assertion that not enough is known about output measurement in non-business organizations, the conclusion of Drebin *et al*. will tend to be, first, that we adopt what is known for the present; and secondly, for the future, we do more research to improve our knowledge.

This kind of contrast between different approaches to user needs is starker when other versions are considered. Professor Holder (1980), in another study for the NCGA, considered all the user groups that had been offered by eight previous studies. He then said that his study would be concerned primarily with those users who:

1   had limited authority over the reporting entity;
2   possessed a relatively intense need for financial information.

This is a well-recognized solution to the problem of the manageability of many user groups. Typically in the business sector, it is the information needs of shareholders which are considered paramount. Holder concludes that the primary users of government financial statements, after applying the above two criteria, are present and prospective, short- and long-term creditors. The parallel is obvious; and of course the tendency to emphasize the similarities of business and non-business reporting is so much greater. In fact, Holder concludes that governments should adopt the basic business model of financial reporting.

The GASB subsequently adopted an approach that is closer to the integral approach than the differential approach, though it is perhaps fair to say that the resulting list of user needs is closer to maintaining the status quo in governmental accounting while leaving the door open to the adoption of business accounting ideas in some areas.

A key paragraph from the GASB (1994, p. B7) is:

> Financial reporting is not an end in itself but is intended to provide information useful for many purposes. Financial reporting helps fulfil government's duty to be publicly accountable. Financial reporting also helps to satisfy the needs of users who have limited authority, ability or resources to obtain information and who therefore rely on the reports as an important source of information. For that purpose, financial reporting objectives should consider the needs of users and the decisions they make.

By beginning with the 'duty to be publicly accountable' the GASB is allowing that financial reporting can be defined in part without explicitly referring to users' needs. This is important in practice because there are elements of traditional financial reports of governments that are not easily rationalized in terms of explicit users and their needs. For example, intergenerational equity between taxpayers (or inter-period equity) could be seen as a public policy, that is implemented in part by using financial statement numbers to influence the level of taxation. In this case, the financial reports are imposing norms rather than passively providing information for users' benefit.

The GASB (op. cit., pp. B15–16) identifies three groups of primary users:

1   those to whom government is primarily accountable (the citizenry), which includes taxpayers, voters, service recipients, the media, advocate groups and public finance researchers;
2   those who directly represent the citizens (legislative and oversight bodies), which includes members of state legislatures, county commissions, city councils, boards of trustees, school boards and those executive branch officials with oversight responsibility over other levels of government;
3   those who lend or participate in the lending process (investors and creditors), which includes individual and institutional investors and creditors, municipal security underwriters, bond-rating agencies, bond insurers and financial institutions.

The needs identified are (op. cit., p. B16):

1   comparing actual financial results with the legally adopted budget;
2   assessing financial condition and results of operations;
3   assisting in determining compliance with finance-related laws, rules and regulations;
4   assisting in evaluating efficiency and effectiveness.

These conclusions were partially based on an attempt to identify users and their needs empirically (Jones *et al.*, 1985), though that exercise was somewhat disappointing because of the very low response rate (reportedly around 10 per cent). This is perhaps symptomatic of a continuing problem with the user/user needs approach to financial reporting theory: we are still not clear that substantial numbers of users exist (Jones, 1992a).

The 1980s witnessed a new development: conceptual frameworks for national governments. They too use the user/user needs approach. Notable examples are *Financial Reporting by Governments* by the Canadian Institute of Chartered Accountants (1980), the *Federal Government Reporting Study* by the Auditor General of Canada and the Comptroller General of the US (1986), *Financial Reporting by National Governments* by the International Federation of Accountants (1991), *Objectives of Government Financial Reports* by the International Organization of Supreme Audit Institutions (1992) and *Objectives of Federal Financial Reporting* by the Federal Accounting Standards Advisory Board in the US (1994).

It is not useful to analyse the differences of detail between these documents because in principle they all take the same approach. Perhaps it suffices to outline the views offered in the last of the list, not least because in dealing with the US Federal Government it is clearly setting the background for the most significant development in accounting standard-setting for national governments in the world.

FASAB offers four major user groups: citizens (including news media, pressure groups, state and local legislatures and executives, analysts), the legislative branch (including their staff), and two groups in the executive branch, namely the senior members and the program managers. In terms of federal financial reporting, they are assumed to have four 'needs':

Budgetary integrity: the report should assist in fulfilling the government's duty to be publicly accountable for monies raised through taxes and other means and for their expenditure in accordance with the government's legally adopted budget and related laws and regulations.

Operating performance: to assist report users in evaluating the service efforts, costs, and accomplishments of the reporting entity; the manner in which these efforts and accomplishments have been financed; and the management of the entity's assets and liabilities.

Stewardship: to assist report users in assessing the impact on the country of the government's operations and investments for the period and how, as a result, the government's and the nation's financial condition has changed and may change in the future.

Deterring fraud, waste and abuse: to assist report users in understanding whether adequate financial management systems and internal controls are in place.

What is striking about the FASAB analysis is that it offers an integral approach but comes to wholly different conclusions about user needs: in contrast to Anthony (1978), the role of the budget is paramount.

Constraints

The search for more useful financial reports does not, however, necessarily mean a search for the most relevant information. Constraints exist which prevent maximum relevance being attainable. Instead, we aim for an optimal solution, achieving the most relevant reports possible in the light of the uncertainties involved in producing them, and the available resources.

Different views have been offered as to what these constraints might be, but the following list is representative of the main ones:

1   objectivity;
2   consistency;
3   comparability;
4   timeliness;
5   ease and economy of account preparation.

The extent to which accounting information enters into the consideration of relevance and how far it meets these constraints, is determined by an additional concept: materiality.

Objectivity

Perhaps the most fundamental characteristic of financial reports is that they are produced by management, they report on management but they are addressed to owners and others external to the reporting organization. Thus, in familiar terms, ownership is divorced from control.

It would therefore be unhelpful, not to say intolerable, if the controllers were able to report on their performance in any terms they chose. This means that the accounting principles adopted must have an acceptable degree of objectivity in the sense that any accountant would produce an acceptable set of accounts from the same data. This statement is deliberately equivocal. We might wish to say that any accountant would produce the *same* set of accounts from the same data. This would accord with the general understanding of the word objective, i.e. independent of the observer. However, the practice of accounting is not, and probably cannot be, objective in this sense. Therefore, we content ourselves with a degree of objectivity which represents an acceptable narrowing of the areas of difference between financial reports.

In practice, objectivity is the main constraint on achieving more relevant financial statements. For example, in this sense, a gross book value of an item of plant in historic cost terms is objective: in the plant accounts there is a debit which supports the balance sheet item and which is itself supported by an order and a paid invoice recording the historic cost. If it is decided that more relevant information for the balance sheet would be the plant's replacement cost, then that entry becomes more subjective: different accountants might produce different replacement costs from different markets.

In fact, most of the proposals for 'improving' accounting practice have involved more current valuations in the balance sheet at the expense of more subjectivity (compared with historic cost) in generating them. The problem is determining where the balance ought properly to be drawn.

A noteworthy exception to this trend can be found where some writers have proposed that financial reports move away from the relative subjectivity of all accruals accounting (subjective because of depreciation charges, stock valuations, etc.) to the relatively more objective cash flow accounting (which recognizes only cash inflows and outflows).

Consistency

This term is used to refer to the consistency over time of financial reports. Its importance lies in the necessity of being able to compare the current year's report with those of previous years. This is fundamental because, while organizations tend to be long term, financial reports usually cover only one year. Therefore, no matter how sensitive an annual report is, it cannot hope to capture even five years' economic activity.

The annual report artificially parcels up the underlying economic trends into years. It would be very naïve to suppose that one report taken on its own could tell you as much as you might want to know about the organization. By comparing a series of annual reports the chances of seeing the underlying trends are so much greater. But the reports must be consistent over time if this comparison is to be facilitated.

Take a simple example: you are interested in the trend of operating profits over ten years of a particular nationalized industry. Capital receipts would normally be credited to reserves and recorded in the balance sheet. But in one year a capital receipt was credited to the profit and loss account and included in turnover. In another year a capital receipt was credited to the profit and loss account but shown as an extraordinary item. Each treatment might be acceptable but the treatment would be inconsistent and would render the analysis of the series of doubtful validity.

Comparability

Clearly concerned with comparing reports, this term is used to distinguish between comparing over time and comparing the report of one organization with another. Thus comparability means the extent to which the performance of organization X can be compared with that of organization Y, using their financial reports.

This constraint relates to objectivity since the more objective financial reports are the more likely that different reports will be produced on the same basis. However, particularly in the context of public sector accounting, it adds a necessary additional emphasis. This is because objectivity is usually narrowed down to refer only to a homogeneous group of organizations. So that what is acceptable practice for one group might not be acceptable practice for another. Thus each group of accounts might be said to be objective but they are not comparable.

A ubiquitous example would be where the accounts of a government department were being compared with those of a business enterprise to judge whether privatization was worthwhile. Each set might be independently verifiable. However, where the government department does not depreciate plant and machinery but the enterprise does, then the resulting accounts are not strictly comparable.

Timeliness

This constraint refers to the amount of time the organization takes to produce its financial report. The basic idea is that the quicker it produces its report the better. In general, therefore, it constrains the increasing tendency for usefulness to mean more and more information. The more that is desired, the more time it is likely to take to produce the annual report. An example would be where two sets of final accounts were presented for the one organization, the first reporting historic costs and the second current valuations. This might be seen to be more relevant to users but the trade-off would have to be made against the possible effects on the date of publication.

There are also examples of more timely reports being potentially less relevant. For example, some local authorities produce their financial statements very quickly; on the other hand, they are able to do this by including more estimates of accrued expenditure rather than waiting for invoices to come in. The question is whether the gain in timeliness is worth the additional subjectivity involved.

Ease and economy of account preparation

All information provision incurs cost. The more information that is demanded the greater the cost. This cost can be direct, for example in the form of additional accounting staff salaries, or it can be indirect, where other activities are neglected so as to put more effort into the final accounts.

As with any other economic decision, the aim is to achieve the right balance of benefit received from cost incurred, while recognizing that this is usually difficult to measure.

Materiality

Central though this concept is in accounting and auditing, professional guidance on its meaning is typically broad. The essence of it is that information is material if it is likely to make a difference in user evaluations of financial statements. There are examples in the private sector of quantification of what is material, but in most cases materiality is left to individual judgement.

As Tomkins and Barker (1985) point out, the concept has not been enunciated in the public sector context and it may be that, while it remains a matter of individual judgement, the specific applications may be significantly different.

However the concept of materiality is implemented, it provides the 'threshold for recognition' of accounting information. Once information is judged material, we weigh its relevance against the constraints, and balance the costs of reporting it against the benefits.

THE REPORTING UNIT

Until now, we have discussed financial reporting in terms of *the organization*, and it has been implicit that we have understood what the organization is and what its implications for accounting are. This was only a matter of convenience, however, to keep the discussion as simple as possible. However, the problem of what the reporting unit is, and how we define it, is a significant one for business accounting and is even more significant for public sector accounting.

A number of theories of the reporting unit have been put forward. These are the main ones:

1 proprietary theory;
2 entity theory;
3 fund theory;
4 commander theory.

Proprietary theory

This theory sees the organization exclusively in terms of the owners (proprietors). The reporting unit is therefore the organization as the owners see it. This applies most readily to a partnership, for example, where the financial statements are concerned with showing wealth and the change in wealth over the period. But it has also been argued that the proprietary view extends, in theory and in practice, to public limited companies.

In this case, the accounts are addressed to the shareholders and the balance sheet is a statement of shareholders' financial position while the income statement is the change in shareholders' financial position. The accounting equation is:

$$\text{assets} - \text{liabilities} = \text{shareholders' equity}$$

The practical effects of this view on the form and content of the accounts are many. For example, interest on debentures is treated as a cost, so it is deducted from income (because from the shareholders' viewpoint it is a cost). Similarly, salaries and wages paid to employees are seen as costs and deducted from income.

The practical effects on the reporting unit can be seen more readily when a proprietary view is taken of a group of companies. Here, the subsidiaries would be shown in the group's accounts (which means the group shareholders' accounts) in terms of the net investment that the group's shareholders hold; consequently, the reporting unit would be the group (from the shareholders' viewpoint) rather than a consolidation of the reporting units of the subsidiaries.

A modification of the proprietary theory, known as the *residual equity theory*, defines the company in terms of the ordinary shareholders only; thus excluding the preference shareholders who would be considered owners under the proprietary theory.

Entity theory

The entity view of an organization is that it is distinct from any group of individuals associated with it. The reporting unit is therefore the entity and the report is addressed to all those interested in it. *The Corporate Report* represents a good example of the entity view. Here, the corporate report is addressed simultaneously to equity investors, loan creditors, employees, analyst-advisers, business contacts, the government and the public.

Using the above example of a group of companies, the entity view would see the group as a whole, reporting in the balance sheet all the assets that the group owns and all the claims on those assets. The accounting equation under the entity view becomes:

$$\text{assets} = \text{liabilities}$$

The value added statement is an entity view of the income statement. Rather than concentrating on a bottom line which shows the profit attributable to shareholders, the value added statement is concerned with how much value the entity has added through its operations and how that added value has been distributed to the many resource providers.

Fund theory

The fund theory of accounting was developed by Vatter (1947) for the business context. He felt that both the proprietary and the entity views had unacceptable weaknesses: first, that the proprietary view, being personal, was unsatisfactory for a public limited company where the owners change as shares are traded; secondly, that the entity view begged the question of how you define the entity.

Consequently, he proposed that the reporting unit should be defined as the *fund* and that organizations should be seen as one fund or a series of funds. This would mean that if an organization was seen as a series of funds, then the financial report for the organization would be an aggregation of the financial reports of the constituent funds.

Of course, the decision about where the funds are and what areas they cover is artificial. The most commonly quoted definition of a fund is found in GASB (1994, Section 1300):

> a fiscal and accounting entity with a self-balancing set of accounts recording cash and other financial resources together with all related liabilities and residual equities or balances and changes therein which are segregated for the purpose of carrying on specific activities or attaining certain objectives in accordance with special regulations, restrictions or limitations.

A fund could therefore be a photocopying unit in County Hall, it could be County Hall itself (i.e. the administration of the County Council), or it could be the whole of the education service. The fund theory offers the reporting accountant the flexibility to define the reporting unit where the definition is most useful.

Commander theory

This theory is a variant of the fund theory in that it sees the organization not in terms of a series of funds but a series of responsibility centres. Each responsibility centre is controlled by a manager ('commander') and each manager is responsible for the performance of his unit.

Therefore, under the commander theory, the financial report of the organization is an aggregation of all the stewardship and performance reports for each responsibility centre. It provides a specific focus and applies most readily to bureaucracies, where the tasks of the organizations are traceable to responsibility centres. Of course, the fund view and the commander view will coincide where the funds are defined in terms of responsibility centres.

In practice, published financial reports tend to adopt more than one of these views simultaneously. Also, different kinds of organizations lay the emphasis on different views.

The typical accounts of a business would largely be proprietary-based but might include entity influences. Thus, although the income statement and balance sheet will be addressed to shareholders primarily, an employee report might be included which amplifies the accounts as they affect employees. Similarly, including current cost accounts marks a shift towards an entity view because there the income statement shows the current cost profit after maintaining the operating capability of the business as a whole, as well as current cost profit attributable to shareholders.

The accounts of some nationalized industries have been more entity-based than those of public companies. This probably reflects the fact that the equivalent of the owners and long-term creditors is the government, on the public's behalf; and that, although return on capital is of interest, the necessarily wider view of the industry's role in the economy takes precedence.

Probably the best example of the fund view is the US local government. The GASB, which is the standard-setter for governmental bodies, recommends that the reporting model includes seven major types of funds: the General Fund, Special Revenue Funds, Capital Projects Funds, Debt Service Funds, Enterprise Funds, Internal Service Funds, and Trust and Agency Funds.

The main issue involved with fund accounting is the extent to which the fund accounts should be aggregated to produce an overall view of the organization. The idea of fund accounts is, of course, that the organization view is not the most relevant. On the other hand, this is anathema to many accountants, particularly those involved in business, because they are used to seeing a single set of financial statements. Specifically, the problems of unaggregated (or unconsolidated) fund accounts is that the cost of a particular service will not be shown as a single item. For example, the bulk of the operating expenditure for the police department will be included in the general fund but the operating implications of capital expenditure (principal and interest repayments) will be included in the debt service fund. On top of this, there may be areas of the police department which have been financed by special funds, perhaps in the form of trusts; the costs of these areas will appear in a different fund again.

The fund view is flexible enough to give the opportunity for providing this kind of 'additional' information. But its flexibility depends upon the levels of aggregation adopted and the willingness to present different views of the same information. Because of pressure from the business community in the US, many local governments are providing more of this kind of information; indeed there are examples of reports including a set of fund accounts and a set of accounts based on a proprietary view.

UK local authorities report under the fund view combined with the commander view. Their fund is not the same as the US version because, although their reports do include the accounts of the general fund, housing revenue account, trust funds, etc., these are not funds in the strict sense of the GASB definition. They are not self-contained sets of accounts. Local authorities tend to have only one significant cash book. Individual balance sheets are produced for the main funds but the cash figures are balancing entries which taken together will, when the accounts balance, produce the cash book balance. Also, both operating expenditure and the operating consequences of capital expenditure appear together in the funds.

Balance sheets are usually produced for each account, but the operating accounts are in much more detail: the General Fund will be segregated into, for example, education, public health, roads. These are the responsibility centres of local government, representing the functional areas of spending, each with a professional responsible for that activity to the council. The director of social services is the 'commander' of social services and is responsible not just to the council but to the community for social services. The accounts, therefore, are structured to report the revenues and expenditures under his/her control.

Many UK local authorities produce a consolidated balance sheet. On the face of it, this is offering a commander view because it is reporting on the command of the authority as a whole. However, many consolidated balance sheets exclude some fund balance sheets. The best example is where the superannuation fund is not consolidated. The commander view would say that the superannuation fund balance sheet should be consolidated: the authority is responsible for managing the fund, although it is on the employees' behalf, not the community's. Indeed, this management does affect the community because of internal borrowing between the superannuation and general fund since the general fund provides employers' contributions and it charges for administration costs. Where the superannuation fund remains unconsolidated, then a fund/proprietary view is being taken: the fund is not owned by the community, therefore it is not included with the community's accounts.

The reporting entity problem is probably becoming greater as the public sector is being changed into smaller and, in some senses, more accountable units. Once again, the GASB has provided a lead in this. The approach it adopted from its predecessor was concerned with offering criteria to be used in practice in order to determine whether a unit should be included within the overall financial report of what they call the 'oversight unit'. The basic, but not the only, criterion to be used is the ability to exercise oversight responsibility of the unit by the elected officials of the oversight unit.

This oversight responsibility is derived from the power of the oversight unit and includes, but is not limited to, the following:

1 *Financial interdependency.* This relates to the extent to which the unit produces a financial benefit or imposes a financial burden on the oversight unit. Manifestations of this would include responsibility for financing deficits, entitlements to surpluses and guarantees of, or 'moral responsibility' for debt.

2 *Selection of governing authority.* This relates to whether the oversight unit possesses final decision-making authority and is held primarily accountable for decisions.

3 *Designation of management.* This relates to whether the management of the unit is appointed by, and held accountable to, the oversight unit.

4 *Ability to influence operations significantly.* This relates to the ability of the

oversight unit to influence the unit's operations, including reviewing budget requests, signing contracts, approving the hiring of key personnel, exercising control over facilities and properties, etc.

5   *Accountability for fiscal matters.* This relates to matters such as the extent of budgetary authority, the responsibility for funding deficits, the control of the collection and disbursement of funds, and whether revenues collected are determined by the oversight unit.

Using the same basic approach, but changing the nature of the criteria, the GASB (1994, Section 2100) has offered new concepts. The financial reporting entity is said to consist of all the following:

1   *the primary government*: a primary government consists of all the organizations that make up its legal entity;
2   *organizations for which the primary government is financially accountable*: these are known as component units;
3   *other organizations* the nature and significance of whose relationship with the primary government are such that exclusion would cause the reporting entity's financial statements to be misleading or incomplete. These are also known as component units.

The first of these includes each state and local government but also each special-purpose government that meets these three criteria: that it has a separately elected governing body, that it is legally separate, and that it is fiscally independent (meaning essentially that it determines its budget, levies taxes and issues bonded debt, all without the approval of another government).

How the component units (categories 2 and 3) are included in the financial statements of the primary government is determined by the closeness of the relationship with the primary government: most are expected to be 'discretely presented' (that is, presented within the primary government's financial statements but using separate columns to distinguish the component unit's results and providing summary note disclosures), but those that are in substance the same as the primary government are 'blended' (that is, their results are not distinguishable from the rest of the primary government).

Both of the approaches adopted by the GASB are pragmatic solutions sensitive to the complexities faced in public sector contexts. The reporting-entity problem is one of the most difficult faced by accounting standard-setters: organizational relationships are being made more complex, often using complicated legal structures, and then accounting is required to produce a report and accounts that brings all the elements back together.

ACCOUNTING POLICY-MAKING

Traditionally, in the UK, the law has played a considerable part in regulating the form and content of published financial reports. This applies as much to business organizations as it does to public sector organizations. However, against this statutory backdrop, the professional bodies have developed a policy-making role and (following the example set in the USA) with the introduction of the Accounting Standards Board in 1990 we have seen the establishment of a standard-setting body which is neither government nor the accounting profession. Accounting theory cannot realistically be discussed without considering the context of accounting policy-making.

Legal prescriptions

The prescriptions concerning the published accounts of nationalized industries and public corporations are typically embodied in the originating Acts. The Acts include a general clause which says that the corporation should keep proper accounting records and should present its accounts in a form laid down by the relevant Secretary of State. Subsequent Acts have tended to produce more detailed requirements, but the main thrust has always been for nationalized industries' accounts to produce, as a minimum, the amount and kind of information that a PLC has to produce. On top of this minimum requirement, reflecting the fact that public corporations are not the same as private corporations, regulations typically provide that additional specific information be produced. A good example of this is the requirement to produce disaggregated operating statements, in order to report on the performance of different sectors of a given industry.

Generally speaking, we can say that for nationalized industries and public corporations the accounting standard-setting function of the law relates to the *form* of published accounts; while responsibility for the *content* is abrogated to the accounting profession (because 'true and fair' is defined by professional pronouncements). This seemed particularly true during the 1970s. However, there are two points to make about recent developments. First, the Companies Acts themselves have included more *content*. Secondly, the suspension of mandatory inflation accounting by the profession (in 1985) did not affect some of the nationalized industries, who continued to report current cost accounts, by government direction.

The regulated industries of telecommunications, electricity, gas and water are a case of their own and accounting policy-making for them is different. These are, of course, former nationalized industries that were sold to investors and are now subject to regulation by non-ministerial government departments: the Office of Telecommunications (Oftel), the Office of Electricity Regulation (Offer), the Office of Gas Supply (Ofgas) and the Office of Water Services (Ofwat).

In local authorities, the law plays an equally important part in accounting standards. The law relates to the form of published accounts. But it also, to a greater extent, relates to content as well: for example, the Local Government and Housing Act 1989 effectively determines how local authorities account for capital expenditure.

In the NHS, the law gives the power to the Secretary of State, with the approval of the Treasury, to determine the accounts of health service bodies. In practice, the broad form of these is determined by central direction, but the detailed content is left to the Management Executive of the NHS to determine.

Standard-setting for central government is almost entirely the responsibility of the Treasury, taking the Exchequer and Audit Department Act 1866 as the statutory basis. There are minor exceptions where small units, which are said to compete with the private sector, produce accounts showing a true and fair view. And although these exceptions will grow with the development of Executive Agencies into 'trading funds', the form and content of the overwhelming majority of what are called the appropriation accounts are prescribed by the Treasury.

This form is laid down in *Government Accounting: A Guide on Accounting and Financial Procedures for the Use of Government Departments*, issued by HM Treasury. The most important provision in this manual is that the system of cash accounting, rather than accruals accounting, is used in accounting for the money voted to government departments by Parliament. Since standard-setting, as the private sector knows it, is primarily concerned with accruals adjustments and their effect, the Treasury manual is not strictly comparable. Instead, it takes the form of a guide to bookkeeping; although the manual as a whole is more concerned with financial procedures for controlling departments' finances than with the accounts *per se*.

The government's proposals to change the basis of its accounting and budgeting (Cm 2626, July 1994) have raised questions about whether the Treasury should retain this standard-setting function. The Green Paper states that it will, but other views are that a public sector accounting standards board could be established and that the Comptroller and Auditor General could have an important role.

Professional standard-setting

Until the mid-1970s, what one might call public sector professional accounting practice had been promulgated by the Chartered Institute of Public Finance and Accountancy (which from 1901–73 was known as the Institute of Municipal Treasurers and Accountants). The majority of its work in standard-setting was primarily concerned with the form, particularly standardization of the form, of accounts; although practices that concern content have also been recommended.

However, the environment of professional standard-setting changed as a result of the inception of the Accounting Standards Committee (ASC). Originally formed in January 1970 as a committee of the Institute of Chartered Accountants in England and Wales (ICAEW), it became in February 1976 a joint committee of the Consultative Committee of Accountancy Bodies. Its objective was

> to propose for the approval of the Councils of governing bodies definitive standards of financial accounting and reporting.

This encompassed:

1 fundamentals of financial accounting;
2 definition of terms used;
3 application of fundamentals to specific classes of business;
4 the form and content of financial statements, including presentation and disclosure.

Although the ASC was clearly under the control of the accounting profession, in 1982 its membership was broadened to include representatives from outside the profession.

Under the ASC, Statements of Standard Accounting Practice were not meant to be rigid specifications of acceptable practice but rather 'to narrow the areas of difference' between accounting practices. The emphasis of the SSAPs was always on standards for accounts showing a true and fair view; indeed, very often the emphasis was on the accounts of PLCs. The force of SSAPs resided primarily in the fact that under the ICAEW's auditing standards, a true and fair view was generally defined as one which did not contravene extant SSAPs; and that any non-compliance had to be stated and its effect quantified.

In 1990, standard-setting for companies was changed by the establishment of the Financial Reporting Council, the Accounting Standards Board and the Review Panel. The last two are limited companies that are subsidiaries of the Financial Reporting Council. The Council raises the money to finance all three (over £3 million a year) but is prohibited from involvement in the core activities of the Board and the Panel. In the first year, over half the finance came from the Consultative Committee of Accountancy Bodies and the government (mostly from fees charged on companies), while the remainder came from the Stock Exchange and the Bank of England.

The Accounting Standards Board is obviously responsible for setting accounting standards and took over all the extant SSAPs from the Accounting Standards Committee. The Board issues standards (Financial Reporting Standards – FRSs) in its own right, without the approval of the accounting profession. Modelled on the US experience, because accounting standards take time to go through 'due process', an Urgent Issues Task Force has also been established which can deal with problems in the interim.

The primary purpose of these new developments is to distance accounting standard-setting from the accounting profession, in much the same way that the establishment of the Financial Accounting Standards Board did in the USA. Because of the substantial sums of money being provided by the profession and the government, if for no other reason, both can be assumed to continue to have an important say in policy-making, but clearly the effect is in some sense to establish a middle ground.

The relevance of SSAPs to the public sector has never been entirely clear. In 1986, a new Explanatory Foreword to SSAPs was issued which pointed out that they only applied to nationalized industries because the government required them to. For other public sector bodies, the Foreword stated that 'it could be expected' that ASC pronouncements will apply 'except where they are clearly inappropriate'. The ASB's Foreword to Accounting Standards (1993, para. 21) states that:

> The prescription of accounting requirements for the public sector in the UK is a matter for the Government. Where public sector bodies prepare annual reports and accounts on commercial lines, the Government's requirements may or may not refer specifically either to accounting standards or to the need for the financial statements to give a true and fair view. However, it can be expected that the Government's requirements in such cases will normally accord with the principles underlying the Board's pronouncements, except where in the particular circumstances of the public sector bodies concerned, the Government considers these principles to be inappropriate or considers others to be more appropriate.

Other developments made the situation even less clear.

The ASC introduced the Statements of Recommended Practice (SORPs). These were not binding on all members of the ASC in the way that SSAPs were, nor did they require the approval of the councils of the six professional bodies. There were two ways of developing them: first, the ASC produced and issued them; secondly, other bodies developed them and the ASC 'franked' the result.

The Accounting Standards Board has adopted a different approach. It has stated that it will not develop SORPs. However, it has also stated that it will be willing to recognize bodies who will develop SORPs to provide guidance on the application of accounting standards to specific industries, which includes the public sector. This recognition depends on the size of the industry or sector, on the ASB being satisfied as to the representative nature of the body, and on the body agreeing to follow the ASB's code of practice. This code is designed to ensure that the subject matter and general scope of the SORP has the ASB's prior approval, that there is due process, and that exposure drafts are submitted for consideration before publication. When the ASB is satisfied with all these requirements, it will issue a 'negative assurance statement' to a SORP. This will not approve the SORP but will confirm that the SORP:

- contains no unacceptable fundamental points of principle;
- is not in conflict with any existing or contemplated accounting standard; and
- has been prepared in accordance with the code of practice.

The essence of the problem with the accounting standards of the ASC and the ASB is that they have not been established with public sector organizations in mind.

One problem with professional standards, because they do not have the force of law, is ensuring compliance. Under the new regime for companies this problem has been addressed to some extent. There are two main elements to this. First, the law (Companies Act 1985, Schedule 4, paragraph 36A, as amended) now requires companies to disclose whether the accounts are prepared in accordance with applicable accounting standards, and to disclose particulars of any material departure from those standards and the reasons for it (the relevant standards are the SSAPs and FRSs of the Accounting Standards Board). This is the first time that accounting standards have had even this amount of statutory backing. Second (under s.245B of the 1985 Act, as amended), the government has authorized the Financial Reporting Review Panel to apply to the courts in cases where it believes that a company has not complied with the law. It is important to note that the Review Panel is only authorized to apply to the courts on the ground of *legal* non-compliance, not non-compliance with accounting standards.

However, these new powers do not apply to the public sector. Compliance there depends on the preparers, perhaps the sponsoring Minister or other regulating body, and the auditor. This is not unlike the former position for companies and this too produced many circumstances where organizations chose not to follow professional prescription and there did not appear to be the power or the will to enforce compliance.

What remains true is that the responsibility for accounting standard-setting for companies is clear, as it is for the government. In between, there is a host of organizations, including public sector organizations, for which there is no comprehensive set of accounting policies established exclusively for their cases. The result has been that within the legal framework, policies have been chosen on an *ad hoc* basis. This situation might have led to a drive for better theory for public sector accounting, to sustain these *ad hoc* policies – but it has not. Policy makers have, in effect, left the difficult theoretical questions unaddressed about how, or to what extent, public sector accounting should be different.

The situation in the USA, at least for state and local governments, is different. Traditionally, there were many standard-setting bodies for the public sector. The NCGA, supported by the Government Finance Officers' Association, was concerned with state and local government; the Council of State Governments was concerned with state government; the General Accounting Office of the Federal Government has set standards for federal departments and agencies. In the 1970s, the Financial Accounting Standards Board declared its intention to become involved. The result was a considerable power struggle, where huge sums of money were spent to protect the many and various positions: the money was used primarily to produce conceptual frameworks for aspects of governmental accounting which would then be generally accepted and would provide the base for future standard-setting. As a result, an institutional compromise was found whereby the Governmental Accounting Standards Board was established, which, although associated with the FASB, is nevertheless separate. The General Accounting Office continues to cover the Federal Government; the FASB sets standards for non-governmental, non-profit organizations; and the GASB deals with state and local government and governmental non-profit organizations.

Uniquely, then, the GASB is an accounting standard-setting body concerned only with governmental units at the state and local level. The politics of the situation probably means that it has to be sensitive to the traditional concerns of the governments themselves but it also has to provide strong arguments for deviations from generally accepted accounting principles for business. Whether the end result will lead to better governmental accounting is impossible to say, but it seems clear that major steps are being taken and will continue to be taken at least to understand the commonalities and differences between accounting for businesses and accounting for governmental units. Indeed, this effort has been given added impetus by the establishment, not of a standard-setting body but of an advisory board, at national level: the Federal Accounting Standards Advisory Board (FASAB), in 1990. It advises the Secretary to the Treasury, the Office of Management and Budget (OMB) and the Comptroller General (who heads the GAO); when its recommendations are accepted, standards are published by the GAO and OMB, and they become effective. Some of FASAB's work is very radical in the context of accounting for sovereign governments and not only in financial accounting: proposals have been made to re-introduce cost accounting standards as well. It is true to say that FASAB is using the work of the GASB, among others, but it is to be expected that the different context will produce different views of public sector accounting.

In addition to the policy-makers in each country, a number of international standard-setters have started to propose public sector accounting policies. The International Federation of Accountants (IFAC) was formed in 1977 and is made up of the major professional accounting bodies of the world. Now, under its auspices, international accounting standards and international standards on auditing are issued by its International Accounting Standards Committee and International Auditing Practices Committee, respectively. Both sets of standards parallel those of the UK and the US particularly, and although they were developed primarily with businesses in mind some are relevant to the public sector; IFAC has also produced material of direct relevance (1991). A body with a similar but naturally narrower membership, and one which is also involved, is the *Fédération européenne des experts-comptables* (FEE) through its public sector committee.

The other major international example is the International Organization of Supreme Audit Institutions (INTOSAI). At the heart of this organization is a triennial congress of supreme auditors, first held in Havana in 1953; there are also now many regional versions of INTOSAI. It produces a journal, the *International Journal of Government Auditing*, and has issued auditing standards (INTOSAI, 1989). It has also a Committee on Accounting Standards whose terms of reference include identifying and reporting on issues to be addressed for the development of international accounting standards for governments (INTOSAI, 1992).

For all these bodies, the lack of power is even greater than is typical in national accounting standard-setting bodies, because they are in essence challenging the sovereign power of governments. They can only work to persuade governments that their standards should be followed. Nevertheless, it is useful for individuals in specific countries, in lobbying for different practices, to be able to turn to 'international best practice': governments have great expertise in dealing with this kind of lobbying but, from the point of view of the lobbyist, having such standards must be better than not having them.

DISCUSSION TOPICS

1   How, if at all, should business organizations be distinguished from other organizations for the purpose of developing accounting standards?

2   'Before we can decide what to include in public sector financial reports we must first of all determine who uses them and what for.' Critically evaluate this statement.

3   Using a public sector organization, identify the component units that could be included in the financial report and discuss how you would decide which should be included and which excluded.

4   Power and responsibility for accounting policy-making in the public sector is particularly unclear. Discuss the situation for a particular public sector organization.

CHAPTER 8

Financial accounting techniques

This chapter is concerned with the financial accounting techniques adopted in the operating statements and balance sheets of public sector organizations. The accounting practices discussed do not exclusively relate to the public sector. However, our discussion will concentrate on the contribution each can make to public sector accounting.

THE MAJOR TECHNIQUES

Different public sector organizations adopt different accounting practices. The main ones are:

1 budgetary accounting;
2 cash accounting;
3 accruals accounting;
4 commitment accounting;
5 fund accounting.

These five are not mutually exclusive. For example, one organization might adopt budgetary accounting, cash accounting and fund accounting simultaneously. It is also possible for one organization to adopt all five simultaneously!

Strictly speaking, the phrase 'budgetary accounting' refers to the practice (adopted particularly by some US local governments) of including budgeted amounts and actual amounts within the double-entry. Very broadly, what happens is that the budgeted amounts of expenditure are credited to appropriation accounts and then as expenditure is incurred debits are set against these credits. The balance on these accounts therefore continuously represents the amount of the budget still unspent. Without understanding the intricacies of these book-entries we can see the philosophy of the system: namely, that the accounts should present in a systematic and continuous way the comparison of budgeted amounts and actual spending. Since bookkeeping is systematic, then one way of achieving this objective is to include budgeted amounts within it.

The main disadvantage of this practice is its complexity; it is easier and more comprehensible if the accounts reflect actual revenues and expenses, and the budget reflects budgeted revenues and expenses. The UK solution to the need for a continuous and systematic comparison of the two is to keep them separate as far as the double-entry is concerned but to report them side-by-side. Hence, many public sector operating statements do not only show actuals but also budgets and comparisons of actuals with budgets.

This practice is in marked contrast to business organizations where, although the budget is of importance, it is never included in the published financial statements proper; indeed, it would be unusual for it to appear publicly at all. The main reason for this difference, and it lies at the heart of the distinction between many public and private sector organizations, is the central role that the budget plays in fixing the level and distribution of taxation in governments. It is no exaggeration to say that this function of the budget shifts the emphasis away from the 'actual' results as recorded in the financial accounts, towards the budget. The actuals remain of importance but in these kinds of organizations they take an equal place alongside the budget. It seems useful, therefore, to emphasize this difference by referring to the practice as budgetary accounting, while remembering that in the UK it does not have the same implications as in the USA.

Cash accounting, accruals accounting and commitment accounting are distinguished from each other by the point in time when expenses and revenues are recognized in the accounts, i.e. the point at which a given transaction generates a bookkeeping entry.

In the case of revenue recognition, there are basically two steps at which a bookkeeping entry might be generated: when the goods sold have been delivered and an invoice has been issued; and when the goods sold have been delivered and an invoice has been paid. The complete cycle would be as follows:

Order received → goods despatched with invoice → cash received

Because of the accounting principle of conservatism, it is unlikely that an accounting system would recognize revenue merely on receipt of an order. The most common system in business is to recognize revenue when the invoice has been issued. However, there are systems, notably in the public sector and non-profit sector in general, where revenue is only recognized in the accounts when the cash is received.

The same thing can be said about expense recognition, although there is a system of accounting which recognizes a debit earlier than the receipt of an invoice. The cycle for purchases might look like this:

Order issued → goods received with invoice → cash paid

The system of accounting which recognizes the transaction in the accounts at the time an order is issued is called 'commitment accounting'. Its name reflects the fact that the accounts are recognizing commitments said to have been entered into when orders are sent. The system of accounting which recognizes the expense when the invoice is received (and the revenue, when the invoice is issued) is called 'accruals accounting'.

'Fund accounting' refers to the practice of accounting, not in terms of an organization taken as whole, but in terms of its separate, independent, constituent parts (which are called 'funds'). This contrasts with the typical accounts of a business which present the business as a whole.

Strictly, therefore, an organization which adopted fund accounting, accruals accounting and had, say, six funds, would keep six complete and separate sets of accounts: six cash books, six sets of personal accounts, six nominal ledgers, six operating statements, six balance sheets. In practice, however, there are modified versions of fund accounting which achieve the same overall purpose, namely keeping the accounts of the funds separate. Most typically, organizations have only one cash book (and bank account). This is tenable because, with sophisticated and computerized accounting systems, control of the various funds can be exercised without separating out the cash transactions.

Although the concept of fund accounting is relatively simple, specific applications of it can be difficult to understand. This applies, for example, to governmental accounting in the USA, where the adoption of fund accounting has introduced an accounting language of its own. In fact, the 'language' is not of use *per se* to public sector accountants anywhere else in the world, except only as a necessary precondition to understanding the intricacies of US practice. Consequently, we shall be concerned with the concept as it applies generally to public sector organizations.

We can now see how one organization could adopt cash accounting, budgetary accounting and fund accounting simultaneously: only cash transactions are recognized, the cash flows are reported in the same format as the budget, and they are also recorded and reported in individual funds. Similarly, it is possible for one organization to adopt all five simultaneously, by reporting in terms of funds, by comparing actuals with the budget and by adopting cash accounting in Fund 1, accruals accounting in Fund 2, and commitment accounting in Fund 3! We can now look at each of these practices in more detail.

BUDGETARY ACCOUNTING

Budgetary accounting refers to the practice of many public sector organizations, and particularly governments, of keeping and presenting their operating accounts in the same format and alongside their budgets. The main purpose of this practice is to emphasize the budget's role in the cycle of planning–control–accountability. As we have seen in detail in Chapters 2 and 3, the budget is the financial plan against which financial out-turns must be compared to effect control. External accountability is enhanced by taking this essentially management control (i.e. control *by* management) and using it to demonstrate, particularly to taxpayers, the performance *of* management against the budget.

Budgets are important because they are used indirectly and directly to fix the levels and distribution of taxes. For example, central government uses budgets rather more indirectly to fix taxes: they form the basic public expenditure requirements, but how taxes are fixed and whether a budget surplus or deficit is being planned are questions beyond the scope of the budgets themselves. On the other hand, local governments use their budgets directly to fix tax levels, the essential point being that they cannot in law tax for a budget deficit. In both cases, however, taxpayers are likely to be concerned with how actual spending turns out (hence the use of the word 'out-turns' to refer to actuals) against budgeted spending; not least because over-spendings are likely to mean higher taxes and under-spendings lower ones.

The idea behind budgetary accounting is, therefore, a simple one. Complications do arise, however, because different kinds of organizations adopt different formats. This is necessarily caused by the fact that the intrinsic differences between the services provided in different organizations reflect themselves in the respective budgets. In budgetary accounting these differences are perpetuated in the accounts.

For example, the main non-staff cost in a blood transfusion unit might be 'drugs and dressings'; while the main non-staff cost in a school might be 'books and materials'. These two items *could* be classified in the same way as, say, 'equipment and materials' but this would merely hide the intrinsic difference between the items of account. It may lead us to compare the relative increase in costs over a year, believing that we were comparing like with like. We might think that any differences reflected poorer performance but it may just be that they merely reflect the different impact of specific price changes on drugs compared with books.

More meaningful results are obtained by producing budgetary accounts that are classified in a way which is specific to the particular service but this is at the expense of a uniform format for budgetary accounting. Since it is unlikely that the accounts of the Blood Transfusion Services will be compared with those of schools on a regular basis, this problem is of less importance. However, there are more significant problems in that the same kinds of organizations and the same kinds of services are often accounted for differently although they are all adopting budgetary accounting. This arises mainly out of two issues: (a) level of aggregation, and (b) comparisons between budget and actuals.

A good example of where the level of aggregation adopted by the budgetary accounts affects their comparability occurs in local government. One authority may publish its budgetary accounts for the education service as a whole. Another authority may publish total amounts for primary schools, secondary schools, continuing education. Another might publish the expenditure of employees, premises, etc. within primary, secondary, continuing education.

Obviously the problem with providing very detailed information is that financial reports become huge documents, which taken as a whole can be daunting for the reader. On the other hand, by reducing the detail, the document may be much more easily handled but potentially important information may be lost.

Traditionally, local authorities have produced weighty financial reports but over recent years many have adopted much higher levels of aggregation with the consequent reduction in report size. A major impetus has been that users found this detailed budgetary accounting confusing. Of course, the reduction in reports also leads to a lower administrative and production cost.

The British government's accounts adopt very high levels of aggregation. Often a single line comparing budget with actual can represent millions or even billions of pounds. This undoubtedly reflects the complexity and breadth of the government's spending, but for the accounts to be of much use the disaggregated figures have to be used.

The other weakness in the practice of budgetary accounting lies in the extent to which financial reports compare budgets with actuals and explain the differences. Many organizations produce the budgetary accounts alongside the budget but only compare the two in global terms. Thus, for example, the accounts and budget might be presented in detail but only total net expenditure of each division of service is compared with budget, showing the over-under-spending and explaining broadly the reasons for any variance. A more extreme version would be to compare and explain budget and actuals only for an organization as a whole.

Clearly, to compare and explain every line in the budgetary accounts would produce a vast amount of information and would probably benefit few. A compromise might be to show the over- and under-spendings for all heads but only to explain any significant variances. A significant variance could be defined as one amounting to more than a given percentage of the budget but which is not explained by the general level of prices, i.e. inflation or deflation.

However, whichever system is adopted, it is imperative that some comparison and explanation is included. The rationale for budgetary accounting is that the budget and accounts should be continuously compared so that action can be taken to correct variances. This applies as much to external users of the information as it does to internal users. By reporting only two columns of figures (budget and actual), not only is the ultimate purpose of budgetary accounting not achieved but much time can be wasted in answering specific users' questions about variances which could have been avoided by the accounts themselves producing the relevant analysis.

In conclusion, budgetary accounting is primarily concerned with the form of the financial accounts rather than their content.

CASH ACCOUNTING

This accounting system recognizes only cash inflows and cash outflows. The resulting final accounts are summarized cash books. There are no balance sheets because there are no assets or liabilities in the books other than cash balances: sales are only recognized when cash is received (so there are no debtors); purchases are only recognized when cash is paid (so there are no creditors); there are no stock adjustments because the accounts are not concerned with recording usage, only with the fact that cash has been paid for purchases (so there is no closing stock figure); there are no fixed assets, for the same reason.

Cash flow statements are now pervasive in business accounting, but as an addition to income statements and balance sheets. They have progressively replaced funds flow statements, which were in essence re-presentations of accruals accounting figures, albeit to include information that would not otherwise be readily apparent.

There is a very serious and respectable literature on cash flow accounting for the business sector (e.g. Lee, 1984) which argues that the traditional accruals accounting statements are too subjective and hide crucial information about organizations' performance. However, no accounting standard-setting body in the world has recognized cash flow accounting as a replacement for accruals accounting.

Cash flow accounting is practised in many public sector and non-profit organizations. The simple receipts and payments accounts of the small charity are probably the most common example; while perhaps the most important (certainly in terms of the amounts of money accounted for) are the cash accounts of most sovereign governments.

Take for example, the accounts of defence spending by the British government as shown in Fig. 8.1. This is a summary of defence spending and is supported by statements which subdivide the four votes into smaller sections. Nevertheless it can come as a shock to a trained accountant to discover that £24 billion of net expenditure is accounted for in this way: no assets; no liabilities, just an excess of payments over receipts of £24.3 billion compared with a budgeted excess of £24.6 billion.

It would be wrong, however, to assume that these accounts are necessarily unsatisfactory and simplistic. They are certainly *simple* and that is one of the chief advantages of cash accounting: it takes little more than common sense to understand and interpret. Not only that, but because of its simplicity it also costs much less in terms

No. of vote	Service	Gross expenditure	Budget Income	Net expenditure	Gross expenditure	Actuals Income	Net expenditure	(Over-) Under- spending on gross expenditure	Over- estimate of income	Net (over-) under- spending
		£m	£m	£m	£m	£m	£m	£m	£m	£m
1.	Defence: Operational and support costs	13,778	1,109	12,670	13,678	1,096	12,583	100	13	87
2.	Defence: Logistic services	4,407	517	3,891	4,406	517	3,889	2	–	2
3.	Defence: Systems procurement and research	7,544	390	7,153	7,339	382	6,958	205	9	196
4.	Defence: Armed services retired pay, pensions, etc.	1,920	1,060	860	1,909	1,060	850	11	–	11
	Total	27,650	3,075	24,574	27,333	3,054	24,279	317	22	295

Fig. 8.1   UK defence spending, 1993/94.

Source: Adapted from *Appropriation Accounts, 1993/94*, HMSO, London, Vol .1, Class 1, HC670–1, 1994/95, pp. 12–13. All figures affected by rounding.

of administration and accounting expertise. This is not an inconsequential item, particularly when in practice many managers doubt the value of producing more elaborate accruals accounts.

The primary impetus, on the other hand, for cash accounting in the business sector comes from the undoubted subjectivity of accruals accounting. Even when only historic costs are being recognized there are still subjective judgements which have to be made to produce balance sheets and income statements: how much depreciation to charge; how to calculate the closing stock figure; what provision to make for doubtful debts, etc. Cash accounting does not include these adjustments and does not therefore involve their subjectivity. When ownership is divorced from control, reducing the ability of managers to manipulate their reports to the owners is seen to be an important part of accounting policy-making. This is no less important in government where the executive reports to the legislature.

Of course the essential point is not whether the accounts are subjective or objective; it is the extent to which they are useful. The purpose of a set of accounts is to provide useful information; the level of subjectivity is just one constraint of many on fully achieving this. The information which receipts and payments accounts give relates to the amount of cash received and paid. When these accounts are compared with amounts which should have been received and which should have been paid (as shown in the budget) much vital information for a public sector organization is shown. Cash is clearly the life blood of any organization. Budgets determine how much tax is collected. If the government spends less than the budget says it would spend during the year, then it is obviously better off at the end of the year and can then spend more or repay borrowings or reduce taxes. If it spends more during the year than it said it would spend, it is worse off and must either borrow more or raise more taxes.

This information and the decisions which emanate from it are of great importance, politically, economically and socially. We must remember also, however, that there is a vast amount of other information which has equal and greater importance. This relates to questions of public finance and economics, such as: What will happen to interest rates if we increase the Public Sector Borrowing Requirement? What will happen to unemployment if we spend more? What will happen to inflation if we reduce taxes? Accounting information does not attempt to answer such questions.

However, there are other less ambitious examples of the kind of information which the accounts could provide about inputs but which is not provided by cash flow accounting. This relates to the two aggregates which are the primary concern of accruals accounting and about which cash accounting has nothing to say, namely, capital and income. Because there are no assets or liabilities, there is no measure of what the organization is worth, no measure of capital. Since income is the increase in capital, there is no measure of income either. An excess of receipts over payments cannot be called income because receipts might include capital receipts. Similarly, an excess of payments over receipts cannot be called a loss because apart from anything else the payments might include the acquisition of assets. There is no opportunity to compare income with capital to yield a return on capital figure which is typically used as a measure of a business's performance. Indeed there is no opportunity to use an income figure in any way as a comparative measure of performance.

Look again at Fig. 8.1 on defence spending. That account tells us the amount of net payments over receipts compared with the budgeted figures. There is no measure of what the defence services are 'worth' in terms of the assets and liabilities they have. The only measure of performance which can be yielded is the comparison of budget with actual. Strictly speaking, good performance is a matching of budget and actual; bad performance is either an over-spending (for obvious reasons) or an under-spending (because Parliament voted money to be spent, not saved). But this measure of performance is a very narrow one and nothing more than an indication of stewardship. The defence budget might have been spent, nothing more or less, but the money could have been spent more economically, more efficiently, or more effectively. Of course, we know that an income figure for the defence budget could not yield the kind of information that it would yield in a profit-oriented organization, not least because it would simply yield a huge 'loss'! On the other hand, parts of the budget could be set up as profit centres which charged other parts of the budget for using their services.

However, segregating income from capital is not only concerned with producing an income figure which might be used as a measure of performance. It is also concerned with the converse, namely segregating capital from income. The emphasis then is on defining that amount which can be consumed without impairing capital. This is the more important part of the capital/income confusion in public sector organizations: agreement on the irrelevance of income as a performance measure can often be readily obtained because service provision may have nothing to do with the profit motive; on the other hand, all organizations have capital of some sort.

An obvious example of where the accounts could provide information about erosion of capital, but in the case of cash accounts do not, is for the sale of capital assets. Selling off public sector land and buildings can be a highly lucrative activity (in the short term). In receipts and payments accounts, the realized amounts will be shown as receipts and the accounts for the year will appear much healthier. But of course what has happened is that the capital base has been eroded, and the future value of the sold asset will not accrue to the organization. This is not to say that selling public sector assets is an unwise activity; only that cash accounts do not provide the complete picture of what happens when you do. In fact, neither do accruals accounts necessarily, but at least they give some indication that capital has been affected.

Apart from this effect of including capital amounts in receipts and payments, there is also the effect of not recognizing invoices until they are paid. In the example in Fig. 8.2, assume that an organization has a series of purchasing transactions each of which begins with an order and ends with payment of cash. When the results for the financial year are being calculated two artificial lines are drawn, at the beginning of the year and at the end. In this case, the effect is that goods received in the old financial year (Invoice$_1$) are not recognized by the accounts until the new financial year (Cash paid$_1$). Similarly, at the year end, goods are received (Invoice$_n$) but not recognized because the cash is not paid until the subsequent year.

This provides two main difficulties. First, it is hard to accept that the subsequent payments figure reflects what the organization 'cost' to run during the year. Invoice$_n$ might be, for example, the cost of electricity used during the final quarter of the year. There is no question that the electricity was used during the financial year and yet the cost of the electricity is not shown until the next financial year. Of course, it may be argued that the Cash paid$_1$ at the beginning of the year relates to the last quarter's electricity for the old financial year and so this financial year includes four payments for electricity; thus, the year's payments do reflect the cost of electricity. This argument assumes that the amount of electricity consumed in each final quarter is the same and that the price per unit of electricity is the same. Take the following example.

Assume financial year runs 1.1 to 31.12

1996	Last quarter	£1,000	(Payment 1997)
1997	1st quarter	£1,500	(Payment 1997)
	2nd quarter	£800	(Payment 1997)
	3rd quarter	£400	(Payment 1997)
	Last quarter	£1,000	(Payment 1998)
1998	1st quarter	£1,500	(Payment 1998)

Following the earlier example, assume the payment for each quarter's electricity is made in the next quarter.

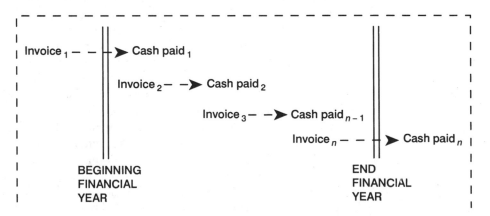

Fig. 8.2

The *payments* for 1997 would total

$$(£1,000 + £1,500 + £800 + £400) = £3,700$$

The *cost of electricity used in 1997* would total

$$(£1,500 + £800 + £400 + £1,000) = £3,700$$

But of course these are equal because the seasonal usage and cost per unit is assumed to be the same.

By making more realistic assumptions, the position changes. Even if we assume that seasonal usage is constant but prices increase by 10 per cent p.a., we produce a difference:

1996	Last quarter	£1,000	(Payment 1997)
1997	1st quarter	£1,650	(Payment 1997)
	2nd quarter	£880	(Payment 1997)
	3rd quarter	£440	(Payment 1997)
	Last quarter	£1,100	(Payment 1998)
1998	1st quarter	£1,815	(Payment 1998)

Payments for 1997 now total:

$$(£1,000 + £1,650 + £880 + £440) = £3,970$$

Cost of electricity used in 1997 totals:

$$(£1,650 + £880 + £440 + £1,100) = £4,070$$

However, the main point does not so much concern the question of whether seasonal usage would be constant or not, or whether costs are rising or falling or staying constant, but that the cash payments method does not record the cost of carrying out the activities for the year.

The second difficulty relates to the potential for deliberate manipulation of the accounts to produce preferred results. For example, the real spending of a department or service might be the same under whatever system of accounting is adopted but in a given year, using cash accounting, the cash payments could be postponed by as little as 24 hours so that the accounts record a lower figure. The likelihood of this occurring increases when budgets are used to control spending. Imagine a department which can see that it is going to over-spend its budget. Rather than reduce its spending it maintains it, but postpones cash payments. Of course, all this is doing is storing up trouble for the subsequent financial year; nevertheless, the financial control through the budget is effectively lost. It could be argued that this is an organization matter, not an accounting one; that a control needs to be introduced which prevents managers artificially postponing cash payments, e.g. a rule that all invoices must be paid within a specific time. However, such a rule might mean that the organization is not taking full advantage of varying credit periods. And anyway, it could also be argued that it is the accounting system which is allowing this manipulation (perhaps even inducing it) and therefore the accounting system should be modified to prevent it.

In summary, we have seen that cash accounting provides essential information, it is more objective than other alternatives and it costs less, in terms of administrative and accounting expertise, to implement. On the other hand, it provides no information about income and capital, nor about the cost of operating the organization during the financial year.

As with many accounting questions, the relative importance of the advantages compared with the disadvantages is a matter for judgement. Some public sector organizations have been through the debate over an agonizing number of years: local authorities in the UK did so at the turn of the century and generally concluded that 'receipts and payments' was not sufficient. On the other hand, most sovereign governments continue to adopt cash accounting though the pressure to adopt accruals accounting has increased and is beginning to have its effect. Influential studies have been: *Federal Government Reporting Study*, Office of the Auditor General of Canada and the United States General Accounting Office, 1986; *Financial Reporting by National Governments*, International Federation of Accountants, Study no. 1, IFAC, 1991; *Better Accounting for the Taxpayer's Money*, HM Treasury, Cm 2626, HMSO, 1994. And the first major application of accruals accounting in the financial statements of a national government has been for New Zealand.

ACCRUALS ACCOUNTING

The definition of the accruals concept as given by SSAP 2 is as follows:

> Revenue and costs are accrued (that is, recognised as they are earned or incurred, not as money is received or paid), matched with one another so far as their relationship can be established or justifiably assumed, and dealt with in the profit and loss account of the period to which they relate; provided that where the accruals concept is inconsistent with the prudence concept, the latter prevails.

The earning of revenues is generally taken to mean that invoices have been issued; costs are incurred when services are received. Thus the recognition occurs one step earlier than under cash accounting.

There are many different forms which accruals accounting can take but the most common is historic cost accounting. Another recognized form in the UK is current cost accounting: the professional version was embodied in SSAP 16, which was finally withdrawn in 1988, but many of its ideas remain influential. The two broad differences between accruals and cash accounting are the calculation of income and capital and the accruing of receipts and payments.

In historic cost accounting, capital is measured as the initial capital invested. Therefore land, which is not depreciated, will be shown at its historic cost in the balance sheet. A depreciable asset would be shown at its cost less any depreciation; we say therefore that these written down amounts are 'unallocated costs', meaning they have yet to be matched with revenues because they have yet to yield revenues. Monetary assets and liabilities are also shown at historic cost, though in many cases the historic cost of a monetary item is the same as its current cost.

In the current cost version, capital is measured in terms of its current value, which in many cases is its replacement cost. Land is shown in the balance sheet at its current replacement cost while a depreciable asset is shown at its current replacement cost less any depreciation to date. Stocks are also most often shown at their replacement cost. Monetary assets and liabilities are shown at their historic cost.

The profit figure is the difference between realized revenues ('realized' in the sense that invoices have been issued) and associated costs, measured either by historic costs or by current costs. This involves accruing any receipts which have been earned in the financial year and accruing any payments which relate to purchases made in the financial year.

The corollary of this is that any receipts received or payments made in the current financial year which relate to accruals made in the last financial year, will not affect the current year's profit figures.

However, there are *modified accruals* accounting systems which are adopted by public sector organizations, most typically some UK local authorities. One version is the 'income and converted payments' method. Under this, all revenues are accrued when they are earned. On the other hand, payments throughout the year are not continually accrued. However, at the financial year end all the invoices that had been received *but had not been paid* would be collected together for each department, say, and a total entry would be put through the books accruing all the payments due to be made. Then the payments made in the new year in respect of these accrued amounts would be debited against the individual expense accounts making the net effect zero in the new year.

The advantage of this income and converted payments method over the full accruals method is that personal creditors accounts do not have to be maintained (why keep a record of the individuals to whom you owe money – they will tell you soon enough if you do not settle) and the bookkeeping effort is reduced.

The 'converted receipts and payments' method applies the same kind of thinking to receipts. Although this method is used, it is less easy to rationalize it. The rationale for not keeping creditors accounts is not only rather shortsighted (because you might lose the goodwill of your suppliers) but it does not apply to debtors accounts – it is for certain that you will want to know precisely who owes you money and how much they owe you. Given then that all public sector organizations will keep meticulous records of debtors, it is hard to see that much effort is saved by not incorporating them in the double entry.

Final accounts under the accruals concept are not produced uniformly. Different public sector organizations adopt different practices. One reason for this is, as we have already discussed, that some adopt budgetary accounting while others do not. What they have in common, however, is that they produce a balance sheet and an operating statement, in marked contrast to the single 'receipts and payments' statement of cash accounting.

We can now examine an example of published accruals accounts.

Here is an extract from the accounts of the Post Office for the year ended 27 March 1994:

THE POST OFFICE

Group Profit and Loss Account

	1994 £m	1993 £m
Turnover	5,568	5,345
Staff costs	(3,340)	(3,295)
Depreciation and other amounts written off tangible fixed assets	(193)	(180)
Other operating charges	(1,735)	(1,606)
Total operating costs	(5,268)	(5,081)

Group Profit and Loss Account (*continued*)

	1994 £m	1993 £m
Operating profit	300	264
Net loss on sale of tangible fixed asset	(14)	(20)
Restructuring provision	(8)	(14)
Profit on ordinary activities before interest	278	230
Net interest receivable	28	53
Profit on ordinary activities before taxation	306	283
Taxation	(111)	(96)
Profit for the financial year	195	187

Group Balance Sheet

	1994 £m	1993 £m
Fixed assets	2,203	2,211
Current assets	2,376	1,904
Current liabilities	(2,289)	(1,917)
Net current (liabilities)/assets	87	(13)
Total assets *less* current liabilities	2,290	2,198
Creditors falling due after more than one year	(5)	(3)
Provision for liabilities and charges	(28)	(41)
	2,257	2,154
Capital and reserves		
Revaluation reserve	299	425
Profit and loss account	1,958	1,729
	2,257	2,154

These final accounts, of course, look very different from the cash accounts of defence spending. The basic difference is that the capital items have been stored separately in the balance sheet, leaving the operating items in the profit and loss account.

We do not know what was paid in cash and what was received in cash by the Post Office; all we know in this regard is the opening and closing cash figure. Nor do we know, because the Post Office has not adopted budgetary accounting, how these 'actual' results compare with its budget.

On the other hand, these accruals accounts have provided much more information than the cash accounts. We can now have a measure of capital employed. For the Post Office as a whole, this was £2,257m for the year ended 27 March 1994; not shown here, but disclosed in the report and accounts were the corresponding figures for the constituent businesses, Royal Mail £1,430m, Parcelforce £22m and Post Office Counters £246m. We can compare performance, for example, by expressing profit as a percentage of capital employed. This is a far from ideal measure but it can be used to compare performance over time and to establish target rates of return. For example, though the government did not set a target for the Post Office as a whole it did for the constituent businesses, and the report and accounts discloses actual performance against these, as follows:

	Target	Actual performance
Royal Mail	15.2%	20.0%
Parcelforce	zero	(8.8)%
Post Office Counters	5.6%	9.6%

These accounts also give an indication that, in producing these returns, the capital base has been maintained so that today's services can be maintained in the future. The accounts of defence spending give no indication at all of this: as a previous example explained, the 'receipts' may well include capital receipts which have eroded our ability to maintain defence facilities. On the other hand, the extent to which the return on capital employed calculation can measure operating capability, given that the accounts are not current cost accounts, is debatable.

Although the above profit and loss account does not show the revenues and expenses separately, supporting statements do break the figures down into much more detail. Because these are accruals accounts, the revenues and expenses shown, subject to measurement problems, 'relate to' this financial year. In other words, there are no revenues included against which we must charge future expenses and there are no expenses against which we must match future revenues: there are ostensibly no hidden liabilities but at the same time there are no hidden windfalls.

A major concern of any user of these accounts must be the extent to which the turnover was earned in a competitive market. In a highly competitive market the returns would be a satisfactory performance measure; for a monopolist it might merely reflect that any inefficiencies in service have been passed on to the customers who have no choice but to pay the higher prices. In practice, the user relies on overall policy control of the government (particularly through the Monopolies and Mergers Commission), as well as consumer controls (e.g. through consultative councils), to help validate 'return on capital'. Having said that, a major recent trend has been to introduce more competition and the Post Office, for example, increasingly competes in all its operating businesses.

A major distinction between accruals accounting in PLCs and accruals in public sector organizations relates to long-term debt. One use of a balance sheet in a PLC may be to help assess the level of gearing (i.e. the ratio of debt to equity) as a measure of the riskiness of future profits. A high level of gearing (relative to others in the same industry) means more risk for shareholders because the possibility of their receiving dividends depends, first of all, upon earning operating profits which will more than cover the interest payments on the debt. Another use, from the lenders' point of view, is in assessing the ability of the PLC to repay its debts with interest. This involves, among other things, comparing the level of debt with operating profits as well as with the value of the assets. The latter is relevant in assessing whether, if the PLC was liquidated, there would be enough funds released to honour the debts. These uses of accruals accounts have little meaning in public sector organizations. This is not to say that they might not be capable of earning enough revenues to repay the debt (far from it) but that the government will not need a published balance sheet to assess financial viability. Instead, data are provided directly and more timely to obviate this need.

The other main group in the public sector which adopts accruals accounting in some form is local authorities. Their accounts look very different from those of the nationalized industries and other public bodies because they adopt budgetary accounting and also because they adopt fund accounting. Therefore, we shall postpone discussion of them until the section on fund accounting.

A final point to make about the adoption of accruals accounting is that in the USA the Governmental Accounting Standards Board has further developed the idea of a set of accounts which are not purely cash-based but are also not full accruals accounting as best commercial practice would envisage it.

A fundamental distinction has been drawn that appears to be useful: between the *measurement focus* of accounting and the *basis* of accounting. The definitions are as follows (GASB, 1994, p. A-10):

> *Measurement focus* refers to *what* is being expressed in reporting an entity's financial performance and position. A particular measurement focus is accomplished by considering not only *which* resources are measured, but also *when* the effects of transactions or events involving those resources are recognized (the basis of accounting).

> *Basis of accounting* refers to *when* the effects of transactions or events should be recognized for financial reporting purposes. For example, the effects of transactions or events can be recognized on an accrual basis (that is, when the transactions or events take place), or on a cash basis (that is, when cash is received or paid). Basis of accounting is an essential part of measurement focus because a particular timing of recognition is necessary to accomplish a particular measurement focus.

The chosen policy for governmental fund operating statements happens to be the *flow of financial resources measurement focus* defined as (GASB, 1994, p. A-17):

> A measure of the extent to which financial resources obtained during a period are sufficient to cover claims incurred during that period against financial resources. This measurement focus considers *financial resources* only and uses an accrual basis of accounting.

Crucial to the above is the definition of *financial resources* (p. A-10):

> Cash, claims to cash (for example, debt securities of another entity and accounts and taxes receivable), claims to goods or services (for example, prepaid items), consumable goods (for example, supplies inventories), and equity securities of another entity obtained or controlled as a result of past transactions or events.

It is important to note that this definition of 'financial resources' has changed since 1988. In the Exposure Draft *Measurement Focus and Basis of Accounting – Governmental Funds* (p. 82), the definition was:

> Cash, claims to cash (for example, accounts and taxes receivable), and claims to goods or services (for example, prepaid items) obtained or controlled as a result of past transactions or events.

The point is, of course, that inventory has now been included in financial resources and therefore, under the flow of financial resources measurement focus, the operating statement includes changes in inventory.

This change in definition helps to pinpoint the essence of the idea of 'measurement focus' as well as the main problem with the idea. Using the measurement focus, we can move up the balance sheet (in the UK) and decide whether changes in each line-item within assets affect the operating statement. Under the original proposal for the flow of financial resources measurement focus, the line was drawn between monetary assets and non-monetary assets, where only changes in monetary assets affected the operating statement. Now the line has moved up to include inventories.

The essence of the idea of 'measurement focus' is, to put it straightforwardly, that by adopting the 'flow of financial resources' a governmental organization can adopt 'accrual accounting' in its operating statement (that is, it can 'recognize the effects of transactions or events on the resources of an entity when they take place, regardless of when cash is received or paid') but does not have to charge depreciation. Depreciation is not relevant because it relates to a non-monetary asset outside the flow of financial resources measurement focus.

The main problem with the idea of 'measurement focus' is that its definition is arbitrary. The original definition of financial resources had the virtue of approximating to a generally understood distinction between monetary and non-monetary assets, though even that distinction can be difficult. But by including inventory in 'financial resources' it is hard to see any rationale for the definition: in what sense is inventory different from equipment, as a 'financial resource'? Nevertheless, though difficulties remain in locating each possible measurement focus, the idea is one that provides an escape from the dominant (if woolly) notion of accruals accounting as an all-or-nothing alternative to cash accounting.

A critique of accruals accounting

The broad benefits of accruals accounting can be summarized as follows. First, the fact that revenues and expenses in the Operating Statement relate to those earned and those incurred respectively, means that accruals accounting provides measures of the economic goods and services consumed, transformed and earned; cash accounting provides measures of cash inflows and cash outflows.

The second benefit is that accruals accounting yields an income figure. When there are no price changes the income yielded in historic cost accruals accounting is an acceptable measure of performance: more profit implies more success. This does not mean that the measure of profit is absolute or objective. Accruing depreciation, stock valuations, provisions for doubtful debts, etc., are subjective judgements which make historic cost profit subjective. Nevertheless, this subjectivity is controlled by independent opinions of auditors and by enforcement of accounting standards and the results are evidently acceptable.

When prices do change, however, the income statement becomes less acceptable as a measure of performance. Inflation, for example, means that the value of fixed assets tends to be understated (historic cost compared with current value) while income tends to be overstated (because depreciation is related to historic cost and not to higher current cost). One of the objectives of current cost accounting is to produce a more acceptable income figure under conditions of rising prices. Having said that, in a public sector context the income figure as a measure of performance can only be as good as the competitiveness of the markets in which it is earned allows. The ability of a monopolist to earn profit, or an organization with social responsibilities to make losses, is hardly to be taken as a signal of economic efficiency.

The Byatt Report, *Accounting for Economic Costs and Changing Prices* (1986), has added an interesting twist to this argument. Following the demise of current cost accounting in the private sector and the apparent determination of the Treasury to retain it for nationalized industries, the fact that Byatt strongly endorsed its retention in the public sector is important, particularly from the policy-making perspective. Essentially, the argument used is that because there is *no* competitive market in the capital of nationalized industries and *no* competitive market in their products, the published accounts have a greater significance in assessing economic performance than in the private sector. Since current cost accounting measures economic performance best, the Report argues, it should be retained in nationalized industries. Put another way, given the government's unequivocal control of nationalized industries, being able to control the industries' current profit provides the best financial control of their behaviour. For similar reasons, forms of current cost accounting are being applied to some of the newly-privatized (regulated) industries, such as the water industry (Regulatory Accounting Guideline 1.02).

The third benefit is that it yields a measure of capital. Historically, the emphasis on maintaining the initial capital invested in a public limited company derives from the *causes célèbres* of the nineteenth century, when creditors were swindled out of their debts by PLCs which distributed capital as income thus leaving insufficient assets to repay creditors. Because of the limited liability of shareholders, creditors had no redress. Consequently, case and statute law was made which prevented distribution of capital invested. However, the idea of capital maintenance also has economic significance: income is only recognized after capital has been maintained intact. If the main asset in a business is a factory, then merely selling the factory does not yield income, only capital in a liquid form. If the receipt is distributed to shareholders as dividends, then the capital base of the business has been eroded.

However, under historic cost accruals accounting, for an asset which was sold for more than was paid for it, then the net gain would be income: only the initial cost would be called capital. In fact, this is the weakness of historic cost accruals accounting. Just as with profit measures, capital measures are affected by changing prices. If the factory was sold for more than it cost, if the net gain was treated as income and if a new factory had to be built at the new (higher) prices, then the capital would have been eroded. Maintaining initial capital intact would be useless if you wanted to remain in the same business. Instead, the accruals accounts would have to be modified to maintain the current cost of assets.

However, we can say that even historic cost accounting, in times of rising prices, does provide *some* indication of the extent to which capital might have been eroded or maintained, which as we have suggested earlier is potentially useful information.

The economic significance of capital maintenance in the balance sheets of public sector organizations has not been a major concern of accountants in the past. Those balance sheets very often do not record the existence of any capital at all, as in the

If the goods delivered and accompanying invoice were for more or less than the amount recorded on the order, a correcting entry would also have to be made. Assume that 100 boxes were delivered at £5.50. This would generate the following entry:

	Dr	Cr
Orders issued	500	
Chalk	50	
Supplier		550

Under this system, the organization is recognizing the issue of an order as a commitment to incur the expenditure and the accounts continuously record commitments.

A critique of commitment accounting

The primary function of commitment accounting is in fact in budgetary control. The idea is that there is little value to a manager of a set of monthly accounts which record only the invoices received or invoices paid. In order that managers are in control of their budgets they need to know how much of that budget has already been committed in terms of the orders issued. By receiving accounts of invoices received or paid, they could easily overcommit their budgets. Of course, sensible managers would know that the accounts did not include any orders issued against which invoices had not been received and would, therefore, keep their own record of these so that they did not over-commit the budget. The response to that is, if this accounting information is so relevant to a manager why is it not included in the accounts?

Because this is its primary function, commitment accounting concentrates on orders issued. Orders received, which relate to revenues, would not be accounted for until invoices had been sent out. The problem of budgetary control does not affect revenues in the same way as expenses.

Although the case for commitment accounting improving budgetary control is a good one, there is a real problem involved in adopting it in the financial accounts. This is simply that the accounts would record, as an expense, an item which is only supported by the issue of an order. There is generally no legal liability incurred and the order could easily be cancelled. It is difficult to accept that this is an expense of the accounting period in which only an order was issued.

On top of this, the kind of problem which has been discussed earlier under accruals accounting becomes more important and potentially more damaging under commitment accounting. Let us return to the example of the manager whose budget is underspent one month away from the financial year-end. The manager knows that the normal level of spending would leave the budget underspent and that this underspending will have to be forfeited with a possible consequent reduction in next year's budget. Under accruals accounting, in order to make sure the whole budget was spent, additional orders would have to be issued and invoices received before debits would be recognized. We have already identified this as a problem, but at least the opportunity for manipulation was constrained by the time it would take to receive the invoice. Under commitment accounting, the manager could simply issue orders a few days before the year-end to 'fill up' the budget. Indeed, there might be little to prevent some of the orders being cancelled when the new year commences. In effect, commitment accounting provides the opportunity for managers and for organizations as a whole to contribute to general reserves at the year-end and to treat the contributions as expenses.

In fact, professional practice in this area is to exclude from the final accounts all orders issued where invoices have not been received. This means that, although commitment accounting can improve budgetary control and as such may be used for periodic reports to managers, professional practice in the UK precludes its use in the final accounts.

If commitment accounting is adopted during the financial year, the conversion to ordinary accruals at the year-end involves the following book entry:

	Dr	Cr
Orders issued	x	
No 1 Expense a/c		x
No 2 Expense a/c		x

in respect of all the orders issued for which invoices have not been received at the year-end. The entry would be reversed in the new financial year so that the accounts would once again be recording commitments.

FUND ACCOUNTING

Fund accounting is a practice we were introduced to in Chapter 7. It refers to the method of accounting which reports in terms of funds rather than in terms of organizations. The practical effects of adopting fund accounting depend upon the extent to which different funds are utilized and the form and extent to which the individual fund accounts are consolidated in the final accounts. If ten funds are used but they are all consolidated into one operating statement and one balance sheet, then the results might well be the same as the accounts for a business. Indeed, the parallel is very close to the consolidation of the accounts of a group of companies, although this will depend upon the manner in which the consolidation is effected. On the other hand, if there is a profusion of funds which are not consolidated, then the fund accounts will be very different from the accounts of a business.

The reason for this difference is that businesses see themselves as having a pool of resources which can be used in any aspect of their business to achieve their overall objective, e.g. to achieve a satisfactory return on capital. Thus this pool of resources could be invested in working capital, in fixed assets, or in financial assets; or it could be spent on wages, supplies, or overheads; or it could be distributed as dividends or used to repay debt. In other words, there is one fund and the accounts do not divulge the whereabouts of specific monies paid into it, only the whereabouts of the monies in the fund as a whole.

The problem with applying this practice to local government, for example, is that the monies which are paid in cannot be used indiscriminately. If central government is to finance 100 per cent of a local authority's programme for maintenance of motorways, the authority cannot charge other, unrelated expenditure to that programme. If an ex-pupil of an education authority bequeathes £10,000 on the condition that the money is invested and the interest earned is awarded as a prize to the best academic performance each year, the money cannot in law be used to keep local taxes down. Similarly, if an authority sells a piece of land, the capital receipt also cannot be used to keep local taxes down. There are many other examples of these kinds of restrictions on how specific monies paid into a local authority can be spent. The American expression for this position is to say that the resources of a local authority are not 'fungible', meaning that we cannot treat them as one mass.

There are different extents of this fungibility. A useful two-way distinction can be drawn between those monies which are unrestricted and those which are restricted. These categories would correspond to those which are fungible and those which are not. Then the restricted monies can be further categorized into broad areas of restrictions, so that one area represents specific grants while another represents bequests, for example. The point being that the more detailed the categorization of the restrictions becomes, the more likely it is that qualitatively different kinds of restrictions will emerge. For example, monies could be restricted because the governing body has put them aside for a specific purpose, such as for renewal of a fleet of cars. This does not mean, however, that they could not easily become unrestricted by a future change in policy: if the fleet of cars subsequently becomes superfluous then it would be nonsensical not to put the fund back to where it originated.

Another degree of restriction might take the form of a bequest. The bequest must be adhered to, but adherence depends upon interpretation of the bequeather's wishes. If a bequest to a school was specified in terms of 'the best performance in the School Certificate' it would be unreasonable not to release that restriction when the School Certificate was abolished. It would be a matter of judgement as to how broadly any new restriction was imposed.

An extreme form of restriction relates to a specific government grant. The terms of the grant would most typically specify precisely which expenditure qualified for grant and that any underspending had to be relinquished to the government. The restriction in this case would be in law and would be an absolute one.

Let us now examine the published accounts of a simplified local authority to see the effects of adopting fund accounting. This authority accounts using the following funds:

1   General Fund;
2   Housing Accounts;
3   Trust Funds.

Each fund accounts for specified items of income and expenditure. Each produces an operating account and a balance sheet. We will concentrate on the General Fund and the Housing Accounts.

Here are the summarized final accounts of the General Fund which is the fund for all expenditure that is properly chargeable to local taxes:

GENERAL FUND

Revenue account for the year

	£000	£000
Income (not allocated to specific services)		
Taxes		32,395
Other government grants		22,700
		55,095

	£000	£000
Expenditure (net of specific income)		
Recreation	2,400	
Education	40,200	
Environmental health	3,000	
Housing	900	
Social services	7,300	
Planning	700	
		54,500
Transfer to Revenue balances		595

Balance sheet as at end of the year		
Fixed assets		55,600
Current assets		26,420
Other balances		15,700
		97,720
Current liabilities	7,220	
Other balances	18,000	
		25,220
		72,500
Financed by:		
Long-term borrowing		61,800
Fund balances		10,700
		72,500

Let us now introduce the Housing Accounts. This fund is concerned with the provision and maintenance of the stock of houses owned by the authority and rented out to tenants. It is maintained seperately from the General Fund because the policy has been, and particularly in recent years, to try to cover operating expenses by rents charged and housing grants. In other words, if there is to be a contribution from taxes to balance the operating account, then it should be explicit and calculation of it should also be explicit as should a contribution from Housing to the General Fund. The current jargon has it that the Housing Revenue Account is 'ring-fenced'. These are the summarized final accounts for housing:

HOUSING REVENUE ACCOUNT FOR THE YEAR

	£000	£000
Income		
Rents		8,260
Subsidies		8,880
Miscellaneous		580
Transfer from General Fund		900
		18,620

	£000	£000
Expenditure		
Supervision and management		
Administration	1,590	
Repairs and maintenance	3,320	
Special services	940	
Capital financing costs	12,280	
		18,130
Surplus of income over expenditure		410
Surplus brought forward		–
Surplus carried forward		410

Housing balance sheet as at year-end		
Fixed assets		134,500
Current assets		1,670
Other balances		380
		136,550
Current liabilities	680	
Other balances	23,330	
		24,010
		112,540
Financed by:		
Long-term borrowing		111,300
Fund balances		1,240
		112,540

The link between these accounts and the General Fund is the contribution of £900,000. The bookkeeping for this inter-fund transfer is a potential source of difficulty because strictly the transaction generates *two* double-entries. The first would be in the General Fund:

	Dr	Cr
Contribution to Housing Revenue Account	900,000	
General Fund Cash Account		900,000

The second would be recorded in the Housing Accounts:

	Dr	Cr
Housing Cash Account	900,000	
Contribution from General Fund		900,000

However, as we noted earlier, most organizations which adopt fund accounting do not keep all their funds completely separate. Instead they keep a common cash book and bank account which serve all funds. Consequently, the above two journal entries could be condensed into one:

	Dr	Cr
GF contribution to Housing Revenue Account	900,000	
Housing Revenue Account – contribution from GF		900,000

Since there is only one cash book for the organization, cash does not pass from fund to fund and so is excluded from the journal entry.

This practice does beg the question of how different cash figures are found for the different fund balance sheets when a single cash book is kept for the authority. The answer is that, in the process of producing final accounts, the cash amounts for each fund balance sheet are balancing figures. As long as the total of the balancing figures for each fund equals the balance on the cash book, then the accounts as a whole are in balance.

We now have two fund balance sheets in this authority's accounts. Each one provides the balance at the year end for the defined area. But what of the organization as a whole?

In order to provide some sort of overall picture this authority, in common with most others, produces a consolidated balance sheet. As with the consolidation of the accounts of a group of companies, this does not only involve aggregation: there is also the elimination of any inter-fund balances to preclude double-counting.

This is the consolidated balance sheet for our authority:

	£000	£000
Fixed assets		190,090
Current assets		15,210
Other balances		16,000
		221,300
Current liabilities	11,100	
Provisions	5,680	
Other balances	41,450	
		58,230
		163,070
Financed by:		
Long-term liabilities		152,025
Fund balances		11,045
		163,070

This balance sheet does not consolidate all the funds. The trust funds are reported only in the fund accounts. The reason for this is that the trust funds are not owned by the authority, they are being administered on behalf of the bequeathers. Consequently, the authority has decided that it would be misleading to include these amounts in a balance sheet which provides some measure of what the authority is 'worth'. Some authorities operate superannuation funds on behalf of their past and present employees and these fund accounts are often not consolidated for the same reason.

A critique of fund accounting

Fund accounting explicitly recognizes the political, economic and legal differences that exist between the services provided, and the activities carried on, within public sector organizations. In the above example, the political differences between the General Fund of a local authority and the Housing Accounts relate to the fact that the former is financed by taxes and the latter is financed by housing rents. Taxes are paid by all owner occupiers (among others), including substantial contribution from commercial property owners; while rents are paid by council house tenants. Therefore, for example the pressure groups relating to each fund are different and their demands are also different.

The economic differences are that taxes are not related to the services which taxpayers might receive from the authority; whereas rents paid by individuals are directly related to their occupancy of council houses. The legal differences reflect the political and economic differences in that different services are provided under the authority of different statutes. These laws require different (specific) standards, different methods of finance and cite different government departments as having overall responsibility for parts of the services. The laws often also mean that specific committees and specific departments are set up within local authorities to administer the services.

These political, economic and legal differences between services define the extent to which a local government's resources are fungible. The objective of fund accounting is to reflect this lack of fungibility in two ways:

1   by ensuring that all debits and credits are maintained separately for funds which are not fungible;
2   by producing a separate operating statement and balance sheet for each non-fungible fund.

In practice, many local authorities do not fully achieve these, for a variety of reasons. For example, many do not publish separate fund balance sheets, only separate operating statements. We have also noted that all debits and credits are not maintained separately because authorities tend to keep only one cash book.

In fact, with sophisticated computer programs available, there is no reason why any organization of any size need maintain separate cash books and bank accounts for separate funds. Indeed, it can be argued that a profusion of cash books and bank accounts would provide more problems than it would solve, particularly to financial managers concerned with managing the organization's cash resources as a whole.

On the other hand, if the arguments for accruals accounting are accepted, then fund accounting requires an operating statement and a balance sheet for each fund.

The most pervasive (and persuasive) argument against fund accounting is the increased costs involved in producing published accounts compared with the business method. These additional costs are of two kinds. First, there are the physical costs of production. The second cost associated with producing fund accounts relates to the investment of time and skill needed to understand them. Most professional accountants have been trained to expect only one set of financial accounts for each organization. They are trained to search for the overall picture so that they can advise on overall financial policy or make an overall judgement on the truth and fairness of the accounts. Judgements about profitability, net worth, and creditworthiness are judgements about the PLC taken as a whole. The idea that an accountant is examining only one set of accounts, of many, is anathema because it carries the implication that unwanted debits and credits might have been secreted away in these other accounts. This is the other side of fungibility. If resources are fungible then judgements must be made in the light of all debits and credits.

Some critics have taken the argument against this second cost to the extreme and suggested that the mere fact of fund accounting not being the norm within the accounting profession as a whole should prohibit its use.

The criticism that fund accounting does not provide an overall view of the organization has partly been countered by local authorities in the UK producing a consolidated balance sheet. We have seen that this does not tend to include funds such as the superannuation fund and trust funds. Nevertheless, it does provide a view of the bulk of the authority.

When this is not as a substitute for the individual fund balance sheets, the argument about incomprehensibility still applies.

However, producing a consolidated balance sheet without the fund balance sheets is hardly a satisfactory solution. Potentially important information can be lost in consolidating the balance sheets of just two funds. If eight were consolidated and the individual ones were not published, then the loss of information would be that much greater. Not only that but it is difficult to see how useful a consolidated balance sheet really is when funds are not fungible. The balance sheets of public sector organizations are not relevant for making judgements about creditworthiness anyway, so the consolidation adds nothing in this respect.

The net assets of the organization are shown but it is hard to imagine what use can be made of this figure. Who owns the asset? What could be done with any realizations? What does the debtor figure relate to? Rent, taxes, government grants, other local authorities, miscellaneous charges?

The accumulated surplus on operating account is shown; but what could this be used for? Reducing taxes, reducing rents, awarding more prizes on the trust fund, reducing administrative charges, reducing insurance fund contributions?

A recent development is the requirement to include a consolidated revenue account. As with the consolidated balance sheet, this excludes the superannuation and trust funds. It is in addition to the revenue accounts of some individual funds, such as the Housing Revenue Account and that for Direct Service Organizations. The Code of Practice on Local Authority Accounting in Great Britain (1993, p. 26) describes this as reporting 'the cost for the year of the major functions for which the authority is responsible, and compares that cost with the finance provided from central government and local taxpayers'. It is clear that the consolidated revenue account cannot serve as a substitute for the individual fund accounts and publishing it does help to counter potential criticism that fund accounts do not provide an overview of the authority as a whole. Yet it only helps to counter the criticism: it does not invalidate it, because the account is not comprehensive. And as with the consolidated balance sheet, it is not easy to see the usefulness of the information it provides over and above the fund accounts that are, or otherwise would be, provided.

We conclude that the political, economic and legal reality demands fund accounts but that many users (particularly business accountants) do not understand them.

There are many analogies in accounting as a whole for this paradox. The published accounts of PLCs are becoming more and more complicated because of the increased number and complexity of footnotes; yet those footnotes reflect the increased awareness of the need to provide more relevant information. Fund accounting is merely one more attempt by accountants to report on a complex reality more sensitively; although this seems inevitably to be at the expense of general understandability.

DISCUSSION TOPICS

1   Fund accounts merely confuse the user. If they were aggregated to produce a consolidated operating statement, balance sheet, and cash flow statement a clear overall position for the organization would be shown, comparable with that of a PLC. Discuss.

2   What are the relative strengths and weaknesses of commitment accounting and cash accounting for budgetary control and accountability in government?

3   In thinking about accruals accounting for a national government, examine the relevance and reliability of each of the possible accrual adjustments (e.g. debtors, creditors, stock, depreciation, etc.).

CHAPTER 9

Capital accounting

This chapter develops our previous discussion about cash accounting and accrual accounting, concentrating on capital assets. It uses a numerically simple example to explain what the different capital accounting techniques yield, from traditional business accounting models to those used by central government, local government and other public bodies. Because local authority accounting has been unique, a more detailed discussion of its development is offered.

THE FORMS OF CAPITAL ACCOUNTING

In business balance sheets, the distinction between capital accounts and operating accounts is mostly unclear. This is because the funds in a business are fungible. The cash figure in the balance sheet might include both capital and operating cash: if a debenture is issued but the resulting cash has not yet been invested in fixed assets, then the cash will perhaps be shown in the cash book – this is capital cash; if profits were made in the current year, some of these profits might take the form of cash – this is operating cash. But in the accounts of the business the distinction is not made.

Nevertheless, it is important as a matter of law and could be important as a matter of economics, that a limited company can distinguish between the original capital invested and the rest. The law attempts to ensure that the original capital invested is maintained within the limited company, particularly so that the rights of un-secured creditors are protected: the original capital, if maintained, is assumed to provide their security. As a matter of business economics, if the capital originally invested is eroded, for example by distributing capital amounts in the form of divi-dends, then the business's ability to carry on will be diminished. In general terms, inflation accounting methods have been concerned with ensuring that capital is being maintained in economic terms.

Consequently, business balance sheets do distinguish between revenue reserves and capital reserves, the former being distributable while the latter are not. More-over, current cost accounting strictly demands that a business's cash book be segre-gated into capital and revenue cash. The capital/revenue distinction is therefore important in business accounts even though the published balance sheets tend to understate it – a fact now emphasized in the Cash Flow Statement.

In public sector organizations, the distinction sometimes takes on a lesser and sometimes a greater importance. In the appropriation accounts of the government, the distinction is almost non-existent. Some votes are for capital items, such as expenditure on new buildings, while others are for revenue items, such as staff salaries. Each are accounted for in the same way: budgeted expenditure is compared with actual spending, budgeted income with actual income, and any net under- or over-spending on the vote as a whole is paid over to, or collected from, the Consolidated Fund. This latter fund simply collects together all the appropriations of expenditure made by Parliament and is financed broadly by taxation and borrowing in proportions which bear little or no relationship to the underlying 'capital' and 'revenue' spending. Simply, as far as the accounts are concerned, spending is spending.

In other public sector organizations which adopt the cash basis of accounting, the capital accounts are essentially the same as the revenue accounts although the two are kept separately. The accounts of the National Health Service as a whole offer a good example. These authorities are ultimately financed by a grant from the government. However, there are current grants (for operating expenditure) and capital grants (for capital expenditure). Although there is some latitude between these grants, in that part of the capital grant can be transferred to be used on the current grant, the distinction between them is maintained and is important. However, the accounts do only compare actual expenditure against grant for both categories.

Although this is true of the appropriation accounts presented to Parliament in respect of the NHS as a whole, the way that the constituent health service bodies account for capital has been the subject of substantial change. Commercial accounting has been introduced for the new Trusts. For the NHS-managed hospitals, a form of accruals accounting has been introduced, including depreciation charges and an opportunity cost of capital charge. In principle, this accounting is no different from commercial accounting except that the depreciation charges are being made into cash flows from each hospital to the Regional Health Authorities, who then reallocate the cash flows back to the District Health Authorities and the GPs, who in turn buy services from the hospitals. This radical treatment (radical at least in the UK – it has distinct echoes of the accounting used in the old centrally planned economies of Eastern Europe) is a result of grafting on depreciation accounting (and including the depreciation in prices) to a cash accounting system.

Capital accounting in a nationalized industry is in essence no different from that in a limited company. Capital finance takes a different form and the Government has overall control of it (in the form of upper limits to the amount the organization can borrow – known as 'external financing limits'). But once the finance has been raised, it is fungible. It has always been the policy of the government for nationalized industries to adopt best commercial practice at least.

The primary reason for differences in how we account for capital is that, in different organizations at different times, there have been and are different relationships between 'accounting' and 'finance'. The traditional and continuing role for the accountant is to keep financial control, which includes keeping records of the money coming in and going out of the entity. What has progressively been changing (over more than a century) is the extent to which accountants can use these records as the basis of other measures, most importantly measures of what the entity costs. Such measures are constrained by their transaction-based origins: one effect is that there is a great reluctance to escape the constraints by totally severing the connection between finance and accounting in adopting opportunity cost measures. For while these may be theoretically the most relevant they are not the most reliable.

At the opposite extreme from opportunity costs is cash accounting, in which finance and accounting are bound up with each other: we account only for the financial flows in and out of the entity. Business accounting is somewhere between cash accounting and accounting for opportunity costs. It has to a large extent, though by no means completely, separated accounting from finance: we take the records of the transactions of the entity and adjust the numbers to provide the best measure we can of what the entity cost and what the entity earned, in many ways regardless of how the entity was financed. This separation can be seen as part of a trend towards emphasizing the need to account for the costs of the entity providing the services it provides. It gives us more meaningful measures of cost. But what must also be remembered is that this additional information is probably not neutral: it affects the basic financial control of the entity.

CAPITAL ACCOUNTING TECHNIQUE

In order to expand on the discussion offered in Chapter 8, let us take a numerically simple example that compares the important elements of the cash basis and forms of the accrual basis of accounting; and compares the local authority models.

Assume that a unit buys a minibus for £10,000 that lasts for four years and at the end of Year 4 is worthless. The financial objective is to break even, either by charging for use of the minibus or by taxing: in a private sector context, we assume charging; in a governmental context, taxing. We abstract from real-world problems of uncertainty (so that the above data are all known) and, in the first instance, from changing prices.

Running costs (e.g. fuel, insurance, tax, driver's wages, etc.) are £5,000 p.a., on both the cash basis and the accrual basis. In other words, there is either no opening and closing working capital for each year or the two balances for each year are the same. Assume also that running costs are financed with credit until receipts are received.

The financial accounting question comes down to this: which year(s) bears the £10,000? There are an infinite number of ways of dividing it up; indeed, there are an infinite number of ways of dividing it up systematically.

The government's cash basis reports the cash payments and the cash receipts at the time they take place. In the first year, the payments for the running costs (£5,000) and for the minibus (£10,000) would be recorded in the appropriation accounts, against a particular vote. The amount for the capital asset may or may not be disclosed separately but otherwise the two payments would be treated in the same way. Sovereign governments are not currently required to balance their budgets and therefore there is no necessary, direct relationship between the annual cost of the minibus (£15,000 in year 1; £5,000 in years 2–4) and how this cost will be financed. If taxes were collected to cover the cost, the cash basis would record the cash receipts when they took place. If the cost were to be financed in part by borrowing, the cash basis would record the cash receipts from the lenders when they took place; in addition, if interest or principal were to be payable during the four years, the accounts would record the cash payments to the lenders when they took place.

Just as a cash flow statement for a business classifies cash flows differently depending on their nature, so the cash basis in government does the same. The Public Sector Borrowing Requirement, for example, which is a measure of the annual shortfall between spending and taxes, would include in year 1 the £15,000 for buying and running the minibus and the cash paid for interest in that year but would not include the cash receipt from borrowing or any principal repayment. Any cash receipts and payments relating to the principal of loans would be added to or deducted from measures of public sector debt and general government debt.

The records of these transactions are an important part of the financial control of government. They provide reliable data on which to base decisions. What they obviously do not do is provide an economically meaningful measure of what it cost to run the minibus in year 1. But this is not to say that governments do not generate aggregate measures of income and capital, which do provide meaningful measures. Such measures are provided through national income accounting. Traditionally this has emphasized income measures but increasingly capital is being measured too. From an accountant's point of view, there are two aspects to these measures that cause difficulty. First, the measures are much closer to statistics than they are to accounting records: they may be more relevant but they are significantly less reliable. The second is that the measures are used less to balance the government's accounts than to balance the economy. Thus, returning to our minibus, it is not the records of transactions that determine how the minibus will be financed: there is no distinction between the running costs and the capital costs that might trigger a view being taken about financing by taxes or by borrowing; there is no balanced budget requirement that even suggests the accounting should determine the financing. Instead, and particularly since the impact of Keynesian economics on government policy, the financing decisions depend on macro-economic factors, such as the effect on inflation, interest rates, and exchange rates: in other words, how will the economy as a whole react to a decision to finance the minibus from taxes.

The main reason why accountants would have difficulty with this is that, while an important part of financial control (namely, probity) can be maintained, it is not clear how financial control (in the sense of living within your means) can be maintained. This difficulty might properly be put down to the arrogance of accountants in thinking that they are the best people to maintain this kind of control but this contribution to financial control is a natural point of the work of accountants in most, if not all, other contexts.

Nevertheless, the criticism that the cash basis does not provide managers with measures of the cost of providing government services is being addressed. Forms of accrual accounting are needed for this. Let us, therefore, develop our example into a business accounting context and return to the question of which year(s) should bear the cost of buying the minibus.

Business accounting invented the notion of 'depreciation', eventually as a systematic allocation of cost or value over the economically useful life of an asset. Commonly-used methods of calculating this depreciation include the following:

Straight-line (divide by asset life)

Year		
	1	2,500
	2	2,500
	3	2,500
	4	2,500
		10,000

Reducing balance   (calculate a percentage that, if applied to the opening balance of each year, will write asset down to zero; an approximation can be obtained by dividing asset life into 100 and doubling the answer; for 4 years, 50%).

Year		
	1	5,000
	2	2,500
	3	1,250
	4	1,250
		10,000

In the context of companies, there is nothing in law or in accounting standards that requires or forbids one or other of these methods to be used. Disclosure of the method adopted is required by SSAP 12; the same standard requires disclosure of the reason for any change in method and the effect of the change. The important point about this is that, however sensitive the depreciation calculation may try to be to the 'reality' of a depreciating asset, the choice of method (and the ultimate charge) is arbitrary. In the following, we will choose the straight-line pattern.

Business Accounting No. 1   (assuming the business begins with £10,000 in capital)

	Years				£ Total
	1	2	3	4	
Running costs	5,000	5,000	5,000	5,000	20,000
Depreciation	2,500	2,500	2,500	2,500	10,000
Charges	7,500	7,500	7,500	7,500	30,000

Opening capital (t_0) £10,000
Closing capital (t_4) £10,000 (because the minibus is worthless, and the surplus cash resulting in effect from the charges made for depreciation remain, say, in the bank account)

Now we can introduce one more element. The unit may not have the capital in the beginning and has therefore to borrow £10,000 at an annual percentage rate (APR) of 12 per cent (otherwise known as the 'internal rate of return'). There are many possible schedules of repayment of this loan but the following two will be used here (both assume cash flows at the end of each year):

Equal instalments of principal

		Principal	Interest	Total
Year	1	2,500	1,200	3,700
	2	2,500	900	3,400
	3	2,500	600	3,100
	4	2,500	300	2,800
		10,000	3,000	13,000

Equal instalments of interest, principal on redemption

		Principal	Interest	Total
Year	1	–	1,200	1,200
	2	–	1,200	1,200
	3	–	1,200	1,200
	4	10,000	1,200	11,200
		10,000	4,800	14,800

Business Accounting No. 2   (assuming the business borrows £10,000 and repays using the equal interest method)

	Years				£ Total
	1	2	3	4	
Running costs	5,000	5,000	5,000	5,000	20,000
Depreciation	2,500	2,500	2,500	2,500	10,000
Interest on debt	1,200	1,200	1,200	1,200	4,800
Charges	8,700	8,700	8,700	8,700	34,800

Opening capital (t_0) 0
Closing capital (t_4) 0   (because the minibus is worthless, and the surplus cash resulting in effect from the charges made for depreciation was used to repay the loan)

We can see, therefore, that using the business accounting model (No. 1 and No. 2), the opening capital position was maintained. Had charges been made in excess of the ones recorded here, these excesses would have been called 'profits' or 'surpluses', after maintaining initial capital intact. This is particularly important because in practice we assume that 'accounting' for the business and 'financing' it are distinctly different issues.

It follows from the above that the principal repayments of loans are not costs of running the minibus that have to be passed on in charges to the users. Put another way, the financing and refinancing of the business are accounted for as balance sheet movements. For example, in No. 2, capital would still be zero even if the surplus cash was not used to repay the loan: when the loan is repaid the two balance sheet items of 'long-term creditor' and 'cash' are written out.

But this accounting abstracts from changing prices. There is one important sense in which company accounting in the UK can modify historical cost accounting in order to reflect price change. The law allows the revaluation of tangible fixed assets at 'market value' or 'current cost' and accounting standards require that any associated depreciation charge must be based on the revalued amount. The effect on Business Accounting No. 1 of assuming that the minibus was revalued in Year 3 to £14,000 would be to increase the depreciation charge in each of Years 3 and 4 from £2,500 to £4,500, in order to recover the additional £4,000 resulting from the revaluation.

Business Accounting No. 3   (assuming the business begins with £10,000 in capital)

		Years			£ Total
	1	2	3	4	
Running costs	5,000	5,000	5,000	5,000	20,000
Depreciation	2,500	2,500	4,500	4,500	14,000
Charges	7,500	7,500	9,500	9,500	34,000

Opening capital (t_0) £10,000
Closing capital (t_4) £14,000   (because the minibus is worthless, and the surplus cash resulting in effect from the charges made for depreciation remains in the bank account)

Under historic cost accounting, the business only maintained £10,000 intact whereas the modification allowed for maintenance of the ability of the business to buy another minibus (assuming the 'market value' or 'current cost' of £14,000 is still the replacement cost at t_4).

In addition to modified historical cost accounting there are other methods available, which have been the subject of much controversy (Tweedie and Whittington, 1984). A comprehensive system of current cost accounting was the subject of SSAP 16, but this was withdrawn in 1985. But the Accounting Standards Committee did issue guidance (and it has not subsequently been withdrawn) on accounting for changing prices (1988), which encourages disclosure of the current cost of fixed assets and of stocks, and what the consequent effects on profit and loss would be.

The guidance also recognizes that both a financial concept of capital maintenance and an operating (or physical) concept of capital maintenance provide relevant information. In our example, when the additional amount of £4,000 is treated as capital, theory recognizes this modification as an important step in moving from a financial concept of capital maintenance to a physical (or operating) concept of capital maintenance. The accounts are telling the reader what the effect would be of assuming that the business is attempting to maintain its ability to keep buying minibuses rather than to keep investing 10,000 one-pound coins.

A further consideration is not the effect of specific price change (that is, relating to specific goods and services such as our minibus) but the effect of general price change (that is, relating to a chosen basket of goods and services). Clearly, the purpose of adjusting for the latter is to approximate changes in the purchasing power of money. For example, we could stay with a financial concept of capital maintenance under historical cost accounting (maintaining our £10,000) but adjust for the effects of inflation (which strictly means general price inflation). Taking a particular measure of inflation, say the Retail Price Index, and assuming that it had risen by 20 per cent from t_0 to t_4, we might want to charge an additional £2,000 to the users of our minibus so that over its life we recover not £10,000 but £12,000, thereby maintaining intact the purchasing power of our initial capital. The guidance does not suggest that companies do this but it does suggest that, when a time-series of financial data is presented, this could be shown in 'constant purchasing power' terms: more specifically, that all data should be shown in terms of purchasing power at the same date, usually the latest date (hence, *current* purchasing power accounting).

Setting aside price change, there is another important issue raised by Business Accounting Nos 1 and 2: the annual costs are different because of the two different methods of financing adopted. In practice, the costs of different methods of finance might be assumed to be different. For example, we might assume that debt costs less than equity, because of perceived differences in risk. But in our example (and in accounting practice) the reason for the difference in annual costs is that the accounting convention is to record the cost of debt as an annual expense but not to recognize the cost of equity as an annual expense. The consequence is that when a business reports 'profit for the financial year' this could be said to include two elements: interest on equity capital and profit. Business accounting would then deduct from 'profit for the financial year' any dividends payable, emphasizing that the accounts are transaction-based.

Whether interest on equity capital should be an annual expense in a business has been discussed in the literature, for example by Anthony (1975). The essence of the argument is that economics would insist that the cost of equity is as much a cost to the business as the cost of debt: capital, in whatever form, has been invested and, just like labour and material resources, incurs cost; economists would say that this cost is the opportunity cost of capital. Accounting traditionally does not record opportunity costs, being transaction-based, and would argue that the business is not required to pay any dividend to ordinary shareholders and that the cost of equity capital involves too subjective a judgement to be included in the financial statements. Moreover, in terms of the effect on the balance sheet, charging this cost to profit and loss would not have a significant effect: retained earnings would probably only be distinguished between that which was the cost of capital and that which was profit. But there is no doubt that the income statement, and the management accounts underpinning it, would be very different. Indeed, it is this effect that is at the heart of Anthony's proposal to make the charge: managers are given curious incentives when the cost of debt is charged against them but not the cost of equity. We can see this clearly in our example because we have assumed that the accounting completely determines prices: in No. 1, users of the minibus pay significantly more than they do under No. 2, notwithstanding the fact that, assuming the costs of equity and debt capital are not markedly different, the economics of the two circumstances are the same.

Taking the assumption that the cost of equity capital was 15 per cent, we can see in the next box the effect on No. 1 if we charge this cost to each of the years of operation.

Now we can see that by making a charge for the cost of equity the annual cost of running the minibus would vary between £9,000 when there is no gearing, and £8,700 when there is no equity; differing ratios of debt to equity would produce annual costs within this range. And of course, the range is determined by our assumptions about the relative cost of debt and equity.

'Cost of equity' accounting   (assuming the business begins with £10,000 in capital)

	Years				£ Total
	1	2	3	4	
Running costs	5,000	5,000	5,000	5,000	20,000
Depreciation	2,500	2,500	2,500	2,500	10,000
Interest on capital	1,500	1,500	1,500	1,500	6,000
Charges	9,000	9,000	9,000	9,000	36,000

Opening capital (t_0) £10,000

Closing capital (t_4) £10,000   (because the minibus is worthless, the surplus cash resulting in effect from the charges made for depreciation remain in the bank account, and the £6,000 charged for the cost of equity is recorded as retained earnings: this would raise questions about what our policy of 'break-even' was intended to mean)

The measurement difficulties of this accounting should not be under-emphasized. There is a substantial literature on the problems of measuring the cost of capital. Moreover, that literature has the benefit of being able to observe financial markets in debt and equity. In most public sector contexts, no such equity markets exist. Anthony (1975), reflecting his background in government, is concerned with many public–private examples, including regulation and procurement. His proposal for dealing with the inherent difficulties in measuring the cost of equity, and in measuring it relatively reliably, is to impose a rate of interest – in his case through the Financial Accounting Standards Board. The public sector versions in the UK have a similarly imposed rate – by the government. The main weakness of this is that its arbitrariness adds to suspicions that the resulting charges are artificial and, given that a primary reason for making them is to change managers' behaviour, this has the potential for creating a major drawback.

Nor can the theoretical framework abstract from changing prices. In our example, we assumed that the cost of capital could be calculated using historic cost capital. This is not necessarily invalid but it does mean that implementing this accounting further complicates the historic cost/current cost debate.

All these business accounting models can be, and have been, used in the public sector. The trading funds of the government and the trading accounts of local authorities are probably the oldest versions in the UK, dating back at least to the early decades of this century. The adoption of best commercial practice in nationalized industries has been there for as long as we have had those bodies.

More recently, there has been an explosion in the use of elements of these models. When accounting for direct labour organizations in local authorities was statutorily changed in 1980, professional interest in current cost accounting was at its zenith and the regulation of their returns on capital (although not the financial statements themselves) was based on current cost returns. At the same time, some nationalized industries were required to adopt current cost accounting.

In addition, and perhaps not surprisingly given the withdrawal of SSAP 16 in 1988, there has been increased use of modified historical cost under the Companies

Acts: National Health Service Trusts and the government's trading funds are notable examples. Indeed, this accounting is the basis for the proposals in *Better Accounting for the Taxpayer's Money* (Cm 2626) that are to be implemented throughout government departments, with the probability that in addition some form of charge will be made for the cost of capital.

UK LOCAL GOVERNMENT

Local authorities account for capital expenditure in a unique way. (For a discussion of local authority capital expenditure, see Chapter 3.) There is no counterpart in any other kind of organization, business or non-business. In fact, new accounting arrangements were introduced with the implementation of the poll tax legislation in 1988 and subsequently. The overall effect of these new arrangements is the same as it was under traditional accounting but there are important differences also.

Before 1988, there were two legal requirements that effectively determined the form of capital accounting:

1   Schedule 13, para 7(i), Local Government Act 1972 required that where expenditure was defrayed by borrowing, a sum equivalent to an instalment of principal and interest was debited to the relevant operating statement so that the loan was repaid over a specified period of years.
2   Local authorities were not allowed, in law, to budget for an operating deficit. In other words, having debited principal and interest for loans raised to operating statements, rates had to be collected at least to cover those repayments (s. 2, General Rate Act 1967).

The effect of these two prescriptions was that the principal repayments of loans raised were taken off the balance sheet and put through the revenue account. In a business, for example, only interest on loans is put through the profit and loss account as an operating expense; principal repayments involve taking one balance sheet item, i.e. cash, and using it to reduce another, i.e. long-term liability. Thus, in a business which finances the purchase of a depreciable asset by issuing a debenture, the operating expense of that machine is:

1   depreciation – the allocation of a proportion of the total cost to the year;
2   interest on the loan.

The redemption of the debenture is either refinanced by another debenture issue or it is repaid from any surplus cash.

In local authorities, the principal repayments were forced through the revenue account: the law was in effect saying that provision must be made annually for repayment of debt. In practice, therefore, these principal repayments took the place of depreciation.

The effect was inextricably to combine matters of capital cost with capital finance – since the annual 'cost' of the asset was defined by the annual cost of finance, the principal repayments. This link also influences accounting for capital expenditure that is financed other than by borrowing. Whether assets are financed from reserves, from grants or from revenue, they are not depreciated. If there are effects on the revenue account, these will be accounted for when the revenue finance is required. Therefore, in the case of capital expenditure out of reserves, the revenue effect is recorded only when the contributions were made from revenue into the reserve accounts. Where capital is financed from grants, there will be no direct revenue effect. Obviously, when capital is financed from revenue, the accounting takes place at the same time as the financing.

This accounting method has been used in local government throughout its modern context in the UK, i.e. since 1835; indeed, it was used before that as well. But since the early 1970s, there has been a great deal of controversy about it and the prevailing mood in the accounting profession appears to be that the system is archaic and needs replacing.

In fact, accompanying the introduction of the poll tax in 1988 (and surviving it with the move to the 'council tax') traditional accounting was changed. The balanced budget requirement is now enforced under Part VI of the Local Government Finance Act 1988. Debt charges (principal and interest) still have to be included in budget revenue expenses and therefore, in the end, local taxes have to be raised to finance these debt charges. However, there are important changes in how this is achieved.

In place of the requirement to debit debt charges to individual operating statements, the law now requires that the local authority makes a 'minimum revenue provision' for the accounts as a whole. This provision is a percentage of the authority's overall outstanding debt and is prescribed by the government (Part IV of the Local Government and Housing Act 1989). As a consequence, whereas before the government used to control the amount of loan redemption by setting a maximum redemption period for each category of asset, now it has a global control. By setting the percentage at 4 per cent (as it did), it is requiring local authorities to spread loan redemption for its *aggregate* borrowing over approximately 50 years at maximum (which equates to 4 per cent on a reducing balance basis). Among other things, this means that the traditional connection between loan redemptions and the lives of associated assets has been broken. Now loan redemption is a matter for the government to decide (at least as to minima), and presumably comes down to a judgement about how much the government thinks local authorities as a whole can afford to redeem in any year.

There is another possible consequence of this change, which may or may not have been intended. The minimum revenue provision is defined in terms of the authority as a whole. This raises the question about whether we still need to allocate debt charges to individual operating statements. In fact, the arguments in response to this question are no different from the pervasive arguments in the whole of accounting about spatial allocations, from a central pool to smaller units. It is just that, since the law has shifted the focus from a disaggregate control to a central control, the question naturally raises itself. The additional attraction of moving to a central control, for some, is that it has often been argued, and increasingly so over the past 20 years, that debt charges do not measure 'cost of service' and should not be charged to detailed revenue accounts anyway.

Returning to our earlier example of the minibus, the existing method of accounting would be applied as shown in the next box.

Local Authority Accounting No. 1   (no depreciation and assuming the authority borrows £10,000 and repays using the equal instalments of principal method)

		Years			£
					Total
	1	2	3	4	
Running costs	5,000	5,000	5,000	5,000	20,000
Depreciation	–	–	–	–	–
Interest on debt	1,200	900	600	300	3,000
Principal	2,500	2,500	2,500	2,500	10,000
Taxes	8,700	8,400	8,100	7,800	33,000

Opening capital (t_0) 0

Closing capital (t_4) 0   (because the minibus is worthless, and the surplus cash resulting in effect from the taxes collected to redeem the loan was used to repay it)

The effect here is that, by requiring taxes to equal spending (as defined), the accounting model inextricably binds the accounting to the financing. If we extend the method to include depreciation as well as principal repayments, the effect is shown in the next box on Local Authority Accounting No. 2.

Local Authority Accounting No. 2   (including depreciation and assuming the authority borrows £10,000 and repays using the instalments of principal method)

		Years			£
					Total
	1	2	3	4	
Running costs	5,000	5,000	5,000	5,000	20,000
Depreciation	2,500	2,500	2,500	2,500	10,000
Interest on debt	1,200	900	600	300	3,000
Principal	2,500	2,500	2,500	2,500	10,000
Taxes	11,200	10,900	10,600	10,300	43,000

Opening capital (t_0) 0

Closing capital (t_4) £10,000 (because the minibus is worthless, and surplus cash resulting in effect from the taxes collected to redeem the loan was used to repay it, and the surplus cash resulting from the additional depreciation is available, say, in the bank)

Now it is obviously possible, because of the way we have constructed this example, to use depreciation to *replace* the charge made for the principal repayments of the loan and to show that the result (in Local Authority Accounting No. 3) will be the same as in Local Authority Accounting No. 1.

Local Authority Accounting No. 3 (including depreciation, excluding principal on loan and assuming the authority borrows £10,000 and repays the loan)					
			Years		£ Total
	1	2	3	4	
Running costs	5,000	5,000	5,000	5,000	20,000
Depreciation	2,500	2,500	2,500	2,500	10,000
Interest on debt	1,200	900	600	300	3,000
Principal	–	–	–	–	–
Taxes	8,700	8,400	8,100	7,800	33,000
Opening capital (t_0) 0					
Closing capital (t_4) 0 (because the minibus is worthless, and the surplus cash resulting in effect from the taxes collected for depreciation was used to repay the loan)					

As long as the balanced budget requirement remains, the accounting remains bound up with the financing. In this example, No. 3 is the same as No. 1, but it is easy to imagine many circumstances in which they would be different in practice. For example, an asset such as land would not normally attract a depreciation charge but it would result in principal charges to revenue if it was financed by loan. All depreciable assets would attract depreciation but only those assets with debt outstanding would produce, in effect, a charge to revenue for principal repayments.

Moreover, in all these examples we have assumed historic cost accounting. Local Authority No. 1 method always uses historic cost accounting. If depreciation was based on current values and these values were different from historic costs that would of itself produce differences. For example, replacement costs of economically useful assets (e.g., Case 3 assets under deprival value accounting) could be significantly higher than the book values of assets with related outstanding debt. This would produce significantly increased charges for depreciation, which in Local Authority No. 3 would simply lead to significant cash surpluses. As was pointed out earlier in this chapter, this is not necessarily bad, particularly when extra resources are needed for capital investment programmes. The point is only that this is as a direct result of the accounting method adopted rather than any policy decision.

There are other issues involved in comparing No. 3 and No. 1. An important question relates to the potential to manipulate the charges for the minibus. As the law and accounting standards currently require for companies, any systematic charge can be made to the income statement. In our example, Year 1 could have been charged with £5,000, £4,000 or £2,500.

Under local authority accounting practice, the minimum revenue provision for the local authority as a whole is a fixed percentage, determined by the government. Why these two methods of accounting are controlled so differently is a complex matter, but a factual difference is that in the context of companies depreciation is purely a matter of accounting, whereas for local authorities it is a matter of accounting *and* finance. Perhaps this opens up the idea of the government substituting depreciation accounting in place of principal repayments of loans but imposing the same control over the depreciation charge that it imposes on the minimum revenue provision. This would be anathema to the Anglo-American tradition of business accounting, but would fit with the Continental European tradition. Depreciation accounting, in that way, could be used to raise additional taxes, perhaps for the explicit purpose of providing further investment. We might be tempted also to say that other benefits of depreciation accounting would ensue, such as producing a charge in revenue accounts for the use of assets, rather than as at present for the financing of assets. This raises many questions about the extent to which *any* depreciation charge could yield a useful measure of this use but, given the policy of fixed depreciation charges imposed by government, it would be hard to see how these charges would be capable of measuring actual usage of assets (a point which is at the heart of the difference between the two accounting traditions).

This might lead us to conclude that in the case where taxes cannot bear the additional charges resulting from depreciation accounting (which is another way of saying that there is not the political will to impose them), in order to retain control of the charge to revenue accounts, the existing system will remain. It is theoretically possible to divorce the balanced budget requirement from the accounting for the cost of individual funds or individual units within funds, by having two sets of accounting numbers. So, for example, the cost of the minibus to the budget-holder is based on a depreciation charge whereas the cost of the minibus to the taxpayer is based on a minimum revenue provision. This solution is familiar to accounting textbooks but the political and other behavioural consequences have hardly been addressed.

A critique of local authority capital accounting

Let us begin by trying to understand the rationale for the system; after all, it has been used for many years and must presumably have had some point to it. We can see it in its most elemental form in its historical context where, for example, an influential group in a community on the Thames decided, in the 1830s, to build a new bridge over the river. The capital cost is to be financed from a local property tax. The community cannot afford to pay the required tax in one year so the immediate finance is by borrowing. The financial decision is taken, in the light of current market conditions, to issue stock redeemable in equal annual instalments of principal and interest over the ten years following completion of the bridge. The property tax will be levied, on the predictable base of immovable property, to yield the required annual debt repayments.

In this case, it would seem natural to establish an accounting system that records the annual debts (principal and interest), in which each year's debt charges signal the property tax rate (having taken account of rateable value) and which subsequently accounts for the actual expenditure and actual revenues (to determine whether next year's taxes need adjusting). If we now introduce the idea that the control and management of this bridge, including its finances, were in the hands of periodically elected local politicians, the system appears in sharper relief. For the community, the bridge is a good thing but the taxes are bad. The borrowing facility severs the relationship between the two things: it allows the community to have all the good things but in the short run to suffer a much smaller amount of the bad. *In extremis*, if the community defaulted on the debt, the relationship would be completely severed. But as long as the politicians are forced to levy annual taxes to make annual debt repayments, there is some control over their fiscal integrity.

This is the essence of local authority capital accounting. By retaining the link between finance and accounting, local politicians are forced to bear some of the cost of their programmes in the annual taxes that they have to levy in the short run. Politicians are endowed by law with finite, and short, time horizons. The capital accounting system is a method of forcing some of the financial consequences of their actions into those time horizons.

We might argue, albeit anachronistically, that best commercial practice could also have been adopted in accounting for the bridge. The asset is capitalized, interest is expensed and principal repayments do not pass through the revenue account. Depreciation may be charged, if the bridge was judged to be depreciable. The tax-financing decision would be severed from accounting. The tax might still be based on debt charges, or might not. The revenue account would match the taxes due with depreciation and interest charged. This would yield a measure of the annual cost of the bridge. But would it provide the same control over the politicians' fiscal integrity? The answer must be that it could not since the fact of adopting depreciation accounting severs the link with finance.

This is not to suggest that the existing system does not have its problems. Because the revenue account is determined by matters of finance, it does not account for the annual cost of running the authority. This is particularly poignant in cost comparisons between local authorities. Differences can be affected as much by different financing requirements as by differences in resources consumed.

Traditionally, controversy has centred around the question of whether local authorities should adopt best commercial practice, i.e. depreciation accounting, *instead of* the existing system. The first major privatization debate (as we would now call it) in this country took place in the first decade of this century. Because the major public sector bodies (outside the government) were local authorities, the debate involved local government accounting (see Jones, 1985). Indeed, a significant part of it concerned the relevance of depreciation accounting. More recently, Sidebotham (1966 and 1970) concluded many years of his own research by proposing, among other things, a *Consolidated Capital Fund* that would include all capital assets of an authority and would charge fund revenue accounts for the use of those assets. The Consolidated Capital Fund would sever the link between finance and accounting.

We can be sure that the debate is, therefore, a long one. In its modern context, we can now examine the issues involved.

We know that local authorities are forced by the law to charge loan redemptions (principal repayments) to revenue. These redemptions are, therefore, in lieu of depreciation in the case of depreciable assets. Indeed, with two assumptions, they will be *equal* to depreciation charges.

Assumption 1: that the whole of the capital cost is financed from loan.
Assumption 2: that the loan redemption period is the same as the estimated useful life of the asset.

If these apply and if, for example, the loans are redeemed using equal annual instalments of principal, then the revenue charge will be exactly the same as if an asset was depreciated using straight-line depreciation and any loan repayments were merely balance sheet transfers. Consequently, the argument about depreciation producing more correct costs in the revenue account applies equally to principal repayments in lieu of depreciation.

The debate about whether local authorities should adopt depreciation accounting is concerned with the following issues:

1   the reasonableness and generality of the above Assumptions 1 and 2;
2   the relevant concept of capital maintenance.

On the first issue, the problem with Assumption 1 is that a significant proportion of capital expenditure is not financed from loan. Particularly, we have seen that it is often financed by revenue, either explicitly (by recording it as an asset with an equal figure of capital discharged) or implicitly (by expensing it). This means that in future years the revenue accounts effectively treat the use of these assets as being free. Whereas, if depreciation was charged on all depreciable capital assets, then a more correct cost would be recorded.

Assumption 2 could be equally unrealistic. One reason is that the government has always set upper limits to loan redemption periods. With a minimum revenue provision based on, say, 4 per cent of outstanding debt, this means that assets as a whole cannot be financed over more than 50 years, assuming that 4 per cent is constant. Since, demonstrably, local government assets have in the past lasted, and continue to last, more than 50 years, for those assets the assumption is mistaken. Another reason is that many local authorities, as a matter of policy, accelerate their loan redemptions so that loans are repaid long before the end of the assets' useful lives. This decision is taken primarily as a matter of finance. Increasing loan redemption periods cannot be done without incurring costs in the form of interest charges. In money terms, therefore, it is cheaper to repay loans quickly because interest will be saved. Of course in real terms, this 'saving' depends upon the relationship between nominal rates of interest and rates of inflation – not to mention the community's rate of time preference. But in practice some authorities judge that this relationship has meant that loans should be repaid quickly. Again, this means that revenue accounts are not recording the more correct cost of the capital assets once the loans have been repaid.

The second issue involves the concept of capital maintenance adopted. We have said that depreciation in business can perform the function of maintaining capital. If depreciation is provided for in terms of replacement costs, this means that the business will set aside out of profits enough funds to replace its expired assets. (This does not mean that the replacement funds will be available in liquid form on expiry since they could be locked up in other fixed asset purchases.)

Charging principal repayments in lieu of depreciation does not perform the same function in a local authority. If we think of an individual asset to be purchased and financed from loan, then the authority begins with no capital. It then borrows the capital required and invests it in the asset. As the loan is repaid the asset depreciates until, when the asset expires, the loan has been repaid (if Assumption 2 is correct). Consequently, the authority is still left with no capital. If it decides to replace the asset, it has to borrow again. And so the cycle goes on. The underlying concept is what has been called 'zero capital maintenance' (Jones, 1982). The rationale for this is that the generation which uses the asset should pay for it.

The extent to which this inter-generational equity is achieved in practice depends upon Assumptions 1 and 2 as well as upon the extent to which *any* pattern of principal repayments is capable of reflecting assets usage. If depreciation is to be substituted for loan redemptions, then first of all the law must be changed, to take the principal repayments out of the revenue account so that they become balance sheet transfers as in business. If the depreciation charges were not controlled in any way, then this would mean that local authorities could do one of three things:

1 They could hold permanent debt. This would arise where depreciation charges were less than principal repayments would have been. The difference between these would be unredeemed debt. In effect, this would mean that capital could be reduced, perhaps from zero to being negative. The starkest example would be unlimited life goods, where depreciation presumably would not be charged at all.
2 They could maintain the status quo, by charging the same in depreciation as would have been charged in principal repayments.
3 They could increase their holdings of capital, by charging more in depreciation than they would have charged in principal repayments. After the principal had been repaid, through the balance sheet, surplus funds would be recorded as increases in capital.

Options 1 and 2 would affect the concept of capital maintenance, and the argument would then include opinions on the relative merits of each. If agreement was reached that inter-generational equity existed under the present system, then option 1 would mean that current taxpayers were benefiting in relation to future taxpayers, on the other hand, option 3 would mean that future taxpayers were benefiting in relation to current taxpayers.

But these conclusions depend upon depreciation being a substitute. If it was to be provided in addition to principal repayments in the revenue account, then local authorities' capital would increase. If agreement was reached that inter-generational equity existed under the present system, then this would mean that the change in accounting policy would lead to future taxpayers benefiting relative to current taxpayers.

The judgements that have to be made are complex, not least because local government has existed for a long time and the opportunities for building up capital or depleting it have been great. The judgement we make today must make allowance for this.

In fact, there is a real example of depreciation accounting being practised alongside payments in lieu of depreciation. This occurred in the old water authorities. When the water industry was reorganized, following the Water Act 1973, the local authority system of capital accounting was adopted throughout. Perpetuation of this system would have meant, as we can predict from the above reasoning, that when the nation's sewers finally collapsed, having been built in the last century, a huge financing requirement would have been forced upon the industry. The local authority system provides no capital for replacing assets; the capital must be reborrowed.

Now, on the face of it, the problem of obtaining the finance is no different from that faced by local authorities every day. However, if we look more deeply, we can see that this massive refinancing would be very inequitable. The reason is that probably for the last 50 years the sewers have been provided free: they have outlived any associated loans and so no charge has been made to the revenue accounts. On top of this, the replacement costs of sewers (indeed of any building and plant) have increased enormously.

In other words, in this case, we cannot assume that the position in 1974 represented inter-generational equity. The then current ratepayers had received substantial bequests from the ratepayers of 50 and 100 years previous. In the light of this, the addition of depreciation charges to water revenue accounts is justified. It could be argued that it came too late to correct the inequity completely, but at least it was a partial correction. The current situation could be interpreted this way: the additional depreciation is building up capital but not so that the sewers can be replaced without the need to borrow; rather, that the smaller future borrowing requirement will recompense future generations for the unwillingness of pre-1974 ratepayers to share the burden of the capital cost of sewers.

Whether local government would be allowed to go through the same process is difficult to say. It is likely that there would be significant opposition to the idea that local taxes should bear the burden of redeeming the old debt as well as building up new capital. There is no doubt that in the past this is where depreciation accounting has floundered, as an addition to the existing system: local taxes were judged to be incapable of bearing the additional burden.

In summary, substituting depreciation accounting for the existing method would make revenue accounts more relevant for cost comparisons but less reliable for financial control. Adding depreciation accounting to the existing system has, in the past, not been affordable.

Perhaps the future lies in the compromise of adopting the old management accounting adage: *different costs for different purposes*. In this, we might keep the existing loan redemptions for the tax calculations but substitute depreciation charges for cost comparisons and management information generally. As a matter of accounting technique, it is easy to see how this would work, though in practice the extra administrative work would not be insubstantial. This has been the broad approach adopted by a number of professional recommendations, through the 1980s. The latest one (of 1993) requires all fixed assets to be valued in the consolidated balance sheet at replacement cost, other than 'infrastructure' assets and 'community' assets, and vehicles, plant and equipment, which should be shown at historical cost. As for the impact on the revenue accounts, the Housing Revenue Account maintains the statutory loan charges system. And, in terms of setting local taxes, the statutory loan charges are the relevant charges. But in the revenue accounts of most of the other accounts (e.g. General Fund, County Fund, Central Support Services, Direct Service Organizations) a 'capital charge (or assets rent)' should be included for all fixed assets used in the provision of the relevant services. These charges should at least equal the sum of any provision for depreciation plus a 'capital financing charge'; this latter is determined by applying a specified notional rate of interest to the amount included in the balance sheet. Further, an element of depreciation must be included for all assets that are expected, at the time of acquisition or revaluation, to have a finite useful life unless it can be demonstrated that repairs and maintenance extend the asset's useful life in its existing use.

In terms of our discussion of business accounting earlier in this chapter, these provisions are a recognizable amalgam of elements that we identified: some revaluations, a charge for the cost of capital, depreciation charges. The significant difference (other than the fact that this accounting is to be used in parallel with the differing statutory framework) is that all fixed assets yield a charge in the revenue accounts, not just depreciable fixed assets. Hence the need to refer to the charge as either depreciation or an asset rent: the rent will be charged for the use of land, for example, where depreciation would not. The most important problem for theorists is whether politicians, officers, the government and others will accept two information systems. For while it is true that 'different costs for different purposes' is an accepted part of textbooks, it is not clear that the idea has been successfully communicated to non-accountants.

DISCUSSION TOPICS

1   What relevance does business accounting have for governmental organizations?

2   What is the effect of, and what are the issues involved in, charging profit and loss accounts with the cost of equity?

3   'It is recommended that the framework of accounting principles and conventions for resource accounting in departments should be based on UK Generally Accepted Accounting Practice, in particular the accounting and disclosure requirements of the Companies Act (1985) and accounting standards, supplemented where appropriate to accommodate the particular requirements of central government. This should ensure broad consistency with accounting practice in the rest of the public sector and the private sector' (Cm 2626, p. viii). Discuss.

4   'In the case of a municipal concern, it may have to bear the double burden of renewing its plant *and* replacing its capital. For example, if £1m is borrowed and spent on £1m worth of plant, at the end of 30 years when the plant is worn out they ought to have in hand £1m for replacing it and also to have repaid the £1m of debt. Frequently, however, they only perfectly achieve one of these objects, and the whole or part of the exhaustion of "subscribed" capital falls to be reborrowed . . . (therefore) . . . the borrowing capacity of a municipality is constantly being repaired, even if the municipality does not grow in size.' (Sir Josiah Stamp, 1935).
    Discuss this quotation and the implications for municipal financial reporting.

5   Should depreciation be charged in the accounts of local authorities?

CHAPTER 10

Financial reporting and performance measurement

This chapter is concerned with the published annual report and accounts. There has been a significant increase in the use of this medium by public sector organizations in recent years. Probably the most dramatic context is in government: formerly 'reporting' and 'accounting', while pervasive, typically did not focus on relatively small groups of civil servants; now, each Department and each Executive Agency produces an annual report and accounts. Included in these reports, and many others, is a profusion of performance measures.

We begin the chapter by introducing the essential parts of these annual reports and accounts, including their relationship to the statutory audit. We then discuss accounting uniformity as a core issue in comparing the accounts of different organizations. We then turn to the use of unit cost statistics to report on performance and finally to wider accountability issues.

ANNUAL REPORTS AND ACCOUNTS

Companies have long produced a single document called the annual report and accounts. It satisfies statutory and other requirements but also includes material at the discretion of management. Some financial statements are required by company law to be published (profit and loss account, balance sheet), some are required by accounting standards (cash flow statement, statement of total recognized gains and losses); together with their accompanying notes, these are known as the financial statements. They are audited (as part of the statutory audit) and the consequent audit report is published in the annual report and accounts and specifically refers, by page numbers, to the financial statements covered by the audit report.

In addition, the law requires the directors of the company to publish a report and prescribes many disclosures in it, including financial disclosures; the law does not require this directors' report to be audited but it does require the audit report, when information is included in the directors' report that is not consistent with the accounts, to state that fact.

The final element of the annual report and accounts is a statement from the chair of the company, which is at management's discretion in terms of form and content, and indeed in terms of whether one is published at all. Companies listed on the London Stock Exchange are required to produce an annual report and accounts but only a few details are prescribed. Listed companies do publish a statement from the chair; unlisted companies tend not to. There is no legal requirement, but there is a requirement of auditing standards for auditors to consider, in making their report on the accounts, whether there is any inconsistency between those accounts and any other information in the annual report and accounts, including information in the statement from the chair, and in certain cases to comment on any inconsistency.

Although the outlines of this model have been introduced into many public sector contexts, some of the details are different and more vague. For example, the 'report' element may be published separately from the 'accounts'; this is now quite common in local government. For companies, the directors' report tends to use 'boiler-plate' language (no doubt reflecting the statutory requirements) whereas the statement from the chair tends to read more like a public-relations piece, and the distinction between the two reports tends to be clearer. In the reports and accounts of Executive Agencies, for example, experience has not yet produced a clear separation: the audited accounts are separate but the rest of the information tends to be commingled.

This is not at all to suggest that the company model is the best. It is far from clear how readers use company reports and how significant the audited pages are in comparison with the unaudited. It is even less clear how the reports of public sector organizations are used. But the issue of publication of performance measures is complicated, perhaps severely complicated, by the form of annual reports and accounts. Are these measures a part of the financial statements? The answer is in practice usually negative, but since one thrust of the measures is to provide information in lieu of 'return on capital', the question becomes, should they be? Because if the measures are unaudited, how reliable can they be? Moreover, if the measures are judged by auditors not to be a part of the financial information, does this mean that auditors do not even review the measures for consistency with the accounts?

Notwithstanding the growth in publication of performance measures, we are still in the development stage and no doubt refinements will be introduced to address some of these issues as we gain experience with them. In addition to these questions, it is also important to observe how the measures are being used. Most striking, perhaps, is their link to performance-related pay and, more widely, the link between performance-related annual reports and accounts to other changes that are being made in the accountability of public sector organizations.

But before we address some of these issues, we need to rehearse longer-standing concerns of accountants in thinking about organizations' annual reports and accounts. One important example is their approach to comparability.

ACCOUNTING UNIFORMITY

In the developed countries of the world, the UK and the USA represent the 'flexible' view of financial reporting: accounting standards exist to narrow the areas of difference; they do not exist to eliminate them.

This is in marked contrast to Continental European countries and the old Eastern bloc. Those countries adopt 'uniform' accounting, the explicit goal of which is to eliminate differences in accounting practice.

We can characterize this polarization of views in the following way: *flexible accounting* is concerned with accounting in accordance with the facts; *uniform accounting* is concerned with accounting in accordance with the rules. On the face of it, it may seem that these two approaches can be made to coincide as long as the rules are drawn up to reflect the facts. In practice, however, they are contradictory, because the purpose of the rules is to produce a single solution to any accounting problem while economic reality, with which accounting purports to be concerned, is far too complex for unique solutions.

Take the example of calculating an annual depreciation charge for a vehicle. Under uniform accounting, the rules will specify, for example, that a given vehicle will be depreciated on a straight-line basis over seven years throughout a particular industry. This produces a uniform depreciation charge (or a standard depreciation charge) and is calculated according to the rules.

The problem is that plainly this depreciation charge cannot reflect the periodic benefits expected to accrue from using the vehicle. Different industries will use vehicles more or less efficiently. An industry which uses the vehicle on long haul will derive different periodic benefits from an industry which uses it over many, short journeys. Different loads will produce different vehicle lives and different repair bills. Different repair schedules will produce different repair costs and different vehicle lives. The economic reality of each organization is likely to be different.

The flexible approach is therefore to allow organizations to account for their own economic reality. Asset lives are not specified, they must only be fair. The depreciation method can be straight-line, reducing balance, sum of the digits, economic, or indeed any other, so long as the periodic charge is fair.

But the more immediate problem in this context is that a totally flexible approach would prevent comparison of the reports of different organizations and the reports of the same organization over time. Since little in accounting is absolute, some comparability is a necessary (though not sufficient) condition for financial reports.

The law has always been reluctant to prescribe the content of accounting, in all kinds of organizations. The impact of the European Economic Community (as it then was) was translated into Companies Acts that prescribe more than they used to, but in essence the problem has been left to the accounting profession and bodies such as the Accounting Standards Board to make the policies. The absence of a single standard-setter for the whole economy has contributed to the lack of uniformity in the financial statements of different organizations, as we saw in the last chapter. But equally importantly, standard-setting for businesses in the UK and the US has increasingly emphasized not uniformity in measurement or presentation but disclosure. Given a significant impetus by the Efficient Markets Hypothesis (and tests of it), an influential argument is that as long as the necessary information is disclosed the capital markets can be left to digest its meaning. Thus, whereas standard-setters may previously have been concerned to prescribe some accounting methods and to proscribe others, they are now more likely to prescribe disclosure of the effects of more than one method. The consummate example in the UK is FRS 3, *Reporting Financial Performance* (Accounting Standards Board, 1992). This made a number of significant changes to company accounting but the most fundamental one was to require disclosure of a new 'earnings per share' – using the 'bottom line', which is profit after all deductions. But FRS 3 does not forbid the publication of other measures of earnings per share: it requires only that these should be presented on a consistent basis over time and should be reconciled to the measure that it does require. In addition, the required measure should be at least as prominent in the financial statements as any discretionary measure and the reason for calculating more than the required one should be explained.

Moreover, the requirements relating to these additional measures have had important effects in practice. The Accounting Standards Board's argument in support of FRS 3 was not that its 'bottom line' measure of earnings per share is the correct measure but in fact the exact opposite: '(i)t is not possible to distil the performance of a complex organisation into a single measure. Undue significance, therefore, should not be placed on any such measure which may purport to achieve this aim' (para. 52). Thus the ASB is saying that much relevant information for measuring financial performance is now available 'above the line' and users can now calculate as many earnings per share figures as needed.

However, there was considerable irony in the response of investment managers and others in the capital markets: they wanted, and developed, an alternative measure that is closer to the old one and that is used to calculate price/earnings ratios. What this shows, among other things, is that even in the circumstance in which most is known about the use of financial reports there is still considerable disagreement about the approach that those financial reports should take.

When we translate the context from public companies to the public sector, the use of disclosure to solve reporting problems takes on a different hue. The capital markets are not investing equity and are much less concerned with the risk of default on the debt they invest in. Thus there is not the same incentive to scour the public sector's financial statements. The capital market may be hypothesized to be efficient in respect of the information that is provided by public sector organizations but there is little information that is relevant. Indeed, we would be more likely to look to politicians, electors, taxpayers and others to identify 'owners'. However, the conclusion is effectively the same: accounting information and the assumptions upon which it is based are not used in elections, for example, and while specific pieces of information may be of use to specific lobby groups, it is not necessarily in the interests of electorate as a whole for this information to be provided. Disclosure has, for the most part, been the 'solution' to the reporting 'problem', although it is significantly less clear in the public sector context just what that problem is.

Nevertheless, there has been one major attempt to produce accounting uniformity in the public sector. In 1955, the then Institute of Municipal Treasurers and Accountants (now CIPFA) produced *The Form of Published Accounts of Local Authorities*. This has been updated a number of times since then, but the philosophy remains the same. Government, particularly, sees the need to have standardized returns of what local authorities cost and, although the need has not resulted in the government taking over the policy-making role necessary to impose standardization, pressure has been felt by the profession to make recommendations. The publication of unit cost statistics has subsequently been based on these standard classifications of accounts. Indeed, the intractable problems involved in fully standardizing have been a recurring source of difficulty.

The current standard classification is broadly as follows (different services have different nuances):

1   *Services* – these are the main services, such as education, health, highways, etc.

2 *Divisions of service* – for example, education will be divided into primary, secondary, continuing education, etc.

3 *Subdivisions of service* – which provides a further breakdown of the division.

4 *Standard groupings* – for each division of service, these groupings represent the main areas of expenditure and income, e.g. employees, premises, transport, etc.

5 *Sub-groupings* – a subdivision of the above standard groupings.

6 *Detail heads* – a detailed analysis of the sub-groupings.

The document produces a revenue account with standard headings which it expects will be adopted by most divisions of service, although it recognizes that the detail heads adopted by a particular division will be different (detail heads are not shown):

Standard grouping	Sub-group
(1) Employees	Employee types
(2) Premises-related expenditure	Repairs, alterations and maintenance of buildings, fixed plant and grounds
	Energy costs
	Rents
	Rates
	Water services
	Fixtures and fittings
	Cleaning and domestic supplies
	Apportionment of expenses of operational buildings
	Premises insurance
	Contributions to premises-related provisions
(3) Transport-related expenditure	Direct transport costs
	Recharges
	Contract hire and operating leases
	Public transport
	Car allowances
	Transport insurance
(4) Supplies and services	Equipment, furniture and materials
	Catering
	Clothing, uniforms and laundry
	Printing, stationery and general office expenses
	Services
	Communications and computing
	Expenses
	Grants and subscriptions
	Miscellaneous expenses
	Contributions to provisions
(5) Third party payments	Independent units within the council (includes DSOs/in-house contractors)
	Other local authorities
	Health authorities
	Government departments

Standard grouping	Sub-group
	Voluntary associations
	Other establishments
	Private contractors
	Other agencies
(6) Transfer payments	(There are no sub-groups recommended)
(7) Support services	(There are no sub-groups recommended)
(8) Capital financing costs	Loans pool/consolidated advances and borrowing pool (CABP)
	Debt serviced by other authorities
	Contribution to capital provision (not Scotland)
	Finance leasing charges
	Direct revenue financing
	Debt management expenses
	Revenue appropriation adjustments (not Scotland)
(9) Income	Government grants
	Other grants, reimbursements and contributions
	Customer and client receipts
	Interest
	Recharges

The above form is essentially *objective*, in that it relates to the objects of local government, e.g. education, health, highways, etc. These objects are then dis-aggregated to produce an analysis over divisions of service. But then, for each division of service, a *subjective* analysis is provided, e.g. salaries, premises, etc. This analysis relates to the kind of expenditure incurred rather than the purpose for which it was incurred. It may be useful to provide a subjective analysis of expenditure for the whole of the local authority. This ignores the objects and would appear as:

Expenditure
    Salaries and wages
    Running expenses
    Capital financing costs
Income
    Government grants
    Other grants, reimbursements and contributions
    Sales
    Fees and charges
    Rents
    Interest
    Recharges

This could be analysed in more detail to include, for example, sub-groupings. It would be in addition to the objective classification and provide a broad analysis of expenditure which could be useful in making broad judgements, for example, about the percentage of total costs paid as salaries and wages. Similarly, it also explains how much is paid in capital financing costs by the authority as a whole.

These are only recommendations and may not necessarily be followed by all local authorities; but even if they are followed there are significant problems in using the costs accumulated from the accounts as a basis for comparing different authorities. As we saw in the previous two chapters, the statutory measurement focus and basis of local authority accounting does not yield economically meaningful measures of cost. Further, the new recommendations to use asset rents or depreciation charges have within them significant arbitrariness. This is exacerbated by the fact that different local authorities have different organizational structures, which means essentially that uniform accounting is being imposed on non-uniform organizations. Accountants can and do make allocations to adjust for these, but it is the allocations that are arbitrary. Moreover, the accounting profession does not have the power to force each local authority to produce comparable accounts and neither has the government appeared to want to take over the policy-making role to use its power to force comparability (Jones and Pendlebury, 1991). So, while this exercise in producing uniform accounts has yielded useful and influential information, it has not resolved the inherent tension between uniform accounting for comparability and flexible accounting to account for the underlying economic reality.

PERFORMANCE MEASUREMENT

Financial accounting techniques have traditionally been concerned with the stewardship function, narrowly defined. The financial reports provide a picture of the resources entrusted, how the resources were employed during the year, and in what form the resources are now held. The emphasis has always been on producing verifiable statements of income and expenditure, balance sheets and, latterly, cash flows. The position taken by the accounting profession is that the function of the accounts is to provide verifiable information: what users of that information choose to do with it is a matter for them.

In business organizations the increasing tendency has been to use the basic financial statements as a measure of performance. The income figure, particularly expressed as a ratio of net investment, has come to be the ultimate test of a company's success or failure. Indeed, the pervasive appeal of the term 'bottom line' is such that it is often used as the ultimate test of success in any aspect of society; in sport, how well the game is played is irrelevant, what matters is the final score – the bottom line is winning or losing.

It is not difficult to pinpoint this appeal. If a firm is operating in a good, competitive market then, notwithstanding the problems associated with accounting measurements, profit does give an indication of how well it produced goods: the market was willing to pay more for the finished goods than it cost the firm to produce them, if the firm made a profit.

In practice, however, many organizations produce and sell goods in markets which are not competitive. Even in the private sector there are many and various impediments to the free flow of goods and services: government subsidies, import controls, export incentives, tax inefficiencies, transaction costs, cartels, etc. In the pluralist economies of the UK and the USA unregulated markets are in the minority.

Taking account of this, and remembering that profit figures are produced by accountants who have an array of alternative treatments of the basic debits and credits, it is not surprising that expert financial analysts are not satisfied with a profit figure alone. Indeed, the profit figure that is required is not likely to be the one in the financial statements: that is forever a bygone. It is the profit in the next financial statement, and the one after, that matters. The past figure is useful as a predictor of the future ones.

But in order to predict the future, one past figure is not enough. A series is required. To make sense of the series, trends have to be identified. In complex businesses, these trends are not stable because they are made up of complex interactions of diverse circumstances. Firms do not produce one kind of product, they produce many kinds. A single profit figure is an aggregation of many, earned from completely different markets. The aggregation cannot be used sensibly as a predictor. Disaggregated data will not merely be by product but also by geographical area. They will also include vast quantities of physical as well as financial data about every aspect of the different markets. Stock market prices do not simply move every half-year when interim profit figures are announced.

Profit figures may be used in banner headlines; but for anyone with any expertise and any money to lose, it is the beginning of an analysis of performance, not an end.

As well as this, the trend over the past few years has been towards greater accountability from business in the form of information about matters other than profits and loss. Representative of this is *The Corporate Report*'s statement (p. 38):

> Business enterprises can survive only with the approval of the community in which they operate and they have an interest in revealing information which displays how differing interests are being balanced for the benefit of the whole community.
>
> Because neither business organizations nor the public regard the maximization of owners' profit as the only legitimate aim of business, distributable profit can no longer be regarded as the sole or premier indicator of performance. This would be so even if accountants were able to agree that 'profit' is one certain figure which can be measured with precision.

The report concludes that there is a need for the following additional statements to be published (p. 79):

1   a statement of value added;
2   an employment report;
3   a statement of money exchanges with government;
4   a statement of transactions in foreign currency;
5   a statement of future prospects;
6   a statement of corporate objectives.

However, these recommendations have yet to be taken up by the profession, and corporate reports in the business sector have largely remained concerned with fulfilling the statutory duties relating to reporting profit and loss.

This is true of nationalized industries too, although there have been exceptions. The statement on value added has been reported in some cases. Take, for example, an old annual report of the Post Office. Although produced outside of the audited financial statements, and therefore not audited, a value added statement was produced:

THE POST OFFICE

Group Value Added Statement for year ended 1 April 1987

		£m
TURNOVER		3,473.3
Less Bought-in materials and services		607.5
		2,865.8
Add Interest receivable		40.1
		2,905.9
Applied to:		
Employees and sub-postmasters		2,408.7
Providers of capital		
Interest payable	15.3	
Dividend	2.1	
		17.4
Central and local government		
Employer's social security contributions	170.0	
Corporation tax	21.8	
Rates (property taxes)	48.8	
Non-recoverable VAT	41.7	
Vehicle excise licences	4.5	
		286.8
The Post Office, for maintenance and expansion of assets		
Depreciation and other amounts written off		
tangible fixed assets	62.2	
Profit retained	130.8	
		193.0
		2,905.9

As *The Corporate Report* (1975, p. 49) says, value added statements of this kind offer an alternative view to the profit and loss account, showing the Post Office as 'a collective effort by capital, management and employees'; it also identifies the financial flows into government. The value added statement is now not published. One interpretation of this is that as the nationalized industries move closer to some form of privatization so their published financial information appears to become closer and closer to the commercial practice of publishing only that which is required, and no more.

Performance measurement in the private sector is almost wholly limited to financial measures, under the tacit assumption that competitive markets are the best judge of the relative value of the goods and services provided. How well a company performs is judged by customers at the point of sale, not by reading financial reports. This is not to say that financial reports should be restricted to financial measures, of course, only that in practice they are.

The use of internal markets and the purchaser/provider split lead, among other things, to financial measures having more to say about a public sector organization's performance than would be the case without them. In the terms of cost/volume/profit analysis, a revenue line is being introduced. This may not necessarily produce better organizations but it undoubtedly means that accounting numbers make a greater contribution to their management. It is well recognized that these internal markets are not by definition as competitive as arm's-length markets and, therefore, that there is an even stronger case than in the private sector for requiring non-financial measures of performance to supplement the financial statements. Ultimately, however, what makes government different is that it is financed by taxation. The balances on their operating statements cannot be called profits or losses, rather they are called surpluses or deficits. Financial accounting reverts to what it traditionally was for businesses: producing verifiable statements of the organization's stewardship.

There is one significant exception to this and that is the use of budgetary accounting. This practice continuously compares budgeted amounts with actuals and as such is providing some measure of performance against a predetermined standard. When employed in the financial reports it provides external users with some measure of performance. This will only be as good as the standards employed and the quality of the audit in detecting whether wasteful expenditure was incurred simply in order to meet budgets. Nonetheless, it does provide some measure.

The basic problem for governments, even with budgetary accounting, is that there is no measure of output in the stewardship accounts: there is no sense in which taxation measures the organization's output.

In recent years, the response to the lack of satisfactory measures of output has been to provide more and more measures, in the belief that more information is better than less and that research will provide better measures. Research has not yet resolved the substantial difficulties involved. The most substantial piece of work was undertaken by the Governmental Accounting Standards Board, resulting initially in a series of reports on particular services (e.g. police, fire, road maintenance, hospitals, mass transport, education) and an overview of these (GASB, 1990). Subsequently, the Board has issued Concepts Statement No. 2, *Service Efforts and Accomplishments Reporting* (1994).

It cannot be expected that this statement will solve the difficulties involved in performance measurement in government and how the resulting measures should be reported. But it does state that the Board believes such measures would represent a significant improvement in annual reports and accounts although further research is needed:

- to determine whether SEA measures that meet the (qualitative) characteristics (in the Statement) can be developed for governmental services; and
- to explore how externally reported SEA information is used and the effects its use has on the quality, effectiveness, and efficiency of the services being reported on.

In other words, notwithstanding the extensive generation and reporting of these measures, in the opinion of the GASB we do not know which measures to report and how any measures that are reported are used, by management or anyone else. Indeed, an important contribution that the Concepts Statement makes is to spell out the details of just how difficult this area is.

Having said that, there is nothing new in the provision of performance measures by governments. The most pervasive examples have always been unit cost statistics and it is to these that we now turn.

Unit cost statistics

In our discussion in Chapter 1 about economy, efficiency and effectiveness, the technical problem was how we can meaningfully compare inputs and outputs to produce a measure of efficiency when outputs are not automatically valued by the market price. A practical solution to this problem has been to compare the monetary inputs (costs) with non-monetary outputs. These can be unit cost statistics which provide some, albeit limited, information about performance. They provide broad indicators of deviant performance which pinpoint areas for more detailed research. This is the sense in which they do little more than 'raise red flags'. Unfortunately, this also means that they are of value only to those users who have the expertise and the authority to make more detailed investigations. In the case of the performance of local authorities, the government fulfils both these requirements. It is perhaps for this reason that a Code of Practice was issued by the Secretary of State for the Environment in 1981 which requires that authorities produce a minimum number of specified unit cost statistics. Examples are:

For each service:
1   Net cost per 1,000 population
2   Manpower per 1,000 population
Supplemented by:
Primary education
1   Pupil/teacher ratio
2   Cost per pupil
Secondary education
1   Pupil/teacher ratio
2   Cost per pupil
Highways
1   Maintenance cost per kilometre: principal roads
2   Maintenance cost per kilometre: non-principal roads
Housing
1   Management and maintenance cost per dwelling
2   Construction cost per dwelling completed

These statistics can be used by non-expert readers of accounts as a basis for asking questions of councils, but in themselves provide little clue as to performance. This has not discouraged the increasingly wide dissemination of these kinds of statistics. Given additional impetus by 'Citizen's Charter' developments, the Audit Commission (1992) has determined a set of indicators against which each local authority (in England and Wales) has to measure its performance and publish the results in a local newspaper. There are 225 of these (though they do not apply to every authority) and they include 'net expenditure per head of population' for each of the major services and indeed for some 'subjective headings' such as 'capital charges', 'interest receipts' and 'changes in reserves and balances'. Given the form of publication, the intention must presumably be for readers of newspapers to derive benefit from them. Even with the annual report and accounts, it is hard to see what this benefit will be. The Audit Commission has stated that it will produce a national report covering all local authorities and perhaps this will provide the necessary supporting analyses.

Because of the fact that unit costs only raise red flags, the onus is on any analyst who is comparing statistics between authorities to explore all the possible explanations for differences before coming to conclusions. Finding unit costs which support preconceived notions is easy but ultimately useless.

Hansen (1977) is as good an example as any of a sensitive analysis of unit cost statistics. The paper is an analysis of refuse collection statistics, comparing the local governments of Rochester, Buffalo, and Syracuse in New York State. The basic unit costs were as follows:

	Gross cost per head of population (US$)
Rochester	14.74
Buffalo	9.58
Syracuse	6.73

For local governments which were judged broadly comparable, these statistics show considerable variation and suggest that Rochester was performing badly. The analyst was prompted to try to explain why these differences occurred. She discovered:

1   In Rochester and Buffalo, although the loads per vehicle were approximately the same, productivity in Buffalo was higher than in Rochester. This was measured as tons collected per man-day (Buffalo 2.55; Rochester 1.88).
2   In Syracuse, tons collected per man-day were 3.07. There were two reasons offered for this. First, larger vehicles were used so the tons per load figure was higher. Second, Syracuse operated an incentive system whereby crews which finished early could not go home until all the crews had finished; consequently, those which finished early had an incentive to help the others.
3   Crews in Buffalo and Syracuse were made up of one driver and two labourers. In Rochester, it was one driver and three labourers.

The differences were beginning to be explained, although these statistics still do not say why Rochester was so out of line. Much of the answer lies in the fact that, while Buffalo and Syracuse had curbside pick-up of refuse, in Rochester they picked up from backyards. And although the analyst questioned whether the additional labour in Rochester was completely justified by this, there is no doubt that this fact is at the heart of the differences in unit costs.

What this example shows is that any stark conclusion on the basis of one unit cost statistic that a given local authority is inefficient is not a national conclusion. The statistic does indeed 'raise a red flag' but detailed investigation reveals that there are good explanations. Moreover, the detailed unit cost and physical statistics do not in themselves measure whether the curbside pick-up is more efficient; only that it costs less. The output comparisons have to take into account social, economic and political considerations: it may just be that in Rochester the residents prefer not to have to drag their refuse up the garden path, at any price. In accounting, we simply do not know enough to be able to measure this.

Now we can return to the unit cost statistics provided by local authorities under the Direction of the Audit Commission (1992). One such requirement is to publish the 'net expenditure per secondary school pupil under 16 in LEA maintained schools', for the current and previous years. Clearly, the immediate use is for comparing performance of the authority over time. But why might these statistics change? Because the number of pupils, the age-distribution of pupils, the quality of pupils, the number of teachers, the quality of teachers, and so on, and so on, have changed. Presumably also there is also some intention for this statistic to be compared with that of other secondary schools: LEA schools in other authorities, grant-maintained schools, independent schools. And why might these statistics be different from each other? It may be that different accounting treatments lead to different ways of calculating cost. Even if the costs were entirely comparable, what kinds of things would we want to know before we could judge the performance of secondary education? Cost per pupil may be low because class sizes are high. Cost per pupil may be the same, although one authority spends much more on teachers and less on books and equipment. Cost per pupil may be high because resources are being wasted. Cost per pupil may be low because the pupils are well-educated when they come to the school. Cost per pupil may be high because money is deliberately being diverted from other uses to make a priority of secondary school education.

The necessary next step in assessing performance on the basis of unit cost statistics such as these is to ask the relevant organization why.

Wider accountability issues

Once we move away from the traditional accounting statements and unit cost statistics, the possibilities are unbounded. There is no 'best professional practice'. Guidance has been provided by *The Corporate Report*, as we noted earlier, on the kind of additional statements that might be produced. But since the decision on which to publish, and in what form, is the responsibility of the management, there is a danger that only that which shows the organization in the best light will be published. Since the management is accountable and is producing the information, it would be rather surprising if it were otherwise.

Of course, the same applies with traditional financial reporting. But in this case, there is a body of professional practice which aims to reduce the subjectivity involved and the basic information used is systematically produced, with a minimum possibility for editing: come what may an operating statement, a balance sheet and a cash flow statement will be published. Moreover, the financial accounts are audited.

It is the greatest weakness of this wider view of accounting that there is no system for producing the data, which is verifiable in the way that double-entry bookkeeping is. Probably because of this, there are no professional guidelines and there is no requirement for audit.

Nevertheless, the 1980s have witnessed ever-increasing use of performance indicators, some of which are unit cost statistics but many of which are output measures, albeit usually low-level output measures. Batteries of these indicators are being produced for the NHS, government departments, universities, nationalized industries and local authorities, among others.

British Rail was a notable example for taking an early lead in publishing performance indicators. In the 1990/91 accounts, the indicators are clearly not part of the audited financial statements and have not been audited.

Because BR had no direct competitor in the UK, some performance indicators were compared with the average of 14 European railways:

	BR 1989/90	Average 14 European 1989/90
Train kilometres (loaded and empty) per member of staff employed	3,422	2,301
Average train loading (passenger km, divided by passenger train km, loaded and empty)	92	144
Average train loading (freight tonnes km, divided by freight train km, loaded and empty)	217	311
Support from public funds as proportion of gross domestic product (%)	0.12	0.70

Many more indicators were provided for BR alone.

Perhaps two of the most important statistics for railway passengers relate to the lateness and cancellation of trains. These were reported in a number of ways:

Percentage of trains arriving within 5 minutes of booked time

	1988/89	1989/90	1990/91
InterCity	87	84	85
Network South East	92	90	90
Regional	90	90	90

Percentage of trains cancelled

	1988/89	1989/90	1990/91
InterCity	1.0	2.0	2.2
Network South East	1.4	4.0	2.1
Regional	1.2	3.6	2.7

In addition, within the Annual Report section, some actual performance indicators were compared with quantified objectives. In the 1986/87 accounts:

Percentage of trains arriving	Objective		Performance	
within 5 minutes of right time	1985/86	82%	1985/86	73%
InterCity	1986/87	87%	1986/87	77%

In the 1990/91 accounts, there is a change:

Percentage of trains arriving	Objective		Performance	
within 10 minutes of right time	1989/90	90%	1989/90	84.2%
InterCity	1990/91	90%	1990/91	85%

Setting aside the important caveat about the reliability of these numbers in the absence of an audit, what conclusions can we draw about performance indicators such as these? The *issues* being reported we can fairly assume are relevant, to the customers and to taxpayers. Whether the performance indicators relating to these issues are relevant is more difficult. At such a high level of aggregation, for an annual period, and reported some months after the financial year, it is not easy to see how most customers would change their behaviour because of them. Taxpayers, at least through the political process, might find such hard data useful, as broad rules of thumb to confirm subjective perceptions about performance. If this were true then the fact of having to report the indicators may encourage managers to achieve their targets. In the context of punctuality of trains, it may also encourage the targets to be adjusted. On the other hand, criticism of railways tends not to emanate from statistics but from personal experience. The distinction is important because performance indicators may support personal experience but they may also pre-empt criticisms based on personal experience: the aggregate statistics may look reasonable enough but these might hide specific areas of ineffectiveness. Nor are the reporting issues changed now that performance against some targets triggers discounts on season tickets, for example. One effect might be to short-circuit, as it were, the annual report and accounts to provide season ticket-holders with an additional element to all the other factors that enter into the decision to renew: a discount on the price that otherwise would have had to be paid had performance reached the target. This might suggest that the season ticket-holder would be interested in verifying the trigger performance measures. But the essential difficulty remains the same: however important the chosen method is to the traveller, it cannot possibly take the place of personal experience.

Returning to the question of *reliability* of numbers such as these in the absence of audit, the Post Office addresses this question in its Report and Accounts. Alongside its performance measures ('quality of service' of the Royal Mail letter service) is the following (for 1993/94):

Report of the Post Office Auditors on Quality of Service
We have reviewed the information set out on pages . . . detailing the quality of the first and second class letter service for 1993/94. The scope of our work was designed to ensure that the information on deliveries was obtained in accordance with the stated methodology and sampling programme set out . . . and that the results were correctly calculated and presented.

In our opinion, the quality of service measurements of the first and second class letter service for 1993/94 have been correctly calculated and presented from information obtained in accordance with the stated methodology and sampling programme.

This obviously makes explicit what is generally true of performance indicators: that they are not usually generated from a systematic record (and when they are, the system is not as reliable as a bookkeeping system can be). Consequently, this is not an 'audit report' as Auditing Standards define one, but is instead an 'accountant's report'. What the report does not do is to comment on the appropriateness of the sampling methodology for producing these kinds of performance measures. But it does add some reliability to them.

There are now many more available examples of reports and accounts that include performance measures. As we noted earlier, the Audit Commission (1992) has determined a set of 225 indicators to be used by local authorities in England and Wales, most of which are non-financial measures. Equally, the annual reports of the Departments and Executive Agencies of government are strewn with them. For example, *Next Steps Review 1994* (Cm 2750) surveys 92 entities and reports that in the aggregate they published 745 targets and the performance against each: these targets cover the whole range of measures of economy, efficiency and effectiveness. One of the Executive Agencies included is the Central Office of

Information. This agency is at the heart of government and is one of the (then twelve) agencies operating as trading funds. Its primary function is to provide publicity services for departments and agencies but it may also work for other public sector clients 'where this will result in the more efficient use of its resources'.

Cm 2750 gives an overview of the Central Office of Information but it is to the report and accounts that we need to turn to find more details. This shows that the audit report (which happens to be by the Comptroller and Auditor General) makes no reference to the performance measures: those measures are reported in the narrative part preceding the financial statements. There are five 'key targets' reported:

1   break even in current cost terms;
2   1 per cent (2 per cent subsequently) reduction in unit cost of output in real terms, while maintaining suitable levels of quality;
3   to equal or better the proportion of work delivered in accordance with client specification during 1993/94;
4   to equal or better the proportion of work delivered on time during 1993/94;
5   to achieve an average score of 7.7 out of 10 for the new COI Customer Satisfaction Index.

The first of these could be misleading: according to the financial statements, it does not mean that current cost accounting is used but rather that historical cost is used, modified by revaluations of fixed assets. Notwithstanding, this measure is obviously a good example of how return on capital generated from an internal market is being used by the government to control parts of government. What it means to an external user of this information is hard to say.

But it is the second target that provides the most difficulty. Nowhere in the report and accounts (or in Cm 2750) does it explain, or refer elsewhere to an explanation of, what this means. What can the 'output' refer to when the report states that a group of civil servants providing 'publicity services' have reduced its unit cost in real terms, while maintaining suitable levels of quality? Whatever it means, the report also states that it 'is used to determine whether or not a bonus is payable under COI's group bonus scheme'.

For the last three targets, the primary meaning is clearly in terms of performance as perceived by the buyers in the internal market. All five targets, then, crucially depend on the integrity of this market and on the integrity of those setting the targets (ultimately, the Treasury). As far as one can see from the report, they have not been audited or 'reported on' by accountants. They surely can have no meaning for a taxpayer trying to hold the COI to account.

Summarizing the discussion in this chapter, for all that we might say about the relevance of performance indicators in financial reporting, a fundamental and seemingly intractable problem remains: performance cannot be judged in terms of output alone; economy, efficiency and effectiveness must be judged together. No doubt any organization could improve its performance indicators given unlimited inputs. What is important is the relationship between inputs and outputs. On this, financial reporting practices are silent. This is not a criticism of the reporting organizations because it simply reflects our ignorance of how to measure the causal relationships.

Performance measures were not invented in the 1980s. We have always measured output. Intermediate measures of output have often been used as surrogates for ultimate output: the use of marking in examinations has dominated education for over 150 years. What happened during the 1980s was that we measured more things, more systematically, and published the measurements to an extent not seen before. It could also be argued that we did so despite any better understanding of the essential problem: how do we establish causal relationships between inputs, low-level outputs and ultimate outputs, reliably?

The final point to make is that having weighed the relevance and reliability of information, we then judge whether the benefits of accounting and reporting outweigh the costs. The information system used to collate these statistics is presumably extensive and costly. Whether these costs are worth bearing is another question that must be asked – though, in truth, it is probably unanswerable.

DISCUSSION TOPICS	1 Choose two or more reports and accounts of comparable public sector organizations and evaluate the extent to which useful and reliable comparisons of performance can and cannot be made.
	2 Using the same reports and accounts identify the ways adopted of reflecting wider accountability issues. How could accountability be usefully and reliably increased?

PART 3

Auditing

CHAPTER 11

Institutional and legal environment of auditing

Many auditing techniques are common to the public and private sectors. However, the institutions which administer and execute public sector audits are different; this is mainly because of the effect of specific statutes. This different institutional and legal background has contributed to public sector auditing having different procedures, different responsibilities and a wider role.

THE NATURE OF EXTERNAL AUDIT

The Auditing Practices Board of CCAB Ltd (which is made up of the councils of the Institute of Chartered Accountants in England and Wales, the Institute of Chartered Accountants of Scotland, the Institute of Chartered Accountants of Ireland, the Chartered Association of Certified Accountants, the Chartered Institute of Public Finance and Accountancy, and the Chartered Institute of Management Accountants) has widened the definition of audit. Its predecessor body, the Auditing Practices Committee, defined audit in the traditionally narrow sense as 'the independent examination of, and expression of an opinion on, financial statements' (Explanatory Foreword, APC, 1980). The APB now states (1993, p. 6) that:

> as well as financial statements, audit and related service engagements may involve other financial information, or non-financial information, such as:
> * the adequacy of internal control systems;
> * compliance with statutory, regulatory or contractual requirements;
> * economy, efficiency and effectiveness in the use of resources ('value for money auditing'); and
> * environmental practices.

This wider definition reflects a number of influences, including those of auditing standards in the US and of the International Auditing Practices Committee, but it also reflects the changes of the last two decades in the way that auditing is defined in the public sector; which is to say that, as with accounting, auditing in the private and public sectors have been brought more closely together, both in the way that we think about auditing and the way in which auditing is practised.

Nevertheless, there are important differences between the two contexts, usually as a result of specific legal requirements in the public sector. As the APB (SAS 120, 1995, para. 20) states:

> the responsibilities of auditors of entities in the public sector as regards the law and regulations are similar to those of auditors of limited companies and other entities in the private

sector . . . However, in some ways the responsibilities of auditors of entities in the public sector go beyond those in the private sector by virtue of statutory or other prescribed duties and obligations.

To be more specific about this extent to which public sector audit usually goes beyond the statutory audit of limited companies, we can turn to the definition of the function of governmental audit found in a Green Paper on *The Role of the Comptroller and Auditor General* (Cmnd 7845). This, with a minor modification, states that the C. and A.G.'s work covers:

Financial and Regularity Audit
(a) A financial audit to ensure that systems of accounting and financial control are efficient and operating properly and that financial transactions have been correctly authorized and accounted for.
(b) A regularity audit which verifies that expenditure has been incurred on approved services and in accordance with statutory and other regulations and authorities governing them (sometimes called the 'Compliance Audit').

Economy and Efficiency Audit
(c) An examination of economy and efficiency, to bring to light examples of wasteful, extravagant or unrewarding expenditure, failure to maximize receipts or financial arrangements detrimental to the Exchequer, and weaknesses leading to them.

Effectiveness Audit
(d) An examination to assess whether programmes or projects undertaken to meet established policy goals or objectives have met these aims.

These definitions were themselves heavily influenced by the seminal work on auditing standards in government, *Standards for Audit of Governmental Organizations, Programs, Activities and Functions*, issued by the US General Accounting Office in 1972 (and revised in 1981, 1988 and 1994). Known as the Yellow Book, it has influenced government auditing around the world. Its revisions have amounted to some significant changes, not least because of the negotiations with the American Institute of Certified Public Accountants, whose members are also involved in government audits. Nevertheless, its idea that public sector auditing is wider than auditing of companies has persisted: the US phrase for this is 'expanded scope audit'; in Canada, the term is 'comprehensive auditing'.

We can see now that the typical sense in which public sector audit is wider than the statutory audit of a company is that the Regularity Audit, the Economy and Efficiency Audit, and the Effectiveness Audit are clearly requirements over and above the attestation of financial statements. In historical perspective, the regularity audit has long been at the heart of government audit; how long there has been economy, efficiency and effectiveness auditing is more controversial but it is clear that, in terms of definition and pervasiveness, the Yellow Book was indeed seminal.

But it is important not to conclude from this that the statutory audit of a PLC is only concerned with financial statements. Many of the methods adopted will include testing, and relying on systems of internal control. Many will include consideration of economy and efficiency. This is so, not least because the efficiency of a PLC's operation can affect its financial statements: stores which allow inventory to deteriorate unnoticed will not only lose the company money, they will overstate the stock valuation in the balance sheet. Equally importantly, it would be wasteful to industry as a whole if questions of economy and efficiency were not identified in the course of audit work. In general, it is fair to say that the legally sensitive nature of the statutory audit has tended to encourage the auditing profession to deflate shareholders' expectations of audit. In practice, the audit is far more wide-ranging than official definitions suggest.

Nevertheless, quite apart from making the wider role more explicit, the comprehensive audit has different implications. For example, the effectiveness audit by its nature introduces political issues. Policy goals and objectives are set by legislative bodies, made up of politicians. These goals never are (never can be) so explicit as to exclude all subjectivity in interpreting performance against them. The more measurable and specific they become, the less realistic they become in terms of the legislature's intentions. An analogy can be drawn with the judiciary, which is often involved in 'interpreting' Acts of Parliament in terms of Parliament's intention. Sometimes these interpretations are controversial, so much so that laws have to be passed 'to clarify' the original intention. Interpretations of statute are not unfamiliar to commercial auditors; but they are unfamiliar when they involve overtly political questions.

The necessary condition of audit independence has a different flavour in government. It is more concerned with independence from the executive and, in the case of central government, this introduces significant and quite distinct problems. The most significant one is how anyone in society today can be independent of the executive, given the power that it wields.

The comprehensive audit has been recognized relatively recently. Traditionally, governmental audit has been concerned with the financial and regularity audit. The demand for more public accountability in the 1970s, along with the demand for real reductions in public sector spending in the UK and the USA, has included demands for greater 'value for money' from government. The supreme audit institutions of both countries, as well as of the profession, have responded with a greater application of and greater publicity about economy, efficiency and effectiveness auditing.

THE NATURE OF INTERNAL AUDIT

Internal audit is a large and significant part of the financial control of many organizations. In central government as well as in the National Health Service there are many internal audit sections; in local government all authorities are required by law to have internal audit departments.

The Auditing Practices Committee (*Guidance for Internal Auditors*, 1990) defined internal audit as follows:

> An independent appraisal function established by the management of an organization for the review of the internal control system as a service to the organization. It objectively examines, evaluates and reports on the adequacy of internal control as a contribution to the proper, economic, efficient and effective use of resources.

There are two important aspects of this definition, in contrast to external audit. First, as essential as *independence* is to both, in the context of internal audit it is bound to have a different emphasis because internal auditors are officials of the audited organization. The *Guidance* concentrates on the organizational status of internal audit and the objectivity of internal auditors in achieving the requisite independence. On the former, it states that internal audit should be involved in the determination of its own priorities, in consultation with management, and the head of internal audit should accordingly have direct access, and freedom to report to all senior management. The objectivity of the internal auditor is seen in terms of each auditor having an objective attitude of mind and being able to exercise judgement, express opinions and present recommendations with impartiality. The second important difference between this definition of internal audit and that of external audit is the concentration on reviewing the internal control system. The main objectives of the internal control system are given as:

1   to ensure adherence to management policies and directives in order to achieve the organization's objectives;
2   to safeguard assets;
3   to secure the relevance, reliability and integrity of information, so ensuring as far as possible the completeness and accuracy of records;
4   to ensure compliance with statutory requirements.

It is interesting that the Auditing Practices Board (SAS 500), while it has re-iterated some of the essence of this definition, has dropped the word 'independence': it goes on to state that 'irrespective of the degree of internal audit's autonomy and objectivity it cannot achieve the same degree of independence required of external auditors when expressing an opinion on the financial statements'. As is always the case in the public sector, the government also has a say. For example, government departments must look to the *Government Internal Audit Manual* (HM Treasury, 1988). In fact, the manual's version is essentially the same as the APC's. Internal audit is defined as an 'independent appraisal within a department which operates as a service to management by measuring and evaluating the effectiveness of the internal control system' (para. A.1). In this context, 'management' means the Accounting Officer. Similarly, the notion of independence is stressed and is seen as 'essentially an attitude of mind characterized by integrity and an objective approach to work' (para. B.2.1).

All of the above gives an impression of being uncontroversial, as official standards tend to do, but the practice of internal audit is fraught with difficulties. Historically, the notion of a 'professional' was of a person who was not an employee of the organization but in 'public practice' and in some sense, therefore, perceived to be able to offer impartial advice. The 'accounting profession' has over the years widened to the point where it is not only commonplace but it is expected that 'professional accountants' will be employed by industry, government, local government, health authorities, etc. The dual responsibilities, to the employer and to the profession, remain problematic; the professional response has been to offer on-line access to ethical guidance.

Just because of the nature of the work that internal auditors do on a day-to-day basis, their dual responsibilities provide more difficulty than most. No doubt this is partly why the official definitions of internal audit stress that, while having an independence of mind, internal auditors report to management: 'whistle-blowing' must be internal 'whistle-blowing'. But particularly in a public sector context, where appeals to the public interest could be assumed to be more common, profound questions remain which cannot be resolved by terse definitions.

We can now turn to the specific institutional and legal environment of external auditing in central government, local government, the National Health Service, and other public bodies.

THE GOVERNMENT

The auditor of government is a unique institution. It is the oldest aspect of the auditing profession. The office has substantial authority with a tradition quite apart from the statutory audit of a PLC. If there is one factor which has determined the nature of the office it is that, in theory, it is auditing the executive on behalf of the legislature. He must therefore be independent of the executive and as an officer of the House of Commons is strictly only answerable to the House. The principal Acts of Parliament which set down the audit requirements of central government are the Exchequer and Audit Departments Acts 1866 and 1921 and the National Audit Act 1983.

Section 1(1) of the 1921 Act requires that:

> Every appropriation account (of government) shall be examined by the Comptroller and Auditor General on behalf of the House of Commons.

The Appropriation Accounts are concerned with monies voted by Parliament; but although they cover a vast area they do not contain all public monies. For example, although the central government proportion of the finance of local government is within the appropriation accounts, the locally financed proportion is outside.

Under section 3 of the 1921 Act (amended by the 1983 Act), the C. and A.G. can also be required to audit certain accounts by direction from the Treasury; but these are relatively few and any direction must be approved by the House of Commons. There are also a large number of bodies' accounts which the C. and A.G. audits by agreement with the body and the government department concerned.

The C. and A.G.'s salary is a charge on the Consolidated Fund (which means it does not have to be voted annually by Parliament) and the holder of the office is, *ex officio*, an officer of the House of Commons. Before the 1983 Act, the C. and A.G. was head of the Exchequer and Audit Department which was made up of around 600 civil servants. This department has now been superseded by the National Audit Office and the new staff are not civil servants. There is no statutory prescription about the qualifications of the C. and A.G. and his staff. For example, they do not have to be qualified accountants; indeed, the majority are not, although the proportion that are has significantly increased.

Statutorily, the power of the C. and A.G. resides in his responsibility to audit public accounts on behalf of the House of Commons. In practice, it has been suggested that the C. and A.G. also has a close and effective working relationship with the Public Accounts Committee; this is the committee of the House of Commons responsible for examining those public accounts it sees fit to examine, and has the power to send for persons, papers and records. This relationship takes the form of the Public Accounts Committee basing its investigations on the reports submitted by the C. and A.G.

The 1983 Act established a Public Accounts Commission. Made up of the Chairman of the Public Accounts Committee, the Leader of the House of Commons and seven other members of the House (who must not be ministers), its purpose is to oversee the National Audit Office, in approving the annual budget and appointing the auditor for the Office's own accounts.

Section 1(1) of the 1921 Act defines the role of the C. and A.G. as follows:

> The C. and A.G. shall satisfy himself that the money expended has been applied to the purpose or purposes for which the grants made by Parliament were intended to provide and that the expenditure conforms to the authority which governs it.

And s. 1(2) says:

> The C. and A.G., after satisfying himself that the vouchers have been examined and certified as correct by the accounting department, may, in his discretion and having regard to the character of the departmental examination, in any particular case admit the sum so certified without further evidence of payment in support of the charges to which they relate . . .

These subsections have been interpreted by the Public Accounts Committee (1980, vol. 1, pp. x–xi) to mean that the statutory audit consists of:

1 *Financial audit* – the C. and A.G. satisfying himself as to the accuracy of the appropriation accounts (s. 1(2));
2 *Regularity audit* – the C. and A.G. satisfying himself that money spent has the proper authority (s. 1(1)).

Before the 1983 Act, it had been suggested that these statutory audits were supplemented by economy, efficiency and effectiveness audits. Part II of the 1983 Act has now included specific provision for these audits, calling them economy, efficiency and effectiveness *examinations*. They are not mandatory (s. 6(1)) and the Act stresses that they do not give any entitlement 'to question the merits of the policy objectives of any department' (s. 6(2)).

The audit certificate which is attached to the majority of the Appropriation Accounts says:

> I have audited the financial statements on pages xx to xx which have been prepared in accordance with the requirements of Government Accounting and other Treasury directions.

Respective Responsibilities of the Accounting Officer and Auditors
As described on page x the Accounting Officer is responsible for the preparation of financial statements. It is my responsibility to form an independent opinion, based on my audit, on those financial statements and to report my opinion to you.

Basis of Opinion
I certify that I have examined the financial statements referred to above in accordance with the Exchequer and Audit Departments Acts 1866 and 1921 and the National Audit Office auditing standards, which include relevant Auditing Standards issued by the Auditing Practices Board. An audit includes examination, on a test basis, of evidence relating to the amounts and disclosures in the financial statements. It also includes an assessment of the judgements made by the Accounting Officer in the preparation of the financial statements.

I planned and performed my audit so as to obtain all the information and explanations which I considered necessary in order to provide me with sufficient evidence to give reasonable assurance that the financial statements are free from material misstatement, whether caused by fraud or other irregularity or error. In forming my opinion I also evaluated the overall adequacy of the presentation of information in the financial statements.

Opinion

In my opinion the sums expended have been applied for the purposes authorised by Parliament and the account properly presents the expenditure and receipts of Class xx, Vote x for the year ended 31 March 19x7.

The content of this report has been significantly expanded in recent years, reflecting the longer-form audit report required by the Auditing Practices Board. There is no audit certificate relating to the economy, efficiency and effectiveness examinations; s. 9 says that the C. and A.G. may report to the House of Commons on the results of any examination.

In addition to the Appropriation Accounts, there are many statutory bodies that have responsibilities to produce accounts, to have them audited by the C. and A.G. and to present the result to Parliament. In some cases, the audit certificate will certify that the accounts 'properly present'. But in others, the accounts adopt, at a minimum, best commercial practice, that is, they show a true and fair view. Take, for example, the Welsh Development Agency's accounts for 1993/94. The audit certificate says:

I have audited the financial statements on pages xx to xx which have been prepared under the historical cost convention as modified by the revaluation of certain fixed assets and the accounting policies set out on page xx.

Respective Responsibilities of the Agency, the Chief Executive and Auditors

As described on page x the Agency and the chief executive are responsible for the preparation of financial statements. It is my responsibility to form an independent opinion, based on my audit, on those financial statements and to report my opinion to you.

Basis of Opinion

I certify that I have examined the financial statements referred to above in accordance with the Welsh Development Agency Act 1975 and the National Audit Office auditing standards, which include relevant Auditing Standards issued by the Auditing Practices Board. An audit includes examination, on a test basis, of evidence relating to the amounts and disclosures in the financial statements. It also includes an assessment of the judgements made by the Agency and the Chief Executive in the preparation of the financial statements, and of whether the accounting policies are appropriate to the body's circumstances, consistently applied and adequately disclosed.

I planned and performed my audit so as to obtain all the information and explanations which I considered necessary in order to provide me with sufficient evidence to give reasonable assurance that the financial statements are free from material misstatement, whether caused by fraud or other irregularity or error. In forming my opinion I also evaluated the overall adequacy of the presentation of information in the financial statements.

Opinion

In my opinion, the financial statements give a true and fair view of the state of affairs of the Welsh Development Agency and the Group at 31 March 1994 and of its surplus, net cost of grant administration, total recognised gains and losses and cash flows of the Group for the year then ended and have been properly prepared in accordance with the Welsh Development Agency Act 1975 and with the determination made thereunder by the Secretary of State for Wales.

I have no observations to make on these financial statements

In 1987, the National Audit Office introduced its own auditing standards. There are two. The first is called an *Operational Standard* and has five requirements:

1 The auditor should adequately plan, control and record his work.
2 The auditor should obtain the relevant and reliable audit evidence sufficient to enable him to draw reasonable conclusions therefrom.
3 The auditor should ascertain the audited body's system of recording and processing transactions and assess its adequacy as a basis for the preparation of financial statements.
4 If the auditor wishes to place reliance on any internal controls, he should ascertain and evaluate those controls and perform compliance tests on their operation.
5 The auditor should carry out such a review of the financial statements as is sufficient, in conjunction with the conclusions drawn from the other audit evidence obtained, to give him a reasonable basis for his opinion on the financial statements.

Only the first two relate to economy, efficiency and effectiveness audits.

The *Reporting Standard* gives details of the audit certificate, including situations requiring qualifications.

We have seen that independence is defined, for the audit of the UK government, in terms of the C. and A.G.'s independence from the executive. This is primarily achieved by taking his appointment out of the control of the executive and making his statutory responsibility that of reporting to the House of Commons. There are a number of ways in which this theoretical independence was compromised before the passing of the 1983 Act:

1 the Treasury had significant powers to direct the areas and nature of the C. and A.G.'s audit;
2 the appointment of the C. and A.G. has historically tended to come from the Treasury;
3 the Treasury audited the accounts of the Exchequer and Audit Department;
4 the Executive controlled the staff of the Exchequer and Audit below the C. and A.G.

Indeed, Normanton (1966, p. 372) says that:

> To suggest that this Act [the 1866 Act] established a legislative type of audit would be a gross over-simplification. What it actually did set up was an audit *on behalf of both the legislative and the executive, under the detailed direction of the latter* [Normanton's italics].

One effect of this Treasury influence which has been suggested is that organizations not under direct Treasury control have avoided being audited by the C. and A.G. Hence, some big spenders of government money have adopted other forms of audit. In the National Health Service, for example, all the public money involved is included in the Appropriation Accounts. The expenditure, however, is not under direct Treasury control; the Health Service is administered by Health Authorities which have executives of their own and which receive block allocations of finance from the Appropriation Accounts of the Department of Health and Social Security. The C. and A.G. is given the responsibility for auditing all appropriation accounts by the 1921 Act. But in practice this has come to mean that the C. and A.G. examines, certifies and reports on the annual *summarized accounts* of the

National Health Service taken as a whole, i.e. as the appropriation account presents them. One might assume that this would mean necessarily that the C. and A.G. audited all the Health Authorities. But this would be wrong. The statutory audit of the Health Authorities is now under the Audit Commission's responsibilities.

The 1983 Act reduced Treasury influence. Section 1(2) of the 1921 Act gave the Treasury power to direct the C. and A.G. to examine vouchers in more detail – the new Act has withdrawn this power. Similarly, s. 3(3), which gave the Treasury over-riding authority to arbitrate in any dispute between the C. and A.G. and an auditee, has also been withdrawn.

The Treasury still has the power to make directions about which accounts shall be audited by the C. and A.G.; but that power is now exercised through a statutory instrument which must be placed before the House of Commons. Also, as we have seen, the National Audit Office's accounts are not now audited by the Treasury and its staff are not now civil servants.

This reduction in the Treasury's influence has not, however, affected the coverage of the C. and A.G.'s audit. The National Health Service is still excluded (although not from the three Es examinations), as are the nationalized industries. The original proposals, which in a modified form became the 1983 Act, brought these in. However, there was successful opposition from the industries themselves.

The three Es audit in the public sector receives most attention in the literature. Previously absent from statutes, economy, efficiency and effectiveness are now included in the 1983 Act. Whether they have appeared as part of the C. and A.G.'s *audit* is a moot point. The Act takes pains to refer to them as 'examinations' and they are not mandatory in the way that the certification of the appropriation account is. On the other hand, the 1866 and 1921 Acts also avoid specific reference to 'audit'.

In recent years, there has been much debate about the role of the C. and A.G. The office is an old and distinguished one. The 1983 Act has invalidated many of the previous criticisms about the lack of complete independence from the executive. It remains to be seen whether the other main criticism will re-emerge and whether the House of Commons will demand a legislative audit of *all* the monies it votes.

LOCAL AUTHORITIES AND THE NATIONAL HEALTH SERVICE

The external audit of local authorities was substantially changed by the Local Government Finance Act 1982.

Section 11 established a body then known as the Audit Commission for Local Authorities in England and Wales. This is a body corporate whose members are appointed by the Secretary of State. The Commission appoints a chief officer, known as the Controller of Audit, and subordinates.

Until 1990, the main task of the Commission was to appoint the external auditors of local authorities. The auditor may either be an officer of the Commission or an outside accountant or firm of accountants, although the auditor must be a member of the ICAEW, ICAS, ACCA, CIPFA or ICAI. Before the 1982 Act, the responsibility for appointing the external auditor rested with the local authority itself. The change to appointment by an Audit Commission follows the Scottish model. Section 15 requires that:

1 An auditor shall by examination of the accounts and otherwise satisfy himself
   (a) that the accounts are prepared in accordance with regulations . . . and comply with the requirements of all other statutory provisions applicable to the accounts;
   (b) that proper practices have been observed in the compilation of the accounts;
   (c) that the body whose accounts are being audited has made proper arrangements for securing economy, efficiency and effectiveness in its use of resources.
2 The auditor shall comply with the code of audit practice as for the time being in force.
3 The auditor shall consider whether, in the public interest, he should make a report on any matter coming to his notice . . .

In 1983, a Code of Audit Practice was issued by the Commission and has been continually updated. The first part concerns the general duties of an auditor under the headings of 'independence', 'professional care' and 'audit objectives'. The second part is about conducting the audit. This says that the auditor must comply with the operational standards promulgated by the APC. But the Code also explicitly deals with questions of fraud, corruption and value for money. An appendix is also provided giving forms of audit certificates.

This is an example of a 'clean' certificate:

> I/we certify that I/we have completed the audit of the authority's accounts for the year ended 31 March 19x7 in accordance with Part III of the Local Government Finance Act 1982 [or *Part I of the National Health Service and Community Care Act 1990*] and the Code of Audit Practice.
>
> In my/our opinion, the statement of accounts set out on pages xx to xx presents fairly the financial position of the authority at 31 March 19x7 and its income and expenditure for the year then ended.

A theme that runs through this code is the more exacting requirements of local government or health service body audit compared with company audit. For example, under the code it is difficult for an auditor to provide management consultancy to the same authority – in order to protect audit independence. Also, the auditor has to have 'a reasonable expectation of detecting material misstatements . . . resulting from fraud'. And of course the possibility of direct confrontation of the auditor by the public significantly increases the auditor's burden. A unique feature of local government auditing (which had been in existence long before the 1982 Act) is the power given to the public to inspect the accounts and all supporting documents; and to make copies. Further, local government electors are given the opportunity to question the auditor of their local authority; the elector can also make objections to the accounts (s. 17, 1982 Act).

The auditor is given the power to apply to the courts for a declaration that a given item of account is contrary to law and the court has the power to recover the amount so declared (s. 19): the modern version of the traditional powers of disallowance and surcharge. The auditor has the responsibility to certify that certain sums are due from individuals. These relate to:

1 sums which have not been brought into account;

2   losses which have been incurred or deficiencies caused by wilful misconduct.

The individuals must either pay the sums due or appeal to the courts. Audit fees are determined by the Commission.

The Commission has other significant powers and responsibilities. It has the power to order an extraordinary audit of a local authority. It is also given the responsibility for undertaking or promoting studies 'designed to enable it to make recommendations for improving economy, efficiency, and effectiveness' (s. 26).

In setting up the Commission, one aim was to make the audit of local authorities independent of the authorities themselves. This has always been a source of concern, particularly because of the auditor's power to certify sums due from individuals and apply to the courts for a declaration that an item was contrary to law. In the past, these items have frequently been incurred because of an explicit policy decision taken by a council but which the auditor subsequently felt was unlawful. From the point of view of the public, the criticism was often levelled against the auditors that they were not independent of the council.

But the question of independence in this context has a further dimension. Sometimes the government was seen to support the auditor and this was regarded by councillors as interference with the auditor's independence. Views became more polarized when the council was of a different political 'colour' from the government.

The balance has been achieved by not making the officers or members of the Commission civil servants. So, although the Secretary of State appoints the members of the Commission, he or she does not have direct control over their day-to-day functioning.

There is an argument for saying that the audit certificates on the accounts of local authorities, and the accounts themselves, have less significance to the general public than do their equivalents in PLCs. This is because of the powers given to members of the public to examine all accounts and supporting documents, as well as those given to electors to question their authority's auditors. Because of the natural unwillingness of PLCs to divulge information which might be used by competitors, for example, the audited accounts tend to be the extent of the publicly available financial information. Since members of the public have the right to examine the detailed books of account, anyone with an intense desire to know about local authorities' finances does not have to rely on the published version.

In 1990, the National Health Service and Community Care Act extended the purview of (what it renamed) the Audit Commission of Local Authorities and the National Health Service in England and Wales. The Commission took over the responsibility for appointing the auditors of the health service bodies (including the new hospital trusts) and for carrying out economy, efficiency and effectiveness studies. The Commission chooses from its own auditors (the law allowed for transfer of existing auditors from the civil service) or accountants in public practice.

The 1990 Act extended the role of the Audit Commission by amending the Local Government Finance Act 1982. Many of the important requirements that apply to local authorities have been retained. Section 15, as shown above, is exactly the same for the NHS. The Commission also has the power under s. 26 to carry out three Fs studies, although for the NHS it is required to consult first with the government and the C. and A.G. Similarly, the Commission has been given the power to issue a Code of Audit Practice for the NHS, although the law explicitly allows that this may not be the same as the one for local authorities.

The striking differences between the local authority audit and the audit of a health service body are that the public does not have the right of inspection of accounts or of access to the auditor (i.e. s. 17 does not apply to the NHS), and what remains of the traditional powers of disallowance and surcharge in local government, whereby auditors can apply to the courts, also does not apply to the NHS (s. 19 and 20 do not apply).

As was pointed out earlier, these developments leave unchanged the fact that other auditors audit the accounts of each health service body but when those accounts are summarized and presented as appropriation accounts to Parliament it is the certificate of the C. and A.G. that is appended.

The establishment and growth of the Audit Commission has raised questions about whether it could usefully grow further. It has been suggested that it provides a good model for companies, as a way of increasing the independence of auditors from management. More immediately, the expansion of the role of the Commission has also raised the question about its relationship with the National Audit Office. For example, the Commission's responsibilities for the National Health Service could in theory have been given to the NAO. It is not useful to speculate how their respective roles might change except to say that they did announce in 1995 that in a number of ways they intend to work more closely together in the future.

NATIONALIZED INDUSTRIES, PUBLIC CORPORATIONS AND OTHER PUBLIC BODIES

This is not a homogeneous group of organizations, and the requirements for audit of their accounts are a part of the heterogeneity. Practices are as much a matter of history as of principle, and such principles as may have been applied in the past are not too clear. As far as nationalized industries and public corporations are concerned, the arrangements adopted for that seminal body, the BBC, have been broadly replicated: the law that establishes the body gives some form of power to the government to appoint auditors, or to regulate the appointment of auditors, from the private sector, who in turn do a company audit but with additional responsibilities.

In the case of the BBC, its powers and responsibilities are above all determined by Royal Charter. The first was issued in 1926 and Article 16(1) required that the accounts must be 'audited annually by an auditor or auditors, who shall be chartered accountants, and shall be appointed by' the government. There were subsequent revisions to the Charter, including Cmnd 8313 (July 1981) which also extended the charter to 31 December 1996. Article 18(1) requires:

> The accounts of the Corporation shall be audited annually by an auditor or auditors to be appointed by the Corporation with the prior approval of Our Secretary of State, and a person shall not be qualified to be so appointed unless he is a member of a body of accountants established in Our United Kingdom and for the time being recognised under [the Companies Acts].

The Charter requires the auditors to certify the accounts and requires the BBC to present its report and audited accounts to the minister for transmission to Parliament. It also gives the Secretary of State, and anyone nominated by that person, 'full liberty to examine the accounts of the corporation and furnish him and them with all forecasts, estimates, information and documents' (Article 18(4)).

The auditors' report on the financial statements for 1993/94 stated:

To the Members of the British Broadcasting Corporation

We have audited the financial statements on pages xx to xx which comprise the consolidated Home Services Group and the World Service and are prepared on the basis set out in the statement of accounting policies on page xx.

Respective Responsibilities of the Governors and Board of Management and Auditors

As described on page x, the Governors and Board of Management are responsible for the preparation of financial statements. It is our responsibility to form an independent opinion, based on our audit, on those statements and to report our opinion to you.

Basis of Opinion

We conducted our audit in accordance with Auditing Standards issued by the Auditing Practices Board. An audit includes examination, on a test basis, of evidence relevant to the amounts and disclosures in the financial statements. It also includes an assessment of the significant estimates and judgements made by the Governors and Board of Management in the preparation of the financial statements, and of whether the accounting policies are appropriate to the Corporation's circumstances, consistently applied and adequately disclosed.

We planned and performed our audit so as to obtain all the information and explanations which we considered necessary in order to provide us with sufficient evidence to give reasonable assurance that the financial statements are free from material misstatement, whether caused by fraud or other irregularity or error. In forming our opinion we also evaluated the overall adequacy of the presentation of information in the financial statements.

Opinion

In our opinion, the financial statements give a true and fair view of the state of affairs of the Corporation as at 31 March 1994 and of its income and expenditure, total recognised gains and losses and cash flows for the year then ended.

As the report states, given that it conforms to the APB's Auditing Standards, there is no substantive difference between it and an auditors' opinion on a PLC: there are no additional legal responsibilities placed on the auditors. More specifically, this also means that there is no power or responsibility for auditors of the financial statements to make judgements about economy, efficiency and effectiveness.

As we move away from the nationalized industries and public corporations into the maze of other public bodies (*Public Bodies 1994*), the audit arrangements may change in two important respects. First, the financial statements of many of these bodies are audited by the C. and A.G. under agreement with the Treasury (under s. 6 of the National Audit Act 1983). Second, the C. and A.G. may have rights of access to these bodies (notwithstanding the fact that the audit of financial statements is done by private sector auditors), giving the C. and A.G. the power to make economy, efficiency and effectiveness examinations. These rights of access apply to the bodies whose financial statements are audited, explicitly by virtue of the 1983 Act, by the C. and A. G. They also apply to the bodies whose financial statements are audited by the C. and A.G. by agreement with the Treasury, as long as the relevant minister agrees. In addition, section 7 of the Act gives the C. and A.G. wide-ranging rights to conduct economy, efficiency and effectiveness examinations into 'any authority or body to which section 7 applies' that 'has in any of its financial years received more than half its income from public funds': the explicit exceptions in the Act are nationalized industries and the BBC, the Independent Broadcasting Authority and the Welsh Fourth Channel Authority. It is interesting to note that these rights relate to private sector bodies too and have had an effect on the management of charities, for example.

As the auditing standards and methodologies of the private sector auditors and the C. and A.G. converge, it is not obvious that their audits of financial statements are significantly different from each other. It is probably more significant that there are important public bodies which are not subject to economy, efficiency and effectiveness examinations, although this statement has to be qualified because the number of these bodies has reduced (following privatization) and also because the bodies are and have been subject to major studies commissioned by government or by the Monopolies and Mergers Commission. Nevertheless, in principle, there is much scope for debate about the extent to which the supreme auditor does, and should, follow public money.

AUDIT INDEPENDENCE

The discipline of auditing derives much of its influence from claims to 'independence'. The most pervasive, and obvious, sense of this refers to the relationship between the auditor and the auditee, although it must also be said that this independence cannot be absolute. Auditing in complex organizations requires some co-operation between auditor and auditee, which itself necessarily compromises independence. The issues surrounding the relationship between auditor and auditee are common to all organizations, public or private, but in the public sector, below the level of a sovereign government, there is often an additional dimension: the institutional arrangements for bolstering this aspect of independence often now include a role for the higher-level government or governmental agency either in appointing, or approving the appointment of, the auditors in the lower-level government or statutory body. This is potentially a source of difficulty because, in a politicized environment, it may bring with it accusations of bias but it does support independence.

However, it is in the context of a sovereign government that the notion of audit independence raises issues that are unfamiliar in the context of business. Independence from the auditee is a very difficult idea when we say instead that this should mean independence of the auditor from the government: in what sense can anyone in the country be said to be independent of the sovereign government – at least independent enough to provide a credible opinion on the government's financial statements and its economy, efficiency and effectiveness? Presumably this suggests that, to obtain true independence, the auditor should be a foreigner. Obviously, we mean this facetiously, but it highlights the fact that complete independence is neither possible nor desirable: the auditor has to be credible to the sovereign government too. In some countries, and indeed Continental Europe includes significant examples, the institutional arrangements are provided by placing the supreme audit in the judiciary, thereby drawing on the same context that secures an independent judicial system. In the countries that have been influenced by the Westminster model, the supreme auditor is placed somewhere between the legislature and the executive but without being outside either.

This is the context of the Auditing Standards of the International Organization of Supreme Audit Institutions (INTOSAI). These include a general standard which boldly states that '[t]he auditor and the supreme audit institution must be independent' and amplifies this in terms of independence of the auditor from the auditee. In the practical case, there are two contexts for this. The first is the obvious one: lack of dependence between the auditor and the executive as a whole. The second one is the lack of dependence between the auditor and the specific, lower-level audited entity: the standards recognize that there are many important issues, and in practice they are probably of greater significance most of the time, relating to the auditor and the department or unit of government that do not involve the grander questions about how the executive as a whole is involved.

But equally interestingly, there is another aspect that the INTOSAI standards emphasize: independence of the auditor from the legislature. Given that these standards are not in the context of a judicial audit, this independence suggests that the officials who are supreme auditors are extremely powerful – to be independent of the executive and the legislature. The formal sense in which this is so in the UK is by making the appointment of the C. and A.G. (but not the staff of the NAO) the prerogative of the Crown.

The reasons the standards require some independence from the legislature is not to deny that there resides the sovereign power but to support the idea that auditors are apolitical. Thus the audit is seen to be of the executive on behalf of the legislature, but the audit is not politically biased.

The concept of audit independence is not easy in any context but perhaps it is most difficult at the level of sovereign governments. It is likely that most supreme auditors around the world would be hard-pressed to claim much independence from their government. The amount in a particular country is presumably a part, perhaps a significant part, of any judgement about the extent to which that country is democratic. Presumably also, any help that internationally promulgated auditing standards can give to support a particular supreme audit institution in asserting some measure of independence is to be welcomed.

DISCUSSION TOPICS

1 Explain the differences between the statutory audit of a PLC and government auditing.

2 Discuss the concept of independence in the context of public sector auditing.

3 The National Audit Office in the UK provides the legislative audit: it audits the executive on behalf of the legislature. Critically evaluate this proposition, particularly contrasting with the old Exchequer and Audit Department.

4 Describe and critically evaluate the audit provisions of the Local Government Finance Act 1982.

CHAPTER 12

Economy, efficiency and effectiveness auditing

The environment of public sector auditing has increasingly included demands for auditors to place less emphasis on the financial and regularity audits and more on value for money. Auditors have responded with auditing standards and have developed methodologies for the three Es audits.

BACKGROUND

Auditors have always been concerned with more than merely reporting on financial statements. Their unique position in relation to organizations has resulted in, and probably necessitated, making recommendations about how performance could be improved.

However, this broader role has not, until recently, been articulated. The trend in auditing for PLCs has been towards narrowing its explicit role, not least because of the upsurge in the number of legal actions brought against auditors. There is also the question of independence: the more involvement in advising companies about better practices, the less the auditor is seen to be independent of the management.

In the public sector, the influence of law on auditing practice has been much greater in terms of specifying duties, responsibilities, and procedures; this has been particularly so in local and central government in the UK. One effect of this has been, as with accounting practice, that there has been less articulation of auditing practices in general, not just of the role of the three Es audits. The 1960s, particularly, saw the development of new techniques in public administration. The US Federal Government was a breeding ground for many of these and the three Es audit is no exception. These new approaches to public sector auditing have been most significantly and comprehensively stated in a publication of the Comptroller General called *Government Auditing Standards*.

First published in 1972, the standards were revised in 1981, 1988 and 1994. They are intended to apply to all governmental audits in the USA and to internal and external auditors alike. There are a number of premises underlying these standards. For example, the term 'audit' means both financial and performance audits. On each of these aspects, the standards have the following to say:

> Financial auditing contributes to providing accountability since it provides an independent opinion on whether an entity's financial statements present fairly the results of financial operations and whether other financial information is presented in conformity with established or stated criteria.

Performance auditing contributes to providing accountability because it provides an independent view on the extent to which government officials are faithfully, efficiently, and effectively carrying out their responsibilities.

A related premise is the following:

To realize governmental accountability, the citizens, their elected representatives, and program managers need information to assess the integrity, performance, and stewardship of the government's activities. Thus, unless legal restrictions or ethical considerations prevent it, audit reports should be available to the public and to other levels of government that have supplied resources.

An interesting change was made to these premises in the 1994 Revision. Whereas statements about holding officials to account were previously restricted to 'public officials', they are now referred to as 'public officials and others entrusted with handling public resources (for example, managers of a not-for-profit organization that receives federal funds)'. This reflects the significant extension of governmental auditing in the US mandated by the executive with effect from 1990 (under Office of Management and Budget Circular A-133): in important respects, the same audit requirements apply to charities that receive government money as apply to government agencies.

The influence of the early versions of these standards on the UK Comptroller and Auditor General is clear to see in the National Audit Act 1983. In local government there has been some recognition of the need for economy, efficiency and effectiveness audits since the early 1970s. At the time of the reorganization of UK local government, the Department of the Environment issued a code of practice on local government auditing. This stated that audit under the Local Government Act 1972 was wider than that of a commercial undertaking:

Over and above the ordinary duties of an auditor he has a number of special concerns.
1   He must satisfy himself as to the legality of items of account.
2   He has a duty to verify that in compiling the accounts different sections of the public whose interests may be affected by them have been fairly treated.
3   He has a special responsibility in respect of loss due to misconduct and it is therefore not enough that he should ensure that systems of financial control and internal audit are sound; he ought also to undertake tests designed for the specific purposes of discovering fraud.
4   He has a duty to submit a report on matters arising from or in connection with the accounts which in the public interest should be brought to the notice of the Council and the public. This means that he must be concerned not only with the form and regularity of the accounts but also with issues of substance arising therefrom, such as *the possibility of loss due to waste, extravagance, inefficient financial administration, poor value for money, mistake or other cause* [emphasis added].

There were difficulties with this code of practice. The value for money audit, although explicitly a part of the auditor's duty, tended to be understated. Since it was only embodied in a code of practice, it was not enforceable. Audit fees did not increase to make a substantial amount of value for money auditing an economic proposition. Consequently, development in this area was slow. Events overtook professional practice and the Local Government Finance Act 1982 made the three Es audit a statutory requirement. The Audit Commission has the power to promote or carry out value for money audits and the basis for audit fees has been restructured. The Commission is also charged with producing a code of practice; in anticipation of this, the CIPFA has offered its own standards which it is hoped will be adopted by the Commission. The main challenge of the three Es audits is to develop robust methodologies. We can now examine the issues involved and the direction of some of the solutions.

ECONOMY AND EFFICIENCY AUDIT

Economy is about least cost. Efficiency is about the best ratio of output to cost; because outputs and costs are measured in different units, this means either the best output for a given level of cost or the least cost for a given level of output. The outputs are low-level outputs; the ultimate outputs of the organization are the concern of the effectiveness audit.

Broadly, there are two ways of treating the outputs. First, they can be treated implicitly and not measured. Thus, for example, an attempt to make an accountancy section more efficient would be concerned explicitly with reducing costs; the assumption that the accounting information was required by the organization in the first place would be implicit. Computerizing the debtors' ledger would produce the same information but would use less resources.

Second, the outputs can be measured. These measurements will typically be in physical units. Common and relatively uncontroversial examples would relate to engineering measures of efficiency such as the efficiency of a school central heating system, a district heating system for council houses or a refuse disposal unit. There are many other more controversial examples such as the efficiency of an old people's home, a school or a refuse collection service.

The General Accounting Office standards (1994, pp. 2–4/5), in considering the economy and efficiency audit, say that the auditor may consider whether the entity:

(a) is following sound procurement practices;
(b) is acquiring the appropriate type, quality and amount of resources when needed at the lowest cost;
(c) is properly protecting and maintaining its resources;
(d) is avoiding duplication of effort by employees and work that serves little or no purpose;
(e) is avoiding idleness and overstaffing;
(f) is using efficient operating procedures;
(g) is using the minimum amount of resources (staff, equipment and facilities) in producing or delivering the appropriate quantity and quality of goods or services promptly;
(h) is complying with requirements of laws and regulations that could significantly affect the acquisition, protection and use of the entity's resources;
(i) has reported measures of economy and efficiency that are valid and reliable.

Question (a) is an example of the first approach. The auditor assumes that purchases have to be made and is therefore concerned primarily with ensuring that the best price is paid and that only authorized purchases are made. In question (b) the output is more explicit. This is concerned with stock control and one element must include consideration of whether obsolete stock or generally unwanted stock is being stored unnecessarily. Hence qualitative judgements about items of stock have to be made.

The important thing is that, although all questions of economy and efficiency involve outputs, some are much more easily handled than others. Where the output is implicit or easily measured, the economy and efficiency audit is no different from the practice of many auditors. For example, question (d) does not require an explicit measurable output for the members of staff concerned if it is self-evident that two people are needlessly doing the same task. The difficulties emerge when the outputs have to be measured. Subjectivity is introduced into the audit judgements and questions of efficiency become matters of opinion.

A rough distinction can be drawn between units, sections, and departments of organizations which are merely servicing the main spending departments, and the spending departments themselves. Paradoxically, the former are the easier to handle: the relationship between their functioning and the ultimate objectives of the organization is so indirect that the manager and auditor would simply not try to make the connection. The more implicit the outputs become, the more the analyst can concentrate on the more easily measurable inputs. With the latter, it is not possible (or alternatively it will be very misleading) to ignore outputs. This situation is paradoxical in the sense that in business it is the service departments (the discretionary costs) which provide the greatest difficulty in performance evaluation.

The procedure for instigating the economy and efficiency audit will be the same as for any other audit. Indeed, although it is important to distinguish between the different kinds of audit, there will usually only be one audit procedure which will result in the different audits being carried out.

The Auditing Practices Committee, the predecessor body to the Auditing Practices Board, produced in 1980 (Auditing Practices Committee, 1980) a useful summary of the various responsibilities of an auditor as follows:

1 *Planning, controlling and recording.* The auditor should adequately plan, control and record his work.
2 *Accounting systems.* The auditor should ascertain the enterprise's system of recording and processing transactions and assess its adequacy as a basis for the preparation of the relevant financial statements.
3 *Audit evidence.* The auditor should obtain relevant and reliable audit evidence sufficient to enable him to draw reasonable conclusions therefrom.
4 *Internal controls.* If the auditor wishes to place reliance on any internal controls he should ascertain and evaluate those controls and perform compliance tests on their operation.
5 *Review of relevant financial statements.* The auditor should carry out such a review of the relevant financial statements as is sufficient, in conjunction with the conclusions drawn from the other audit evidence obtained, to give him a reasonable basis for his opinion on those financial statements.

From these, a general approach to any audit can be summarized as:

1 planning the audit;
2 reviewing the accounting systems and internal controls;
3 testing the accounting systems and internal controls;
4 conducting the audit;
5 producing the report.

In planning the audit, a significant consideration will be the extent to which the financial and regularity aspects and the three Es will be covered. It has always been clear that not every annual audit will include all aspects for all services. Apart from the fact that the resources to do this will not be available, it would also be an inefficient use of those which are available to repeat annually an economy and efficiency audit of a particular unit. Even within the financial audit, the auditor takes account of the detailed checks of previous years. For the three Es audits, it is all the more important that the areas to be covered follow logically from previous years.

It may be that the auditor is directed to a particular activity by events. Pressure from a higher legislative body or from the policy makers may necessitate considering a given area. This is probably anathema to auditors who have always avoided political involvement. But this is just one example of how the expanded scope audit inevitably introduces political considerations. The challenge is to produce independent and dispassionate audit reports in this environment.

Staffing the audit team is an important part of the planning stage. Because the economy and efficiency audit entails much more than financial considerations, it is likely that auditors will need more than financial skills. The extent of this will depend upon the kind of audit being considered. Where outputs are implicit, financial skills sensitively applied will usually suffice. But where outputs are measured in other than monetary units they will not. Take the example of an efficiency audit of a refuse disposal unit. A hefty dose of common sense would enable an auditor to observe and comment upon a system which takes raw refuse and either disposes of it or processes it to yield a saleable product. But this would complement, not act as a substitute for, an engineer's understanding of the process, an O & M consultant's understanding of the management of employees, and a marketing manager's understanding of the market. The efficiency audit, by its very nature, involves more than accountancy and audit expertise; and audit teams must be staffed to reflect the wider specialisms.

The second and third stages of any modern audit involve the review and testing of systems. Systems of accounting will clearly have fundamental importance for the financial and regularity audits. But they are important also to the economy and efficiency audit. The costs of the activity being audited will be one subject of the inquiry. These costs are recorded by the accounting system. Therefore, the ability of the system to produce relevant and 'correct' costs needs to be ascertained. This does not mean that there is no scope for the auditor to modify or challenge the costs, as reported in the accounts, in the efficiency audit. The very notion of relevant costs demands different costs for different purposes; the costs in the accounts may not be relevant to an examination of efficiency. An obvious example would be any allocations of central administrative charges. Professional practice recommends that these are made to all services, primarily for completeness. However, if, from the point of view of the activity being audited, these costs are not variable, then it would be unhelpful to include them in an assessment of efficiency. On the other hand, if the activity is supposed to break even, then the extent to which these allocated costs are covered by charges made will be relevant.

Yet, with these caveats, the auditor will still need to rely on the accounting systems to produce measures of inputs sacrificed.

Internal control systems have equal, if not greater, importance. The Auditing Practices Board (1995, para. 8) states that an internal control system comprises the control environment and control procedures and includes all the policies and procedures (internal controls) adopted by the directors and management of an entity to assist in achieving their objectives of ensuring, as far as practicable, the orderly and efficient conduct of its business, including adherence to internal policies, the safeguarding of assets, the prevention and detection of fraud and error, the accuracy and completeness of the accounting records, and the timely preparation of reliable financial information.

It is the responsibility of management to establish proper internal control systems and clearly, therefore, the efficiency audit must be primarily concerned with whether the controls are sound, whether they are being complied with and whether they are achieving their stated objectives. For example, an important factor in the efficiency of any (labour-intensive) activity is the competence of responsible staff. The internal controls which attempt to ensure that responsible posts are occupied by suitably qualified staff will relate to the system for appointing and promoting employees. Reviewing and testing these systems will be essential in almost all efficiency audits.

The review will include questions such as:

1   Who gives the authority to advertise appointments?
2   Do all posts have to be advertised externally?
3   Who is responsible for drawing up shortlists?
4   Who is responsible for interviewing?
5   Who ultimately appoints?

The main concern in this review will be the extent to which subjective views of interested staff are allowed to intervene in the appointments process. Having established the system as it ought to function the auditor will be concerned with how it does function. This compliance testing will typically be sample-based. It will follow specific appointments from establishing the need to appoint through to the taking up of the post. If exceptions to the established procedure emerge, the auditor must decide whether they invalidate the internal controls or whether there are good reasons for them. The decision will affect the substantive tests subsequently undertaken in the audit proper.

The question of whether the controls are achieving their stated objectives is a difficult one. The objectives may be well-defined or hardly defined at all. In either case, the auditor will need to exercise judgement. In our example it may be that a specific job description requires 'a qualified engineer of five years' standing'. This is as specific as any criterion is likely to be but it still contains substantial room for manoeuvre. What happens if the auditor discovers that the head of the refuse disposal unit is a chemical engineer? This might be within the 'letter' of the criterion but is it within the 'spirit'? How do you discover whether it is or is not? Even if it is, should it be? Might inefficiencies not have crept in because no one ever considered whether a chemical engineer was qualified to manage a refuse disposal unit? Might a chemical engineer not be precisely what is required, but previous holders of the post were mechanical engineers?

Reviewing the accounting systems and internal controls will not only involve studying them but also documenting them. A complete picture is required of all the resources (personnel, equipment, materials, cash) which are used by the activity and the outputs yielded. Tests are designed to ascertain the correspondence between the theoretical flows of inputs into outputs and the practice.

The next step is to conduct the economy and efficiency audit. We have the right audit team and the accounting systems and the systems of internal control have been reviewed and tested. We have been able to draw conclusions about potential weaknesses in terms of higher-than-necessary costs and lower-than-obtainable outputs.

We are faced with a given level of relevant cost for the year under review. But what of the output measurements? Ideally these will have been specified by the organization and will be used explicitly in measuring the performance of managers. It would, at the very least, be dysfunctional if the auditor were to measure efficiency against a criterion which was not used as a goal by the managers. However, in practice, it may be that outputs are not explicit. This would mean that the auditor would have to be instrumental in generating them, although this must be with the co-operation and understanding of the management. The economy and efficiency audit is already potentially sensitive and an auditor who was evaluating performance against measures for which there was no consensus would be placed in an intolerable position.

As public sector organizations are exposed more systematically to the economy and efficiency audit, this problem should diminish.

Let us continue the example of the refuse disposal unit and assume that the agreed measure of output is taken to be 'tonnes incinerated'; there are lower-level surrogate output measures such as 'staff per '000 population'. The first substantive tests will be concerned with verifying the accuracy of these measures. The financial measures will already have been dealt with as a part of the financial and regularity audit. Certainly the accounting principles adopted will be common to the rest of the organization and the data produced have the added advantage to an auditor that they are systematically produced (by the double entry).

More emphasis is likely to be placed, therefore, on verifying the output measures. The system for recording the tonnes incinerated will have been considered, so the audit will now be concerned with tests of the figures produced. These are probably intrinsically unverifiable: how can an auditor check on the amount of refuse burnt? But indirect checks are possible, such as comparing the figures with figures on the amount of refuse delivered to the unit, if these are kept. Or perhaps comparison of the amount of energy consumed with the refuse disposed of.

Given these measures of inputs and outputs, the auditor must decide whether the outputs could have been achieved at a lower cost or whether the costs incurred could have yielded greater output. Comparisons have to be made:

1   with predetermined standards;
2   with previous years' performance;
3   with other refuse disposal units
    (a) in the same organization,
    (b) in other organizations.

One would expect an activity such as refuse disposal to adopt a standard costing system which continuously compares costs against standard costs to highlight and explain variances. If this is so, the standard costing system will already have been reviewed and tested. The auditor will then be concerned with examining particular expenditure heads to test their accuracy. In terms of efficiency, the auditor will be most concerned with significant variances and the explanations of them.

In considering predetermined standards, however, we must recognize that most public sector activities are not amenable to standard costing systems. This is because of the lack of measurable outputs which can easily be correlated with costs.

This is a significant problem for the efficiency auditor and one which has to be faced. Traditionally in public sector organizations the predetermined standard, particularly for costs, is the budgeted expenditure. The budgets are not designed to reflect outputs but to record inputs. These are the line-item budgets, subjectively classified. They tend to be calculated incrementally or decrementally, i.e. the 'base' expenditure is the previous year's and the budget for the next year concentrates on the marginal increase or decrease. The standards then are: spend £X thousand on staff, £Y thousand on equipment, £Z thousand on debt charges. These standards are of little use in the efficiency audit. Any variances simply reflect changes from what was spent last year. If last year's expenditure was inefficient then even if this year's is less, there are no grounds for assuming better performance. Because these budgets are calculated by concentrating on the margin, it is difficult to accept that they can in any sense have been authorized to achieve a defined level of performance. Even when this level of performance is explicit, the efficiency auditor could not be satisfied that this relationship is efficient. For example, a school's budget might include the estimated number of pupils. But the consequent budgeted cost per pupil cannot be assumed to be efficient. It must be assumed to be politically acceptable since the budget will have been approved on that basis. But that does not preclude more efficient ways of achieving the same policy goal. This is so not least because 'cost' is made up of such a heterogeneous group of costs: what contribution to this 'cost per pupil' do books make? Might books be used more efficiently? Is it efficient to require pupils to buy their own books?

The necessity of predetermined standards in many areas of performance measurement in the public sector seems inevitably to lead to the conclusion that budgets should be either programme budgets or zero-base budgets. Both kinds are not without their critics and have not been particularly successful as management tools during the past twenty years in practical applications. However, the important contribution they can make is in producing budgeted and actual input data which are explicitly matched at the budgeting and reporting stages with measurable outputs. Certainly, it is difficult to see how an efficiency audit can be carried out in many public sector organizations without an output-defined budget as a prerequisite. Nevertheless, the majority of budgets do not incorporate any form of output measurement and the inputs consumed are often the only measure of the level of service provision. This means that the inputs are in effect the predetermined standards and it could be argued that this should result in budgets being subjected to an independent audit. It is the budget that provides the authority to spend and the consequent costs cannot be seen otherwise than in the context of the budgets which to some extent generated them.

Returning to our more easily managed problems of the refuse disposal unit, the next comparison to be made is with previous years' performance. This comparison will be enhanced if an efficiency audit has been previously carried out on the unit. The usual caveats would apply to comparing costs over time, not least that some adjustment is necessary for changes in the general level, or more usefully (but less available), the specific levels of prices. The longer the period adopted for comparison the less comparable the figures will tend to be, so the more adjustments will have to be made, although the more useful the extrapolations will be.

Since the comparisons have so far been within the refuse disposal unit, as it were, they are of less value than external validation. This can take the form of comparing this unit with any others that the organization owns and with those belonging to other organizations. Difficulties will arise with the former in that there may be no comparable units. The problem with the latter is likely to be the dearth of detailed statistics: unit cost comparisons could be made but there is likely to be no access to the information required to help explain differences.

The final stage in audit is producing the report. The more public the report is to be, the more difficult it will be to write. The emphasis in a report on economy and efficiency must always be on constructive criticism which will improve future performance, rather than on gratuitous carping about the past. Nevertheless, in the public sector *any* criticism is politically charged. Even if no one else is moved to comment, an opposition is bound to oppose. The report should be clear, dispassionate, constructive, and should contain the evidence to support criticisms. Because of the potential for political use of such a report, the auditor will typically consult with management before it is published. If we envisage an audit report which says that our refuse disposal unit is as economical and efficient as any other unit, this is as 'clean' a report as is conceivable: economy and efficiency are comparative notions, not absolute ones. But is that as much as the expanded-scope audit could say? In fact, it is not. There is the further question of how *effective* the unit is.

EFFECTIVENESS AUDIT

Effectiveness is about achieving objectives. According to the Audit Commission (1986, p. 8) it 'means providing the right services to enable the local authority to implement its policies and objectives'. It is therefore concerned with the ultimate output of the service, i.e. the impact on the consumer. This distinguishes it from the outputs required for measuring efficiency which, as described in the previous section, are low level and clearly defined measures of the level of service provided, such as tons of refuse collected or number of planning applications processed. The initial emphasis of value for money audit work was, not surprisingly, on economy and efficiency, and experience in carrying out effectiveness audits is still quite limited. One reason for the past lack of enthusiasm is that very often there are no explicit goals or objectives embodied in a policy decision to spend public money. And even when there are, they are so hazily stated that good performance and bad performance are difficult to judge.

Without these specific criteria, the effectiveness auditor is inextricably bound up with political questions. How effective is a social services department if neither the government nor the local government has laid down criteria? The answer is, that it depends on what the objectives were. The importance of objectives is acknowledged by Price Waterhouse (1990, p. 76). They identify the following questions as crucial:

1   Is there a clear identification and ranking of goals?
2   Can progress towards goals be objectively assessed?
3   Is the 'target' service level (i.e. how activities contribute to goals) clearly known?

If the answer to all three questions is 'Yes' then an effectiveness audit could be undertaken. However, if the answer to question 3 is 'No' then the evaluation becomes highly subjective and if the answer to question 1 is 'No', and goals cannot be agreed, then the evaluation of effectiveness is a political process. Price Waterhouse admit that 'in both cases, but particularly the latter, the auditors would therefore find it extremely difficult to carry out effectiveness auditing at all'. This is, of course, consistent with the typology developed by Hofstede (1981) for management control. Hofstede's analysis shows that when the objectives of an activity are ambiguous and its outputs non-measurable then the appropriate control model is 'political' control. If the ambiguity can be resolved but outputs remain non-measurable, i.e. acceptable surrogate measures cannot be found, then the appropriate control model is 'judgemental' control. Hofstede then goes on to argue that PPBS and zero-base budgeting are completely unsuitable techniques for those situations requiring political or judgemental control models. Perhaps his analysis and conclusions will, in time, prove to apply equally well to effectiveness audit.

Nevertheless, in spite of the obvious difficulties, effectiveness audits are now a reality. The Audit Commission (1989, p. 6), while acknowledging the difficulty of measuring the 'impact' or 'outcome' of many public services, do point out that even if effectiveness cannot be directly measured it can nearly always be evaluated in other ways. The alternatives they identify are:

1   proxy measures of impact;
2   evaluation by customers;
3   evaluating the process rather than the outcomes.

The Audit Commission suggests that the level of complaints or level of customer demand and customer retention might offer simple proxy measures for many services. Even though many public services are effectively monopolies or are heavily subsidized, it is still argued that customers can be good judges of quality. An example given is the level of attendance at a recreation centre being not only an indicator of utilization but also of quality. It is also suggested that the effectiveness of most services can be gauged by inspection and quality control over the service itself by relating this to accepted standards. For example, rather than test the 'impact' of street lighting on road safety, crime reduction, etc., which is the ultimate test of effectiveness, the evaluation should concentrate on whether the street lighting programme that is being examined actually meets generally acceptable standards of good practice. If so, it can then be assumed that the service is providing the desired impact.

A further acknowledgement of the problems facing the audit of effectiveness can be seen in a joint report by the Audit Commission and the Office for Standards on Education on full-time education for 16–19-year-olds (Audit Commission, 1993). The report points out that:

> Effectiveness in education is difficult to define. A full definition would take account of all the ways in which education affects people's personal fulfilment and the contributions to society throughout their lives. The task for those seeking to monitor effectiveness is to find practical indicators. A number of types of evidence can be looked at in relation to the 16–19 phase: participation rates, because they indicate young people's views of the worth of 16–19 education; number of qualifications in the general population, because a key purpose of 16–19 education is to increase these; proportion of students who succeed on 16–19 courses; 'value-added' by A-level and GCSE courses, because value added

evaluations take account of the progress which students should make; interested parties' views on the quality of the 16–19 curriculum; the quality of students' work as evaluated through inspection.

The procedure for instigating an effectiveness audit is much the same as for economy and efficiency. Planning will take account of the impetus for the audit and any previous experience with the particular activity. Staffing the audit team will depend on the activity but is more likely to need non-accountancy expertise than other audits. Even with established criteria, the auditor is bound to be involved in making judgements about the work of professionals in spending departments.

Accounting systems are likely to be of little importance; the auditor will have to rely on internal (administrative) controls. Reviewing and testing these controls will be an intrinsic part of the audit.

The effectiveness of the activity must be judged against agreed criteria. If these are not available, the auditor must generate them and achieve consensus from top management and the policy-making body. These criteria will, by their nature, be difficult to measure but some attempt must be made, to give validity to the audit.

Let us return to the example of the refuse disposal unit. How could we measure its effectiveness? The objective could be established that it should dispose of all the refuse generated within the area. The basic choice in refuse disposal is between incinerating and land-fill. In terms of measurable costs, incinerating is far more expensive. But taking account of the social costs of tipping rubbish, e.g. nuisance, smell, unproductive use of land, the body has decided that it is worth the extra cash cost to incinerate.

The unit will be effective if all the rubbish that accumulates is burnt. It will be ineffective if it cannot cope with existing levels and refuse is piling up outside. Or if the manager collects refuse less often so that it accumulates in the domestic or commercial situations where it was generated. Or if the manager disposes of the excess by way of land-fill. It will similarly be ineffective if it is under-used and refuse is disposed of on tips. This might occur because the management or a higher-level body has imposed budget cuts on refuse disposal. Because the cash cost of land-fill is less than that of incinerating, the temptation may be to absorb the cuts by diverting some of the refuse. This may have happened without the top management knowing, and identifying it would be a positive and proper contribution of an effectiveness audit.

A methodology for this kind of work would involve direct interviews with, and questionnaires to, not only officers but also users of the service; background material from the media might help; but most of all the auditor would rely on non-financial information systems. Thus, a verifiable system for recording the amounts of refuse incinerated would be paramount.

The reason for choosing to illustrate the three Es audits with the refuse disposal unit is that it is easier to handle. There are many examples which are not. Schools, hospitals, old people's homes, universities, council houses, the armed forces, Parliament, Whitehall are just some of the examples of areas where measures of effectiveness are difficult to agree on and yet the auditor is charged with making judgements about them. Butt and Palmer (1985) provide an example of the kind of performance indicators that might be used as a basis for evaluating the effectiveness (and also the efficiency and economy) of a more 'difficult' activity, i.e. a vocational training scheme for the blind. This is reproduced in Fig. 12.1. It

Department: Education
Activity: Training of blind
Period: Six months to October 19XX (Period 12)
Objective of function: To provide functional training to blind citizens to enable them to find appropriate long-term employment.

Indicators	Period 12		Target		Period 11	
	No	%	No	%	No	%
Effectiveness/Success						
1 Students completing training						
Number as percentage of starters	29	76	30	80	26	84
2 Number of students who obtain employment						
From Period 12 students	14	48	15	50	17	65
From Period 11 students (cumulative)	23	88	26	100	31	90
Average time before obtaining employment	11.5 weeks		8 weeks		10.4 weeks	
3 Satisfaction with training/survey						
Former students satisfied	13	93	15	100	15	88
Employers satisfied	14	100	14	100	30	95
4 Students withdrawing from training before completion	8	22	6	16	12	33
Efficiency and Economy						
5 Number of courses offered	6		8		6	
6 Student/teacher ratio	6.4/1		5/1		5.7/1	
7 Average class size per training course offered	8.1		6.0		7.2	
8 Costs						
Teaching costs	£26,800		£32,000		£25,400	
Other costs	£12,900		£14,000		£12,200	
Teaching costs per student course attended	£291		£296		£264	
Other costs per student course attended	£140		£130		£127	

Remarks:
This report does not include all the possible indicators, only those that we decided were essential to this organization's performance. Lower-level indicators could be produced particularly if certain courses were either not in demand or costly to present.

Fig. 12.1   Special educational services performance (value for money) report.

can be seen from this example that the evaluation of effectiveness makes use of two distinct types of data. First, there are 'neutral' performance indicators, such as the success of students in finding employment. Secondly, there is the use of data, which attempt to obtain opinions about the service. In the example this is achieved by a survey of the level of satisfaction of users of the service and the user groups identified are students and employers. All of this leads the auditor well away from the more familiar confines of financial data and emphasizes the need for different types of expertise. The question that then arises is just how far along this route should the auditor go. Surveys of perceptions of effectiveness, for example, must first of all identify the different groups who may have an interest in the service. Tomkins (1987, p. 55) points out that:

> Once one admits the relevance of different groups, one must allow for the emergence of competing interests. Indeed, even within well-spread groups of doctors, ratepayers, patients etc. it is likely that competing views will emerge.

The possibility of conflicting sets of values leading to conflicting positions among the surveyed groups does of course make the results of the surveys themselves difficult to interpret and in such a situation they probably add little to the evaluation of effectiveness.

However, surveys of interested parties are not the only means of obtaining opinions about effectiveness. Other approaches might be to make use of the judgement of experts (e.g. the Office for Standards in Education) or the use of special enquiry panels. In the USA, publicly funded social programmes are subjected to a regular system of evaluation by expert evaluators. Programme evaluation is essentially concerned with examining the four key issues of: (a) whether the programmes are relevant and realistic; (b) what the impacts and effects of the programme will be; (c) whether the programme achieved the stated objectives; and (d) whether there are better ways of achieving the results. The US experience of setting aside for evaluation purposes a small amount, say 1 to 1.5 per cent, of the revenue budget of a publicly funded programme, is that this led to a substantial growth in evaluation activities. Not surprisingly, the benefits of all of this were soon questioned and Schmidt (1983, pp. 171–88), for example, whilst drawing attention to the high costs of evaluation, contended that 'evaluation studies are read by few people and acted upon by even fewer'.

The requirements of an effectiveness audit suggest that it too is likely to be a high-cost exercise, and in the UK there has been much debate over whether the audit of effectiveness is achievable and whether existing auditors are the appropriate group to carry out effectiveness audits. In a study of the attitudes of auditors to these and related issues, Pendlebury and Shreim (1990) surveyed a sample of auditors drawn from the National Audit Office, the Audit Commission and a major private sector firm of accountants. All three groups were of the opinion that effectiveness auditing is achievable and that it is appropriate for auditors to be involved, but the support was discernibly stronger from the National Audit Office respondents than from the other two groups. The more positive attitude that the National Audit Office respondents had to effectiveness auditing was also clear from their belief that their part in the evaluation of effectiveness was more important than that of service specialists or service department managers. The respondents from the Audit Commission and the firm of accountants were more prepared to concede that service specialists and service department managers had a more important part to play than auditors. When Pendlebury and Shreim (1991) extended their survey to include local authority service department managers as well as auditors they found somewhat different results. The majority of the sample of service department managers felt that auditors are not the most appropriate persons to make the kinds of personal judgements required in an effectiveness audit and attached a much lower level of importance to the role of auditors in the evaluation of effectiveness. Pendlebury and Shreim suggest that if service department managers 'are to accept the validity and relevance of effectiveness audits, then the audit teams are likely to require a much higher ratio of service experts to accountants than is currently the case'.

Alternatively, it might be more appropriate to follow the suggestion of Tomkins (1987, p. 59) when he states that in order 'to avoid excessive costs, effectiveness reviews should probably be pursued selectively and periodically by the organizations delivering the service, or consultants assisting them'. The role of the auditor would then be to verify that such reviews are undertaken and that they are undertaken properly.

PERFORMANCE INDICATORS

In addition to being subject to a three Es audit, many public sector organizations now include a range of financial and non-financial performance indicators in their annual report and accounts. As was seen in Chapter 10, this is part of the move towards improved accountability and presumably the performance indicators are meant to contribute to the ability of users of annual reports and accounts to assess the value for money provided by the reporting organization. If this is the case, then the extent to which the performance indicators should be subject to some form of independent verification becomes an issue and perhaps this is a further role for the public sector auditor when carrying out a three Es audit.

The financial audit and the three Es audit of the published report and accounts of an organization would, of course, have to be carefully distinguished. At the moment the annual report and accounts of both private sector and public sector organizations contain a lot of information that is not covered by the statutory audit report. For example, the directors' report or equivalent is not audited. Auditing standard-setters have to regulate this circumstance, however, to ensure as far as possible that it is clear to the reader which parts are audited and which not. Moreover, there is usually a requirement for auditors to review the non-audited parts to ensure that nothing is said in them that contradicts the audited financial statements. (UK company audits offer an example of such a requirement.) Measures of economy, efficiency and effectiveness would typically be included in the non-audited part of the financial reports of an organization. They might be covered by the requirement of auditors to ensure that there is no contradiction but more typically they would not. Over recent years, however, auditors have developed more non-audit services, which provide some form of attestation short of that provided by an audit. In the US, these are called compilation and review services and have been distinguished from audits by calling the consequent reports 'accountants' reports' rather than 'auditors' reports'. The International Auditing Practices Committee has issued 'standards on related services'. Similar developments are taking place in the UK to rationalize this reporting, typically but not always referring to the reports as 'accountants' reports'. The essential point is that financial information deriving from a bookkeeping system is different in nature from other financial and non-financial information. Auditors themselves cannot rely on the latter to the same extent and therefore cannot be expected to provide enough assurance to make the two sets of information equally reliable. Nevertheless, what the auditors can provide, of course, is a different view of the data from that offered by management.

DISCUSSION TOPICS

1 Describe how you would conduct the three Es audits of a public sector organization of your choice, in the light of what you know about its management accounting, financial accounting, and other information systems.

2 You have experience as an auditor of PLCs. The Audit Commission has offered you the appointment to carry out an *ad hoc* value for money audit of a local authority. What factors would you consider before you accepted?

3 Explain what is meant by the evaluation of effectiveness. To what extent do you consider that the auditors of public sector organizations can make a contribution towards such an evaluation?

4 'Economy, efficiency, and effectiveness audits can only be undertaken against a background of predetermined standards of performance.' Discuss the above quotation and explain what action the auditor should take if predetermined standards do not exist.

BIBLIOGRAPHY

Accounting Standards Board, *The Objective of Financial Statements and the Qualitative Characteristics of Financial Information*, proposed Statement of Principles, 1991.

Accounting Standards Board, *Reporting Financial Performance*, FRS 3, 1992.

Accounting Standards Board, *Foreword to Accounting Standards*, 1993.

Accounting Standards Committee, *The Corporate Report*, ASC, London, 1975.

Accounting Standards Committee, *SSAP 16: Current Cost Accounting*, ASC, London, 1980.

Accounting Standards Committee, *Accounting for the Effects of Changing Prices: A Handbook*, ASC, 1988.

Aiken, M., 'Parliamentary sovereignty and valuation accruals: uncongenial conventions', *Financial Accountability and Management*, Vol. 10, No. 1, 1994, pp. 17–32.

American Accounting Association, *A Statement of Basic Accounting Theory*, AAA, Sarasota, Florida, 1966.

American Accounting Association, 'Report of the Committee on Concepts of Accounting applicable to the Public Sector 1970–71', *Accounting Review*, supplement to Vol. XLVII, 1972, pp. 77–108.

American Accounting Association, 'Report of the Committee on Not-for-profit Organisations 1972–73, Auditing Issues and Problems', *Accounting Review*, supplement to Vol. XLIX, 1974, pp. 237–45.

American Accounting Association, 'Report of the Committee on Non-profit organizations 1973/74', *Accounting Review*, supplement to Vol. L, 1975, pp. 1–39.

American Accounting Association, 'Report of the Committee on Accounting in the Public Sector 1974–76', *Accounting Review*, supplement to Vol. LII, 1977, pp. 33–52.

American Institute of Certified Public Accountants, *Objectives of Financial Statements* (known as the Trueblood Report), AICPA, New York, 1974.

Anthony, R. N., *Accounting for the Cost of Interest*, Lexington Books, Lexington, Mass., 1975.

Anthony, R. N., 'ZBB – a useful fraud?', *Government Accountants Journal*, Summer 1977.

Anthony, R. N., *Financial Accounting in Nonbusiness Organizations*, Financial Accounting Standards Board, Stamford, Connecticut, 1978.

Anthony, R. N., 'Making Sense of Nonbusiness Accounting', *Harvard Business Review*, May–June 1980, pp. 83–93.

Anthony, R. N. and Young, D. W., *Management Control in Nonprofit Organisations*, 5th edn, Irwin, 1994.

Aronson, J. R. and Schwartz, E. (eds), *Management Policies in Local Government Finance*, International City Management Association, Washington DC, 1981.

Audit Commission for Local Authorities in England and Wales, *Better Financial Management*, Management Papers No. 3, Audit Commission, 1989(a).

Audit Commission for Local Authorities in England and Wales, *Managing Services Effectively – Performance Review*, Management Papers No. 5, Audit Commission, 1989(b).

Audit Commission for Local Authorities and the National Health Service in England and Wales, *Code of Practice for Local Authorities and the National Health Service in England and Wales*, 1990 and updates to 1995.

Audit Commission for Local Authorities and the National Health Service in England and Wales, *Citizen's Charter Indicators: Charting a Course*, undated.

Audit Commission for Local Authorities and the National Health Service in England and Wales, *The Publication of Information (Standards of Performance) Direction 1992*.

Audit Commission for Local Authorities and the National Health Service in England and Wales, *Unfinished Business: Full-time Educational Courses for the 16–19 Year Olds*, Joint Report by the Audit Commission and the Office for Standards in Education, 1993.

Auditing Practices Board, *Accounting and Internal Control Systems and Audit Risk Assessments*, Statement of Auditing Standards 300, 1995.

Auditing Practices Committee, *Auditing Standards and Guidelines*, London, 1980.

Auditing Practices Committee, *Auditing Guideline on Internal Control*, 1990.

Auditing Practices Committee, *Guidance for Internal Auditors*, 1990.

Babunakis, M., *Budgets: An Analytical and Procedural Handbook for Government and Nonprofit Organizations*, Greenwood Press, London, 1976.

Beedle, A., *Accounting for Local Government in Canada: The State of the Art*, Canadian Certified General Accountants' Research Foundation, Vancouver, 1981.

Bellamy, S. and Kluvers, R, 'Program budgeting in Australian local government', *Financial Accountability and Management*, Vol. 11, No. 1, 1995, pp. 39–56.

Berry, L. E. and Wallace, W. A., 'Governmental Auditing Research', *Research in Governmental and Nonprofit Accounting*, James Chan (ed.), Vol. 2, 1986, pp. 89–115.

Berry, R. H., *Management Accounting in Universities*, Chartered Institute of Management Accountants, London, 1994.

Bromwich, M. and Hopwood, A. G. (eds), *Essays in British Accounting Research*, Pitman Books, London, 1981, pp. 337–40.

Bohm, P., *Social Efficiency: A Concise Introduction to Welfare Economics*, Macmillan, London, 1977.

Brown, R. E., *Accounting and Accountability in Public Administration*, American Society for Public Administration, 1988.

Buschor, E. and Schedler, K. (eds), *Perspectives on Performance Measurement and Public Sector Accounting*, Haupt, Berne, Stuttgart and Vienna, 1994.

Butt, H. and Palmer, B., *Value for Money in the Public Sector. The Decision-Maker's Guide*, Blackwell, 1985.

Byatt Report, *Accounting for Economic Costs and Changing Prices,* Vols I and II, HMSO, London, 1986.

Cabinet Office, *Public Bodies*, HMSO, London, 1994.

Canadian Institute of Chartered Accountants, *Financial Reporting by Governments*, CICA, Toronto, 1980.

Canadian Institute of Chartered Accountants, *Local Government Financial Reporting*, 1985.

Centre for Industrial, Economic and Business Research, University of Warwick, *Management of Financial Resources in the National Health Service*, Research Paper No. 2 for the Royal Commission on the National Health Service, HMSO, London, 1978.

Chambers, A. D., Selim, G. M. and Vinten, G., *Internal Auditing*, 2nd edn, Pitman, London, 1987.

Chan, J. L. and Jones, R. H., *Government Accounting and Auditing*, Routledge, London, 1988.

Chan, J. L., 'The Birth of the Governmental Accounting Standards Board: How? Why? What Next?', *Research in Governmental and Non-Profit Accounting*, Vol. 1, 1985, pp. 3–32.

Chandler, R. (ed.), *Auditing and Reporting 1994/95 (of the Auditing Practices Board)*, Accountancy Books, 1994.

Chartered Institute of Management Accountants, *Management Accounting – Official Terminology of the CIMA*, CIMA, 1994.

Chartered Institute of Public Finance and Accountancy, *Financial Information Service*, multi-volumed, regularly updated manual.

Chartered Institute of Public Finance and Accountancy, *Local Authority Accounting 1, Accounting Principles*, CIPFA, London, 1975.

Chartered Institute of Public Finance and Accountancy, *Local Authority Accounting 2, Finance in Management*, CIPFA, London, 1975.

Chartered Institute of Public Finance and Accountancy, *Charging for Local Authority Services*, CIPFA, 1984.

Chartered Institute of Public Finance and Accountancy, *The Management of Overheads in Local Authorities*, CIPFA, London, 1991.

Chartered Institute of Public Finance and Accountancy, *Code of Practice on Local Authority Accounting in Great Britain*, CIPFA, London, 1993a.

Chartered Institute of Public Finance and Accountancy, *Code of Practice for Compulsory Competition*, CIPFA, London, 1993b.

Cm 2626, *Better Accounting for the Taxpayer's Money*, HMSO, London, 1994.

Cm 2750, *Next Steps Review 1994*, HMSO, London, 1994.

Cmnd 7845, *The Role of the Comptroller and Auditor General*, HMSO, London, 1980.

Cmnd 8313, *Broadcasting*, HMSO, London, July 1981.

Cmnd 8616, *Efficiency and Effectiveness in the Civil Service*, HMSO, London, 1982.

Committee of Public Accounts, *The Role of the Comptroller and Auditor General*, Vols I, II, III, House of Commons Paper 115, HMSO, London, 1980/81.

Coombs, H. and Edwards, J. (eds), *Accountability of Local Authorities in England and Wales, 1831–1935*, Volumes 1 and 2, Garland, New York and London, 1990.

Coombs, H. and Edwards, J. (eds), *Local Authority Accounting Methods, 1884–1908*, Garland, New York and London, 1991.

Coombs, H. and Edwards, J. (eds), *Local Authority Accounting Methods, 1909–1934*, Garland, New York and London, 1992.

Coombs, H. M. and Jenkins, D. E., *Public Sector Financial Management*, Chapman and Hall, 2nd edn, 1994.

Coopers and Lybrand Associates Ltd, *Services Provision and Pricing in Local Government*, HMSO, London, 1981.

Copeland, R. M. and Ingram, R. W., *Municipal Financial Reporting and Disclosure Quality*, Addison-Wesley, London, 1983.

Craner, J. and Jones, R., 'Accrual Accounting for National Governments', *Research in Third World Accounting*, Vol. 1, 1990, pp. 103–13.

Davies, J. R. and McInnes, W. M., 'The Efficiency and the Accountability of UK Nationalised Industries', *Accounting and Business Research*, Vol. 13, No. 49, Winter 1982, pp. 29–41.

Dean, P. (with Pugh, C.), *Government Budgeting in Developing Countries*, Routledge, 1989.

Department of the Environment, 'Local government audit – Code of practice', published in *Local Government Finance*, Vol. 76, No. 6, June 1972, pp. 210–13.

Department of the Environment, *Local Authority Annual Reports*, HMSO, London, 1981.

Department of the Environment, *Competing for Quality: Competition in the Provision of Local Services*, 1991.

Department of Health, *Working for Patients*, HMSO, London, 1989.

Department of Health and Social Security, *Report of the NHS Management Inquiry* (The Griffiths Report), HMSO, 1983.

Dittenhofer, M. A., *Applying Government Accounting Principles*, Matthew Bender, 1991.

Drebin, A. R., 'Governmental vs Commercial Accounting: The Issues', *Governmental Finance*, Vol. 8, No. 3, November 1979, pp. 3–8.

Drebin, A. R., Chan, J. L. and Ferguson, L. C., *Objectives of Accounting and Financial Reporting for Governmental Units: A Research Study*, Vols I and II, National Council on Governmental Accounting, Chicago, 1981.

Efficiency Unit, *Improving Management in Government: The Next Steps*, Report of the Efficiency Unit to the Prime Minister, HMSO, London, 1988.

Efficiency Unit, *Making the Most of Next Steps: The Management of Ministers' Departments and Their Executive Agencies*, Report of the Efficiency Unit to the Prime Minister, HMSO, London, 1991.

Ellwood, S., 'Pricing Healthcare under "Managed Competition": The Role of Cost Accounting in the UK National Health Service', in E. Buschor and K Schedler (eds), *op. cit.*, 1994, 163–88.

Federal Accounting Standards Advisory Board, *Objectives of Federal Financial Reporting*, Concepts Statement No. 1, FASAB, 1994.

Fielden, J. and Robertson, D., 'Value for Money and Performance Reviews in Local Government', *Management Accounting*, Vol. 58, No. 9, October 1980, pp. 26–30.

Financial Accounting Standards Board, *Objectives of Financial reporting by Business Organizations*, FASB, 1978.

Fletcher, C. G. A., *Government Accounting*, Institute of Chartered Accountants of Scotland, 1991.

Foster, C. D., Jackman, R. A. and Perlman, M., *Local Government Finance in a Unitary State*, Allen and Unwin, London, 1980.

Freeman, R. and Shoulders, C., *Governmental and Nonprofit Accounting*, 4th edn, Prentice-Hall, Englewood Cliffs, N. J., 1993.

Garbutt, D. and Minmier, G. S., 'Incremental, Planned-programmed and Zero-base Budgeting', *Public Finance and Accountancy*, Vol. 1, No. 11, November 1974, pp. 350–7.

Geist, B. (ed.), *State Audit*, Macmillan, London, 1981.

General Accounting Office (of the US), *Auditing Standards*, GAO, Washington DC, 1994.

Governmental Accounting Standards Board, *Service Efforts and Accomplishments Reporting: Its Time Has Come*, Research Report, GASB, 1990.

Governmental Accounting Standards Board, *Service Efforts and Accomplishments Reporting*, Concepts Statement No. 2, 1994a.

Governmental Accounting Standards Board, *Governmental Accounting and Financial Reporting Standards (as of June 30, 1994)*, 1994b.

Gray, A., Jenkins, B. and Segsworth, B., *Budgeting, Auditing, and Evaluation*, Transaction, New Brunswick and London, 1993.

Gray, R., Bebbington, J. and Walters, D., *Accounting for the Environment*, Paul Chapman Publishing/Chartered Association of Certified Accountants, 1993.

Hansen, Elizabeth, 'Municipal Finances in Perspective', *Journal of Accounting Research*, Vol. 15, Supplement 1977, pp. 156–201.

Heald, D., 'The Economic and Financial Control of UK Nationalised Industries', *The Economic Journal*, Vol. 90, June 1989, pp. 243–65.

Henke, E. O., *Introduction to Nonprofit Organisation Accounting*, PWS-Kent Publishing, Boston, 3rd edn, 1988.

Henley, D., Likierman, A., Perrin, J., Evans, M., Lapsley, I. and Whiteoak, J., *Public Sector Accounting and Financial Control*, 4th edn, Chapman and Hall, London, 1992.

Herbert, L., *Auditing the Performance of Management*, Lifetime Learning, Belmont, California, 1979.

H.M. Treasury, *Government Internal Audit Manual*, HMSO, 1988.

H.M. Treasury, *Government Accounting*, HMSO, London, 4th edn, 1989.

H.M. Treasury, *Economic Appraisal in Central Government – A Technical Guide for Government Departments*, HMSO, 1991.

H.M. Treasury, *Executive Agencies: A Guide to Setting Targets and Measuring Performance*, HMSO, London, 1992.

Herzlinger, R. E. and Sherman, H. D., 'Advantages of Fund Accounting in "Non-profits" ', *Harvard Business Review*, May–June 1980, pp. 94–105.

Hofstede, G., 'Management Control of Public and Not-for-Profit Activities', *Accounting, Organisations and Society*, Vol. 6, No. 3, 1981.

Holder, W. W., *A Study of Selected Concepts for Government Financial Accounting and Reporting*, National Council on Governmental Accounting, Chicago, 1980.

Hopwood, A. G. and Miller, P. (eds), *Accounting as Social and Institutional Practice*, Cambridge University Press, Cambridge, 1994.

Hopwood, A. and Tomkins, C., *Issues in Public Sector Accounting*, Philip Allan, Oxford, 1984.

Inflation Accounting Committee, *Inflation Accounting* (known as the *Sandilands Report*), HMSO, London, 1975.

Ingram, R. W. and Copeland, R. M., 'Municipal Accounting Information and Voting Behaviour', *Accounting Review*, Vol. LVI, No. 4, October 1981, pp. 830–43.

Institute of Municipal Treasurers and Accountants, *The Form of Published Accounts of Local Authorities*, IMTA, London, 1955.

International Federation of Accountants, *Financial Reporting by National Governments*, Study No. 1, IFAC, New York, 1991.

International Organization of Supreme Audit Institutions, *Accounting Statements*, INTOSAI, 1992.

International Organization of Supreme Audit Institutions, *Auditing Standards*, INTOSAI, 1989.

Jablonsky, S. F. and Dirsmith, M. W., 'The Pattern of PPB Rejection: Something about Organisations, Something about PPB', *Accounting Organisations and Society*, Vol. 3, No. 3/4, pp. 215–25.

Jarratt Report, *Report of the Steering Committee for Efficiency Studies in Universities*, Committee of Vice Chancellors and Principals, 1985.

Jones, D. B., *The Needs of Users of Governmental Financial Reports*, Governmental Accounting Standards Board, Stamford, Connecticut, 1985.

Jones, R., 'Accounting in English Local Government: from the Middle Ages to c. 1835', *Accounting and Business Research*, Vol. 15, No. 59, Summer 1985, pp. 197–210, reprinted in Parker and Yamey, *op. cit.*, pp. 377–403.

Jones, R., 'Accruals accounting in UK Local Government: A Historical Context to Continuing Controversies', *Financial Accountability and Management*, Vol. 1, No. 2, Winter 1985, pp. 145–60.

Jones, R., 'Financial Reporting in Nonbusiness Organizations', *Accounting and Business Research*, Vol. 12, No. 48, Autumn 1982, pp. 287–95.

Jones, R., 'The Development of Conceptual Frameworks of Accounting for the Public Sector', *Financial Accountability and Management*, Vol. 8, No. 4, Winter 1992a, pp. 249–64.

Jones, R., *The History of the Financial Control Function of Local Government Accounting in the United Kingdom*, Garland, New York and London, 1992b.

Jones, R., 'An Indictment of Performance Measurement in the Public Sector', in E. Buschor and K. Schedler (eds), *op. cit.*, 1994, 43–57.

Jones, R. and Pendlebury, M., 'What makes public sector accounting different', *The Accountant's Magazine*, Vol. LXXXIX, No. 953, November 1985, pp. 490–4.

Jones, R. and Pendlebury, M., 'The Published Accounts of Local Authorities, Revisited', *Financial Accountability and Management*, Vol. 7, No. 1, Spring 1991, pp. 15–33.

Jones, Reginald, *Local Government Audit Law*, HMSO, London, 2nd edn, 1985.

Jonsson, S., 'Budgetary Behaviour in Local Government', *Accounting Organizations and Society*, Vol. 7, No. 3, 1982, pp. 287–304.

Kaufmann, F. X., Majone, G. and Ostrom V. (eds), *Guidance, Control, and Evaluation in the Public Sector*, de Gruyter, Berlin and New York, 1986.

King, M., Lapsley, I., Mitchell, F. and Moyes, J., *Activity Based Costing in Hospitals: A Case Study Investigation*, Chartered Institute of Management Accountants, London, 1994.

Kloman, E. H., *Cases in Accountability: The Work of the GAO*, Westview, Boulder, Colorado, 1979.

Knighton, L. M., 'Information Preconditions of Performance Auditing', *Governmental Finance 5*, No. 2, 1976, pp. 22–77, reprinted by R. J. Vargo and P. A. Dierks, *op. cit.*, pp. 247–52.

Lapsley, I., 'Income Measurement at a State Railway Corporation: The "Social Profit" Illusion?', *Journal of Business Finance and Accounting*, Vol. 8, No. 4, 1981, pp. 529–47.

Lapsley, I., 'Capital Accounting in UK Non-Trading Organisations', *Financial Accountability and Management*, Vol. 2, No. 4, Winter 1986.

Lapsley, I., 'The Accounting and Organisational Consequences of Privatisation and Regulation', *Financial Accountability and Management*, Vol. 9, No. 2, 1993, pp. 69–73.

Lapsley, I. and Pettigrew, A., 'Meeting the Challenge: Accounting for Change', *Financial Accountability and Management*, Vol. 10, No. 2, 1994, pp. 79–92.

Lapsley, I., Llewellyn, S. and Mitchell, F., *Cost Management in the Public Sector*, Longman, London, 1994.

Lauth, T. P., 'Zero-base Budgeting in Georgia State Government: Myth and Reality', *Public Administration Review*, Vol. 38, No. 5, September/October 1978.

Lee, T., *Cash Flow Accounting*, Van Nostrand Reinhold, 1984.

Lewis, V. B., 'Towards a Theory of Budgeting', *Public Administration Review*, Vol. 12, No. 1, Winter 1952.

Likierman, A., 'The Reports and Accounts of Three Nationalised Transport Industries', Report to the Transport Committee, House of Commons, session 1981–1982, HoC 390.

Likierman, A., *Public Expenditure*, Penguin, 1988.

Likierman, A., 'Management Accounting in UK Central Government', *Financial Accountability and Management*, Vol. 10, No. 2, 1994, pp. 93–115.

Likierman, A. and Taylor, A., *Government's New Department Reports: Challenges and Potential Problems*, Certified Research Report 19, Chartered Association of Certified Accountants, 1990.

Llewellyn, S., 'Linking Costs with Quality in Health and Social Care: New Challenges for Management Accounting', *Financial Accountability and Management*, Vol. 9, No. 3, 1993, pp. 177–94.

Lüder, K., Accounting for Change: *Market Forces and Managerialism in the Public Sector*, Speyerer Arbeitshefte No. 100, Hochschule für Verwaltungswissenschaften Speyer, 1994a.

Lüder, K., *The 'Contingency Model' Reconsidered: Experiences from Italy, Japan and Spain*, in E. Buschor and K Schedler (eds), *op. cit.*, 1994b, 1–15.

Lyden, J. and Miller, E. G., *Public Budgeting – Program Planning and Implementation*, 4th edn, Prentice-Hall, Hemel Hempstead, 1982.

McGuirk, T., *CCT and the Private Sector, Vol. 2: A Clean Sweep – An Overview of Building Cleaning in Local Government*, Institute of Public Finance, Croydon, 1993.

Macve, R., *A Conceptual Framework for Financial Accounting and Reporting*, ICAEW, London, 1981.

Mayston, D. J., 'Non-profit Performance Indicators in the Public Sector', *Financial Accountability and Management*, Vol. 1, No. 1, Summer 1985, pp. 51–74.

Mellett, H., 'Capital Accounting in the National Health Service after 1991', *Financial Accountability and Management*, Vol. 6, No. 4, Winter 1990, pp. 263–83.

Mellett, H., Marriott, N. and Harries, S., *Financial Management in the NHS*, Chapman and Hall, London, 1993.

Mishan, E. J., *Cost Benefit Analysis*, Unwin and Hyman, London, 4th edn, 1988.

Mullen, P. M., 'Which Internal Market? The NHS White Paper and Internal Markets', *Financial Accountability and Management*, Vol. 6, No. 1, Spring 1990.

National Health Service Management Executive, *Manual for Accounts*, Department of Health and Social Security, 1977 and 1986; Department of Health, 1991.

Next Steps Team, *Next Steps Briefing Note*, Cabinet Office (OPSS), 7 December 1994.

Normanton, E. L., *The Accountability and Audit of Governments*, Manchester University Press, Manchester, 1966.

Novick, D. (ed.), *Program Budgeting*, 2nd edn, Harvard University Press, London, 1973.

Novick, D. (ed.), *Current Practice in Program Budgeting (PPBS)*, Crane Russak, New York, 1973.

Office of the Auditor General of Canada and the Comptroller General of the US, *Federal Government Reporting Study* (1986).

Office of Water Services, *Guideline for Accounting for Current Costs (Regulatory Accounting Guideline 1.02)*, Ofwat, London, 1992.

Organization for Economic Co-operation and Development, *Accounting for What? The Value of Accrual Accounting to the Public Sector*, Occasional Paper on Public Management, OECD, Paris, 1993.

Otley, D. T., 'Behavioural Aspects of Budgeting', *Accountants Digest*, No. 49, ICAEW, London, Summer 1977.

Owen, D. (ed.), *Green Reporting: Accountancy and the Challenge of the Nineties*, Chapman and Hall, London, 1992.

Parker, R H. and Yamey, B. S. (eds), *Accounting History*, Clarendon Press, Oxford, 1994.

Pendlebury, M., 'Management Accounting in Local Government', *Financial Accountability and Management*, Vol. 10, No. 2, May 1994, pp. 117–29.

Pendlebury, M. and Jones, R., 'Budget Auditing in Governmental Organisations Financed by Taxation', *Journal of Business Finance and Accounting*, Vol. 10, No. 4, Winter 1983, pp. 585–93.

Pendlebury, M. and Jones, R., 'Governmental Budgeting as Ex Ante Financial

Accounting', *Journal of Accounting and Public Policy*, Vol. 4, No. 4, Winter 1985, pp. 301–16.

Pendlebury, M. and Shreim, O., 'UK Auditors Attitudes to Effectiveness Auditing', *Financial Accountability and Management*, Vol. 6, No. 3, Autumn 1990, pp. 177–89.

Pendlebury, M. and Shreim, O., 'Attitudes to Effectiveness Auditing: Some Further Evidence', *Financial Accountability and Management*, Vol. 7, No. 1, Spring 1991, pp. 57–63.

Pendlebury, M., Jones, R. and Karbhari, Y., 'Accounting for Executive Agencies in the UK Government', *Financial Accountability and Management*, Vol. 8, No. 1, Spring 1992, pp. 35–48.

Pendlebury, M., Jones, R. and Karbhari, Y., 'Developments in the Accountability and Financial Reporting Practices of Executive Agencies', *Financial Accountability and Management*, Vol. 10, No. 1, 1994, pp. 33–46.

Pendlebury, M. W., *Management Accounting in Local Government*, ICMA Occasional Paper Series, ICMA, 1985.

Pendlebury, M. W., *Management Accounting in the Public Sector*, Heinemann, 1989.

Perrin, J. R., 'Accounting Research in the Public Sector', in Bromwich, M. and Hopwood, A. G., *Essays in British Accounting Research*, Pitman Books, London, 1981, pp. 297–322.

Phyrr, P. A., *Zero-base Budgeting – A Practical Management Tool for Evaluating Expenses*, Wiley, Chichester, 1973.

Phyrr, P. A., 'Zero-base Budgeting', in Anton, H. R., Firmin, P. A. and Grove, H. D., *Contemporary Issues in Cost and Management Accounting*, 3rd edn, Houghton Mifflin, Boston, Massachusetts, 1978.

Price Waterhouse, *Value for Money Auditing – The Investigation of Economy Efficiency and Effectiveness*, Gee and Co. and Price Waterhouse, 1990.

Prowle, M., Jones, T. and Shaw, J., *Working for Patients – The Financial Agenda*, Certified Research Report 15, Chartered Association of Certified Accountants, 1989.

Ramanathan, K. V. and Weis, W. L., 'Supplementing Collegiate Financial Statements with Across-fund Aggregations: An Experimental Enquiry', *Accounting Organisations and Society*, Vol. 6, No. 2, 1981, pp. 143–51.

Rockley, L. E., *Local and Public Authority Accounts*, Heinemann, London, 1975.

Rosenberg, D., Tomkins, C. and Day, P., 'A Work Role Perspective of Accountants in Local Government Service Departments', *Accounting, Organizations and Society*, Vol. 7, No. 2, 1982, pp. 123–37.

Royal Institute of Public Administration, *Budgeting in Public Authorities*, Allen and Unwin, London, 1959.

Rutherford, B., Sherer, M. and Wearing, R., *Cases in Public Sector Accounting*, Paul Chapman, London, 1992.

Rutherford, B. A., *Financial Reporting in the Public Sector*, Butterworth, London, 1983.

Sarant, P. C., *Zero-base Budgeting in the Public Sector: A Pragmatic Approach*, Addison-Wesley, London, 1978.

Schick, A., 'The Road to PPB: the Stages of Budget Reform', in Lyden, J. and Miller, E. G. (1982).

Schick, A. (ed.), *Perspectives on Budgeting*, American Society for Public Administration, 1987.

Schultze, C. L., *The Politics and Economics of Public Spending*, Brookings Institute, 1968.

Sherer, M. J. and Kent, D. B., *Auditing and Accountability*, Pitman, London, 1983.

Sherer, M. and Turley, S., *Current Issues in Auditing*, 2nd edn, Paul Chapman, London, 1991.

Sidebotham, R., 'An Accounting Framework for Local Authorities', *Abacus*, Vol. 2, September 1966, pp. 24–40.

Sidebotham, R., 'The Consolidated Capital Fund', *Local Government Finance*, Vol. 74, No. 2, February 1970, pp. 42–50.

Skousen, C. R., 'Budgeting Practices in Local Governments of England and Wales', *Financial Accountability and Management*, Vol. 6, No. 3, Autumn 1990, pp. 191–208.

Sorensen, V. E. and Grove, H. D., 'Cost Outcome and Cost Effectiveness Analysis: Emerging Non-profit Performance Evaluation Techniques', *Accounting Review*, July 1977, Vol. LII, No. 3, pp. 658–75.

Sowerby, T., *The History of the Chartered Institute of Public Finance and Accountancy*, CIPFA, London, 1985.

Stewart, J. D., 'The Role of Information in Public Accountability', in Hopwood and Tomkins, *op. cit.*, pp. 13–34.

Surányi-Unger, T., *Comparative Economic Systems*, McGraw-Hill, London, 1952.

Thain, C. and Wright, M., 'The Advent of Cash Planning', *Financial Accountability and Management*, Vol. 5, No. 3, 1989, pp. 149–62.

Thain, C. and Wright, M., 'Running Costs Control in UK Central Government', *Financial Accountability and Management*, Vol. 6, No. 2, 1990, pp. 115–31.

Tierney, C. E., *Governmental Auditing*, Commerce Clearing Houses, Chicago, 1979.

Tomkins, C., 'Value for Money in the Public Sector: (1) Rationality vs Incrementalism in Budgeting', *Local Finance*, June 1980, Vol. 9, No. 3.

Tomkins, C., 'Financial Control in Local Authorities', in Bromwich, M. and Hopwood, A. G., *Essays in British Accounting Research*, Pitman, London, 1981, pp. 323–36.

Tomkins, C., *Achieving Economy, Efficiency and Effectiveness in the Public Sector*, Institute of Chartered Accountants of Scotland, 1987.

Tomkins, C. and Barker, D., 'Materiality in Local Government Auditing', *Public Finance and Accountancy*, 12, 19 and 26 July 1985.

Tweedie, D. and Whittington, G., *The Debate on Inflation Accounting*, Cambridge University Press, Cambridge, 1984.

Van Gunsteren, H. R., *The Quest for Control*, Wiley, Chichester, 1976.

Vargo, R. J. and Dierks, P. A. (eds), *Readings and Cases in Governmental and Nonprofit Accounting*, Dame, Houston, Texas, 1982.

Vatter, W. J., *The Fund Theory of Accounting and its Implications for Financial Reports*, University of Chicago, Chicago, 1947.

Wallace, W. A., 'Internal Control Reporting Practices in the Municipal Sector', *The Accounting Review*, Vol. LVI, No. 3, July 1981, pp. 666–89.

Whittington, G., 'Financial Accounting Theory: An Overview', *The British Accounting Review*, Vol. 18, No. 2, Autumn 1986, pp. 4–41.

Wildavsky, A., *The Politics of the Budgetary Process*, 4th edn, Little, Brown and Co., Boston, Massachusetts, 1984.

Wildavsky, A., *Budgeting: A Comparative Theory of Budgetary Processes*, Little, Brown and Co. Boston, Massachusetts, 1975.

Wildavsky, A. and Hammond, A., 'Comprehensive versus Incremental Budgeting in the Department of Agriculture', *Administrative Science Quarterly*, vol. 19, 1965–6.

Worthley, J. A. and Ludwin, W. G. (eds), *Zero-Base Budgeting in State and Local Government: Current Experience and Cases*, Praegar, New York, 1979.

Young, E. Hilton, *The System of National Finance*, Smith Elder and Co.,1915.

Zimmerman, J. I., 'The Municipal Accounting Maze: An Analysis of Political Incentives', *Journal of Accounting Research*, Vol. 15, supplement 1977, pp. 107–44.

INDEX